The need for active participation in the defeat of a regime he detested led Dr. Hoover into intelligence work during World War II. In the OSS he was responsible for Northern Europe and Poland and the penetration of Germany from those areas. One agent, a Swedish-American professor, was able to obtain a count of German troops on the trains passing through Sweden by putting on a railway worker's uniform and walking through the cars. As an economist and an intelligence officer with specialized knowledge of Germany, Dr. Hoover was selected as chairman of the German Standard of Living Board after the war. This board prepared the Hoover Report on German reparations which established that country's post-war level of production.

After returning to the United States Dr. Hoover was appointed to President Truman's Committee on Foreign Aid. The recommendations of this committee, headed by Averell Harriman, came to be known as the Marshall Plan. In more recent years Dr. Hoover's studies of capitalism and totalitarianism required another visit to Russia. "There had been a great relaxation in tension since the death of Stalin . . . Yet the essential character of the police state remained." Dr. Hoover's **Memoirs** conclude with an assessment of the possibility that further relaxation of controls in Russia could produce sufficient liberties for her citizens while retaining state control of the economy.

In 1946 Dr. Hoover was awarded the United States Medal of Freedom. He holds honorary degrees from Columbia University and Monmouth College, in addition to his A.B. from Monmouth College and his Ph.D from the University of Wisconsin. At Duke University, where he began teaching in 1925, he is James B. Duke Professor of Economics. He was chairman of the department of economics for twenty years and Dean of the Graduate School from 1937-1947.

His previously published works include, **Economic Life of Soviet Russia, Germany Enters the Third Reich, Dictators and Democracies, International Trade and Domestic Employment, Economic Resources and Policies of the South, The Economy, Liberty and the State, Economic Systems of the Commonwealth** (editor), and numerous articles in journals.

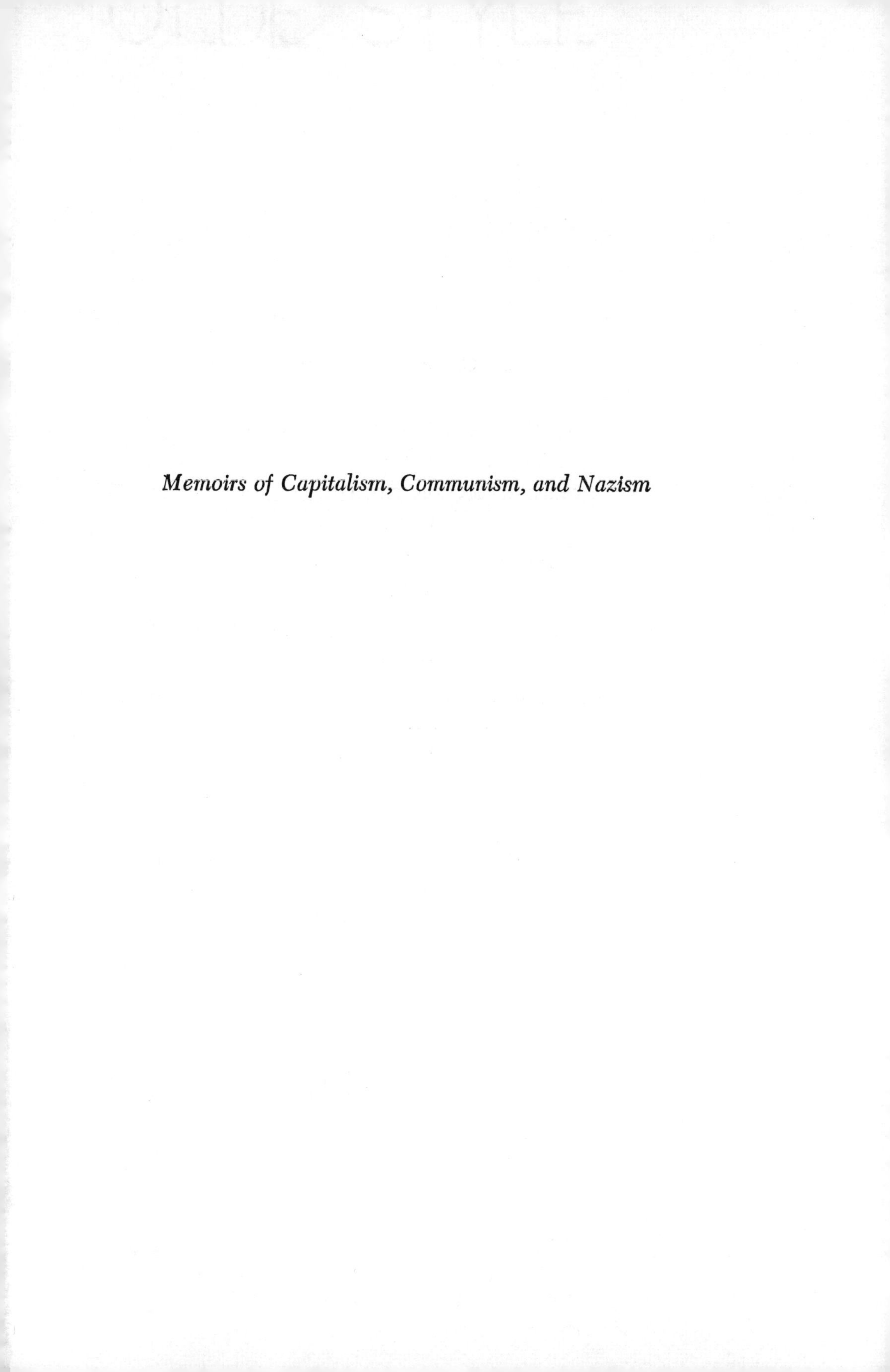

Memoirs of Capitalism, Communism, and Nazism

by Calvin B. Hoover

ECONOMIC LIFE OF SOVIET RUSSIA
(1931)

GERMANY ENTERS THE THIRD REICH
(1933)

DICTATORS AND DEMOCRACIES
(1937)

INTERNATIONAL TRADE AND DOMESTIC EMPLOYMENT
(1944)

ECONOMIC RESOURCES AND POLICIES OF THE SOUTH
with B. U. Ratchford
(1951)

THE ECONOMY, LIBERTY AND THE STATE
(1959)

ECONOMIC SYSTEMS OF THE COMMONWEALTH (*Editor*)
(1962)

* *All things are changed
and with them we too change.*

Calvin Hoover

Memoirs of Capitalism, Communism, and Nazism

Omnia mutantur nos
*et mutamur in illis.**

Duke University Press
Durham, N. C.
1965

Library of Congress Catalogue Card number 65–24926

Printed in the United States of
America by Kingsport Press, Inc.

To

P. HUBER HANES, JR.

Patron of Research
and Friend

Preface

Fundamentally, these memoirs constitute my appraisal of the economic, political and social systems of capitalism, Communism, and Nazism as I have observed them and lived under these systems. The account of my personal life is offered to facilitate an understanding of the change in my attitude from hostility to old-style capitalism to dedicated support of our current form of modified capitalism. The account is also intended to furnish the basis for an appropriate discount of whatever personal and class bias I have developed.

The portion of the memoirs which describes my contacts with Communism and Nazism makes clear the reasons for my abhorrence of these systems. This abhorrence was the primary motivation for my governmental service, which proved invaluable in my understanding of the problems and processes involved in working out a balance between the power of the state and personal liberty.

It has been difficult to write of my experiences in Intelligence without violating security. I have avoided mentioning any person by name unless the connection with Intelligence was already well known. Some aspects of these experiences must remain secret even though they happened over two decades ago. On the other hand, the passage of time has removed the necessity for secrecy concerning a number of events which were highly classified at the time.

These memoirs have not been "vetted" by any governmental official. There is probably no one official who would have the authority to do so. It would have been impractical as well as unfair to request a number of different governmental officials to take the responsibility for particular portions of the memoirs which deal with Intelligence. I do not believe that the national interest has been impaired by any references in this field in the memoirs.

I am grateful to Duke University for allowing me to live this "double life" for such a large part of the forty years I have been a member of its faculty. I was Chairman of the Department of Economics for twenty years, and for ten of those years I was also Dean of the Graduate School in addition to doing my teaching and research. Consequently, extraordinary broadmindedness on the part of the university administration was required to permit a parallel career in governmental service.

I am deeply grateful to those of my colleagues who have so kindly read portions of the manuscript. My particular thanks are due to Mrs. Dorothy Moore, who has not only typed innumerable drafts but has also served admirably as research assistant. My thanks are also due my neighbor Mrs. Sycho Pickett who typed some drafts of the manuscript.

CALVIN BRYCE HOOVER

Durham, North Carolina
September, 1965

Table of Contents

Memoirs of Capitalism, Communism, and Nazism

Chapter one. *Life in Berwick*

Participant-narrators commonly invoke Vergil, who had Aeneas say, "These things I saw; a great part of them I was." The participant-narrator can only recount the events of history with more or less personal bias. Whatever devices one who writes his memoirs may use to attain the appearance of objectivity and avoid the vice of immodesty, neither characters nor events can be portrayed other than subjectively. If I cannot totally disclaim responsibility for influencing historical events during my lifetime, only rarely was the public aware that my advice was a factor in action by our government. It is, consequently, easier for me to review these actions objectively than for those who received the lion's share of praise or blame.

During the contemporary revolutionary epoch, I came in contact with many of its great, temporarily near-great, or notorious historical figures, J. M. Keynes, Henry Wallace, Chester Davis, Rex Tugwell, Leon Henderson; Generals William Donovan, Walter Bedell Smith, Lucius Clay, and William Draper; Paul Hoffman, Averell Harriman, Allen Dulles; even for fleeting moments with Presidents Roosevelt, Truman, and Eisenhower; Harold Macmillan, Winston Churchill, Adolf Hitler, Nicolai Bulganin, Vyacheslav Molotov, Georgi Malenkov, and Nikita Khrushchev. Yet a host of others had much closer contact with any one of these than did I. My reason for writing these memoirs is not the intimacy of my relations to some of the persons who played great roles during the last three decades. I may claim, however, to have had a more continuing responsibility on the advisory level for more varied areas of our national economic, strategic, and foreign policy for a longer period than have most public figures who have played more direct roles. Because of my responsibility in the area of strategic Intelligence for a considerable part of the time, my activities have sometimes been characterized by a "cloak and dagger" atmosphere which seems particularly incongruous for an academic economist.

As an economist, I have also had an almost unique opportunity to observe, either as a participant or as an analyst, at closest hand the development and functioning of contrasting economic and political systems in Soviet Russia, in Nazi Germany, in the United States, and in Western Europe. I have had the opportunity for intimate and continuous observation of the Soviet system over a longer period than any other foreigner. Thus, not too long ago I found myself quoted by Khrushchev:

> The bourgeois economist, Hoover, in his lifetime, wrote that "if the time comes when Communism can offer a higher standard of life, in point of elementary comforts, to the majority in the working classes of the capitalist countries, an exceedingly serious situation will arise."
>
> Yes, the time has now come when socialism, communism, in addition to the unarguable political and social advantages that it brought people from the very first days of its firm establishment in the socialist countries, is affording them more and more material and spiritual blessings.[1]

Some five years ago, in the course of doing the research for writing *The Economy, Liberty and the State,* I determined to re-examine the political and social as well as the economic changes which have taken place since the turn of the century. I came to realize that some of the most fundamental changes which have taken

1. *Pravda,* May 6, 1960, reporting a speech by Khrushchev before the joint meeting of the two houses of the U.S.S.R. Supreme Soviet, May 5, 1960. Khrushchev's quotation is not textually precise but in substance it was quite correct. The last paragraph of my *The Economic Life of Soviet Russia,* published in early 1931, was as follows:

> "The significance to the capitalistic world of developments in the Soviet Union cannot be exaggerated. If the present crisis is passed, the Soviet Union, within a decade, will be in a position to offer a standard of living which will compare favorably with that of the more poorly paid manual workers in capitalistic countries. Unless in the meantime Capitalism has notably improved its technique of marketing and distribution, so that under-consumption and unemployment can be prevented, and unless the standard of living of such workers in the capitalistic world shall have been materially raised, the World Revolution will begin to make rapid strides."

place were neither solely economic nor even solely institutional but reflected profound shifts in attitudes and values. I decided to examine these changes against the background of my early life when for a couple of decades at the turn of the century the capitalistic system seemed to have reached a never-ending plateau, and when the values of national patriotism were rarely called into question.

It is, I know, still sometimes questioned whether the institutions and processes of American capitalistic society have undergone fundamental change.[2] Nevertheless, it seems to me that there is no longer need to pile up evidence of the basic character of the movement away from old-style capitalism. The transformation in attitudes and value judgments which has accompanied the changes in economic institutions both in the United States and throughout the world are less well recognized. This is due in part to attitudes and value judgments being more easily reversible than changes in economic and political institutions. It is often difficult to say whether the changes in attitude were the cause of the changes in institutions or whether it was the other way around, but the existence of the interrelations is evident. It seems probable, however, that the interaction from attitudes to social institutions is in large degree irreversible as new social institutions nourish the cultures in which originally weak attitudes develop the strength of maturity.

As I observe both the changes since the turn of the century, I find myself in the frame of mind of Tacitus, surveying the Roman scene towards the end of the first century A.D., filled with nostalgia for the virtues of the Republic which no longer existed. The changes in our institutions and the attitudes of the American people towards them which have taken place through the two World Wars, the Great Depression, and the advance of World Revolution are as great and perhaps as catastrophic as those of which Tacitus wrote.

To develop perspective for an understanding of these changes from a world in which capitalism was universal and unchallenged, to one in which capitalism has either been overthrown or greatly changed in all countries, I shall deal with the events of my own life span. I shall also try to analyze the profound shifts in public attitudes during this period, with a parallel account of my own reactions to

2. See my *The Economy, Liberty and the State,* published in 1959 by the Twentieth Century Fund. A new edition was brought out as one of Doubleday's Anchor Books in 1961.

these shifts. In this way it may be possible for the reader to appraise the attitudes and no doubt the prejudices of my value judgments with respect to American capitalism and the Soviet and Nazi economic political and cultural systems.

The changes in my own attitudes and value judgments have by no means always coincided with those of public opinion as expressed either in the existing media of communication or by those persons with whom I was in contact at a particular time. I shall try to recall by an account of my early life in a rural village in Illinois how near to pressing poverty, by the standards of our current affluent society, we all lived. I offer this account as a partial explanation of the diverse changes in values and attitudes which have taken place since that time.

My observations began in the village of Berwick, Illinois, where I was born April 14, 1897. My father was born just five years before the outbreak of the Civil War in Rockingham County in the Shenandoah Valley of Virginia, where he lived until he came to Illinois shortly before I was born. This Southern origin of my family was to condition my early life and to make much easier the transition from the Middle West, where I was born and reared, to permanent residence in North Carolina after I had completed my academic training.

The Shenandoah Valley had been settled, not from "Tidewater Virginia," but by immigrants, mostly "Dutch" and Scotch-Irish, from Pennsylvania and Maryland. These "Dutch," of course, were not Dutch at all, but Germans who belonged to the "Plain People"—the Dunkards, Mennonites, and like religious sects. These "Valley Dutch" were simply an offshoot of the Pennsylvania Dutch and had largely the same hard-working, thrifty habits. Very few owned slaves, since slavery was contrary to their religious principles. My father's family had been bilingual, the old folks still speaking their corrupt Low German even though their ancestors had settled in Virginia before the Revolution. When they spoke English in the home it was with an admixture of Low German expressions. A few nursery rhymes in a German which could hardly be recognized as such survived to my own day.

At least one really Dutch family had somehow got into the valley. My grandmother's father was Tunis Van Pelt, which had also been the name of my first ancestor in this country. Early in the seventeenth century he settled on Staten Island and built a house there which has been only quite recently torn down. How a descendant of his happened to settle in Virginia, I have not the least idea. My father's mother was from an Anglo-Irish family, Cherry-Home. Thus, even though the Valley "Dutch," like the Pennsylvania Dutch, clung tenaciously to their quaint customs, the blending of diverse racial strains into standard "Old American" had already begun.

As a boy, I strove to identify myself with the fictional South of beautiful ladies and chivalric gentlemen who had fought for the "Lost Cause." This identification encountered factual obstacles which perplexed and troubled me. My father's family had not, in fact, belonged to the planter aristocracy (even if such actually existed in Virginia). He used to refer with hostility to "the aristocrats." When I asked him about the Ku Klux Klan, for example, he said it had been used by "the aristocrats" to frighten "poor people."

The anti-aristocratic sentiments of my father's family had not interfered with the enlistment of my relatives in the Confederate Army. (My father had been too young to enlist.) I grew up on tales of my Uncle Joe, who had been a courier for Stonewall Jackson. He worshiped the General's memory, in spite of what apparently had been a constant and not always successful struggle of that stern disciplinarian to compel Uncle Joe to conform to the regulations of the Confederate Army.

He recounted with pride how General Jackson had once ordered him to carry dispatches from the lower to the upper Valley. "I want you to make the fastest ride ever made in the Valley to get this dispatch through," said the General. "How fast must I come back?" asked Uncle Joe. "I don't care when you get back," the General said in angry annoyance; "just get there the fastest a man ever traveled on horseback." According to legend in the Valley, Uncle Joe did deliver that dispatch after the fastest ride ever made. Thereafter, he simply went home and visited his family and friends for a leisurely week. When he reported back to General Jackson, the General shouted, "You damned deserter, I wonder that you dare show your face!" Uncle Joe replied, "You told me to make the fastest trip ever made up the Valley, and I did. I asked you how fast I should come back and you said you didn't care. Well, it took me a little over a week to make the trip back."

I tell the yarn about Uncle Joe and his attitude towards authority as a partial explanation of my own instinctive social sympathies, which to this day remain somewhat schizophrenic. I have never been able to identify myself fully with the upper economic and social classes in spite of the fact that in later life I was to be primarily associated with these groups and with the higher echelons of military authority. My father's economic status strengthened this tendency to think of myself as belonging to the working class rather than to the property-owning classes. This failure to identify myself with "the ruling class" was later to be accentuated when I was to serve as an enlisted man and non-com throughout World War I.

I heard the Union side of the Civil War from "Cap" Fordyce, who had commanded a company of Pennsylvania infantry at Gettysburg. He told me many times how "Pickett's Charge" had rushed a stone wall held by Cap's company. Of the attackers, only a Rebel captain remained alive to reach the wall. "You're my prisoner!" cried Captain Fordyce; and totally unsupported, under Cap's upraised saber, the Confederate captain had surrendered. We invited Cap Fordyce to call when my Uncle Joe visited us, and the former Union captain and Stonewall's courier got on famously. The call was repeated when Uncle Jack, who had ended the war serving with Uncle Joe in Mosby's Guerrillas, was visiting us. The bitterness of defeat still rankled in Uncle Jack after forty years, and he could hardly endure hearing Cap's reminiscences of Gettysburg.

These stories of the Civil War supplemented my reading to foster my patriotic sentiments and yearnings for military adventure, which were considered normal for any boy in the days before World War I. Abstract ideas were little discussed in Berwick, Illinois, anyhow; but pacifism had not really begun to play an important role even in intellectual circles in the United States at this time.

There were not many books, apart from school books, in Berwick. Itinerant book sellers, following some spectacular earthquake or other natural catastrophe, peddled books like one we had at home entitled *The Disaster of Mont Pelee*. There were perhaps a dozen books in the school library in Berwick. These included Prescott's *Conquest of Mexico*, which I read enthralled. A neighbor had a copy of Conan Doyle's *Micah Clarke*, a tale of the rebellion led by the Duke of Monmouth against James II, which I devoured. The son of the largest owner of land in the village loaned me many of the Henty books. The history which I learned thereby may not have been accurate, but these books bred a love for history and provided a historical background which was to be of greatest value to me. I reveled in *King Solomon's Mines* and the other books of Rider Haggard, and in Richard Harding Davis' stories when they later became available.

Berwick had about 150 inhabitants when I was growing up in it. It had once had a somewhat greater number. There were two general stores, a blacksmith shop, and a post office grouped around the village square. There had also been two churches, a Baptist and a Methodist. The congregation of the Methodist church dwindled away, and it was transformed into the Christian church. When I was still a child, this church building was finally closed up and eventually moved away to become a barn. There had also once been two "fraternal societies," the Modern Woodmen and the Odd Fellows. The Odd Fellows finally gave up the ghost like the Methodist church, but the Modern Woodmen, to which my father belonged and which was always referred to as "the lodge," survived until after I had left Berwick. The village school served the surrounding rural area also.

Berwick had been one of the early settlements in Illinois, with most of the settlers arriving from Kentucky. The local satirical tradition, apparently historically correct, had it that Berwick was exactly the same age as Chicago, but had not grown quite as rapidly. The first settlers had evidently expected the settlement to become the county seat, for it was originally called Bowling Green, after the county seat of Warren County in Kentucky. Our county continued to be called Warren, but for some unknown reason, Bowling Green became Berwick when the village lost out to Monmouth as the seat of the county government.

It is a curious circumstance that Berwick's Southern border-state origin continued to dominate its political affiliations long after any consciousness of Southern affinity had vanished. In overwhelmingly Republican "downstate" Illinois and in a county which was even more Republican in sympathy, and in economic institutions tending toward political conservatism, Berwick township invariably voted Democratic right down to the election of President Eisenhower.

It was the custom on election nights to take up a collection, usually amounting to two or three dollars, to induce the local railway station agent to stay up until about midnight and get the returns by telegraph. On election night in 1904, when Alton Parker was the Democratic candidate against Theodore Roosevelt, all of us boys were violent Democratic partisans. The first returns showed Parker leading Roosevelt by a substantial majority. I organized a demonstration, beating pans, tubs, and so on to celebrate the victory. We were "shushed" in great disgust by the older citizens, who informed us that the first reports always came in from the Southern states and that, since there was never any doubt that the Democrats would win there, these early reports meant nothing with respect to how the election was really going. From this humiliating experience there developed my deep and continuing interest in the analysis of regional voting preferences and trends.

The Democratic political affiliation made all the more incongruous the local hostility which we suffered because the family had moved to Berwick directly from Virginia just a year or two before I was born. I can still recall the taunt of "Virginians! Virginians!" flung at us by the other boys and girls in the village school. This use of "Virginian" as a term of opprobrium naturally had the effect of making me identify myself with Virginia even though born in Illinois.

I frequently came home with blackened eyes and covered with blood from fights with older boys. My nose always bled with disgusting ease. My absorption with tales of war and books of romantic adventure had caused me to embrace a very unrealistic code of conduct when confronted by superior force. This Don Quixote code was the more likely to get me into trouble since it included a sense of duty to intervene to protect the weak from the strong. The really severe beatings which I got in consequence did not cure me while I was in grade school, for I was large for my age. I recall that by the time I was in the sixth grade no other boy in school any longer wanted to try to administer what had become almost routine beatings. So I did not learn to make some sort of accommodation to reality, and I was to suffer a really savage beating later when I was in high school and tried to take on two older boys at once. As I shall relate in its place, a rather crude and dramatic demonstration still later in my life that the weak are not always in the right and, moreover, can be devilishly provocative, did bring me to a belated recognition of the facts of life. Yet to this day, the vestigial survival of the code of Don Quixote sometimes threatens to involve me in trouble.

I cannot be sure when I began to regard private property, and particularly private inheritance, as an inherently unjust social institution, but it was as early as when I began to think about it at all. This critical attitude towards property reflected in part the grim struggle, which I witnessed and in which I participated, of my father and mother to feed, clothe, shelter, and educate a family of six children. Our economic status was indeed no more difficult than that of other families who had no income from property. The fact that the family in Virginia had once been land-owning farmers probably was responsible in part for the ambition, shared by my father and mother as well as by my brothers and sisters, that we must all get an education beyond grammar school. Thus, we would be able to keep above the status of ordinary laborers.

The effort to educate six children greatly accentuated the poverty of our family. The necessity for maintaining a status above that of a propertyless laborer sharpened my feeling that the institution of private property and inheritance was socially unjustifiable. The difference in status between land owners and renters in Berwick was very noticeable. I could find no basis in equity for the customary rental contract by which one-half of the crop had to be given to the landlord. I am sure that my father had never read *Progress and Poverty*, but he was at least vaguely aware of Henry George's doctrine that the receipt of rent by landlords constituted a fundamental social injustice.

There were always more would-be renters than there were farms, and in consequence the customary rent began to rise. When I later became an economist, I could understand that this "rack renting" was quite in accord with the operation of the free market, however unfortunate it might be for tenant farmers. I can remember the painful impression it made on my father when a renter had to pay two and one-half bushels of corn per acre above the customary half of the crop in his desperation to obtain a lease even on a very poor farm in the neighborhood.

I was also greatly troubled by this case, but as I pondered the matter, I could see that there would be no socially acceptable solution if all the renters had suddenly been released from the obligation to pay rent. It was obvious that if this should happen, the renters would now begin to receive an "unearned increment" and would themselves become, in effect, landlords. This would have been of no benefit to agricultural laborers or indeed to laborers in any other occupation who would not share in the expropriation of the landlords.

Nevertheless, I felt deeply the unfairness of private property and inheritance in land, and this led me into the path of a kind of primitive socialism. My father took a weekly socialist newspaper called *The Appeal to Reason*, although he always voted the Democratic ticket. I read this rather feeble sheet avidly in spite of the fact that respectable folk referred to it as *The Appeal to Treason.* Although I never became affiliated with the Socialist party, by the time I was entered in high school, I thought of myself as a socialist. I realized, nevertheless, that many of my ideas and sentiments were not in accord with orthodox socialist doctrine and that this was particularly true of the strong national patriotism which I always felt.

In retrospect, as at the time, it is perfectly clear that differences in economic well-being among the 150 inhabitants of Berwick were primarily due to differences in the ownership of property rather than to differences in intelligence, strength, or skill. These differences in the ownership of property in turn depended almost entirely upon inheritance. One would have thought, since the first settlement of Bowling Green and the area around it had taken place only some sixty years before my birth, that I might have been able to view the privilege of inheritance of the wonderfully productive black soil as delayed compensation for the risks and hardships of the original settlers whose immediate descendants had inherited the farm lands around what was now Berwick. There was, however, simply no folk tradition of the early settlement of the area around Berwick which might somehow have provided a historical background for the inheritance of the land. It is doubtful whether, in fact, a single farm within the township was in the hands of descendants of the original settlers. Certainly no farm family in the area had any tradition of the early settlement of the family upon the land.[3]

3. This was in curious contrast to the situation in Virginia. A farm of 600 acres, shrunk from its original 1,100 acres on which an ancestor of mine had become, in 1773, the first white settler, was, although heavily mortgaged, still in the hands of a Hoover, a distant relative, when I visited him in the Shenandoah Valley in 1925.

As in all small towns, watching the passenger trains come in at the railway station was one of our favorite occupations. I can remember returning from rabbit hunting, carrying my .22 rifle on my arm one day as the train came in. I had unfortunately broken the walnut stock of the rifle and had wrapped it in binder twine as a temporary repair. As I stood in my torn blue jeans, gaping at the train, I must have seemed like a character out of an earlier century. I still remember my embarrassment as one of the passengers stared at me and cried out, "Shades of Daniel Boone!"

The boys who lived in Berwick did indeed play at Daniel Boone. We used to hunt in the wooded lands along the creeks around Berwick where we would nostalgically contemplate an occasional mouldering log cabin, wishing that we had been born two or three generations earlier. The earliest settlers did not take up the rich, black, swampy land, which was then covered with rank prairie grass. Only after the land was tiled at a much later date could a plow break this heavy black soil.

I was passionately fond of hunting rabbits and squirrels with a .22 rifle. I remember one bright, crisp fall morning when I was about twelve years old, I left home around six-thirty in the morning and tramped some seven or eight miles through the woods hunting red squirrels. I shot five that day and returned home about three o'clock in the afternoon without having had any lunch. My mother had just finished baking bread and churning butter. She gave me a loaf of bread, hot out of the oven. It was too hot to slice, so I simply broke it open and ate it spread with fresh butter, washed down with buttermilk. I skinned and cleaned the squirrels and we had them in a stew for supper. For sheer joy of living, few other days in my life have matched that one. I felt that I had been born a century too late, for on the frontier, I might have hunted deer and bear as well.

Since our barn was situated next to the railroad station in Berwick, we got to see the circus in the county seat at Monmouth almost every year. When the advance crew for Ringling Brothers or Barnum and Bailey came through, they never failed to pay tribute to the strategic location of our barn as a billboard. It was the custom to offer two free tickets in payment for this advertising privilege. However, the four of us children who were usually at home always gathered around to watch the marvelous lithographs going up and seldom did we fail to get four tickets. The bill posters simply dared not try to divide two tickets among four children who were all so obviously in need of going to the circus. To me, getting those four free tickets always seemed a magical reversal of all normal compensation procedures. We could not possibly have paid for having put on our barn the gorgeous pictures of lions, tigers, elephants, clowns, acrobats, and lovely ladies riding white horses while standing up, even though we could enjoy them for months after the circus had passed on, so the circus paid us!

My father was the local section foreman on the Iowa Central, later the Minneapolis and St. Louis Railway. In the summer, a full-strength section gang consisted of five men. They replaced worn out railway ties, raised "low joints" in the rails with jacks, and laboriously dug out encrusted gravel and "tamped" in loose gravel under the ties. In order to do this, the handle of the shovel had to be moved back and forth while the foot was kept pressed down hard on the top edge of the shovel. On account of this movement, track workers, either in the small local section gangs or the larger "extra gangs" used on new construction, were called "gandy dancers."

The most time-consuming work was to replace the thousands of wooden ties which wore out annually. To do this, a trench had to be picked out in the encrusted gravel alongside the tie to be removed, the spikes removed from the old tie with a "claw bar," a bed for the new tie dug out, the new heavy seasoned oak tie tamped into place and fastened to the rails. This last was done with steel spikes driven in by a spike maul. Heavier physical labor can hardly be imagined.

The "gandy dancers" on a local section gang also mowed weeds and brush on the right-of-way and punched out weeds which grew among the gravel between the rails with a "scuffle hoe." This last was the most tiring and boring job imaginable. It was also hard on the hands, for pushing the "scuffle hoe" against frequently unyielding rocks among the gravel made the palm of the hand exceedingly sore. My father as the foreman was not supposed to work as a laborer. Yet most of the time he had to do so, since otherwise his gang could not have got the work done for which he was responsible.

I began to work as a "gandy dancer" on my father's section gang when I was thirteen years old. I worked for only about two weeks that summer, punching out weeds with the despised scuffle hoe. The next summer I worked as a regular laborer and continued to work the following summers in order that I might go to school for the nine months of the rest of the year.

We worked from seven to six, six days a week, with an hour out for dinner at noon. No time in my life ever passed as quickly as that dinner hour. We usually found shade under the trees in a neighboring pasture. It was heaven to be freed for that hour from exhausting labor in the glare of a Midwestern sun on the steel and gravel of the roadbed, a heaven always marred by the knowledge that at ten minutes after one (my father almost always gave us those illegal ten minutes of extra respite) we would have to go back to work and endure somehow the endless stretch of time until about five-thirty, when we would start back to Berwick on the handcar.

It requires an effort to remember that there could have been so recent a time in the United States when the value of a man depended so nearly exclusively on his muscles and that these muscles were still used so prodigally as a source of energy. But low wage rates made this economical. The handcar was operated by the alternate pushing down and pulling up by the men on wooden bars on opposite ends of the handcar, which carried our heavy tools as well as ourselves. We always had to keep constant vigil for trains coming around curves, for when a train came, we had to lift the car off the track in order to avoid disaster. Five or six men could lift a car off the track easily enough. In the winter, when the gang was cut to only one or two men, it was a back-breaking job.

For this extremely heavy labor, section hands received $1.50 per day plus time and a half for overtime. Overtime was earned when we were called out at night. We would be picked up by a work train and hauled perhaps fifty or sixty miles to the scene of a flood or a train wreck to repair the roadbed. Often we would work all night without food. I do remember once when one sandwich per man was brought out from a nearby town by the railway supervisor. It seemed an unheard of generosity.

I not only worked "on the section" in the summer months, I often worked in the winter months during Christmas vacation or on Saturdays when school was not in session when my father could not get other labor and particularly when a rail had to be changed. We had to cover at least twice a week, all the six and one-half miles of track for which my father was responsible. In the winter the section gang was reduced to only one or two men besides the foreman.

This was, of course, in order to save money, since the railroad company was continually in bankruptcy or on the edge thereof. The book of regulations provided that when a rail must be replaced, a "flagman" must be sent about a mile in each direction to stop all trains. Obviously this could not be done since at best there would have been only one man to do the heavy work of changing the thirty-foot steel rail. It was indeed an almost superhuman task for two men to do it. Yet, when a rail became seriously defective, it had to be changed with only one flagman out in one direction, relying for the rest on a telegraphed message warning train crews to be on the lookout. If a wreck had occurred, my father would undoubtedly have been fired and perhaps brought to trial. The company rule book would have been invoked to prove that he had been sternly forbidden to take such a risk. Yet every foreman knew that he had to take this risk if he wanted to get the work done and so keep his job.

In winter the temperature sometimes got down to 30 degrees below zero. Our breath froze in a white frosting on our faces. We put on all the old clothes we had and wore our overshoes with two pairs of heavy socks with no shoes inside because the tightness of the leather shoes was likely to result in frostbite. As we trudged along, pushing the heavily loaded handcar, because we could not "pump" the car up hill against the bitterly cold wind, I pictured the advertisements of warm, fleece-lined coats with fur collars for sportsmen. I pondered on the paradox that men doing the kind of work in which that kind of clothing was so badly needed could never afford it.

My father received $55.00 a month as foreman. He did not get paid for the overtime which he often had to work. (Fifty-five dollars a month then would be about the equivalent of $170.00 a month in current dollars, correcting for change in the price level.) How did a family of eight live on this? We had about twenty or thirty chickens. My father customarily bought a pig and fed it up and butchered it in the winter. We always had a cow, which I had to milk. Except when the cow was "dry" for a couple of months before she had a calf, we always had milk. My mother churned butter and made wonderful cottage cheese. She, of course, baked our bread, both "light" and "hot." We had peach trees, which bore lots of peaches with a delicacy of flavor which can no longer be experienced now that only those varieties of peaches which ship well are grown. We had a grape arbor from which we got large quantities of the finest Concord grapes I have ever tasted. We picked gallons of blackberries and gooseberries in the woods, which my mother canned, as she did the peaches and the grapes. We had "pie plant," of which there was always more than sufficient for rhubarb pies. We always had plenty of pumpkins from our garden for pies.

Dandelions along the railroad right of way provided greens. We picked wild crab apples and wild grapes in the woods to make the most delicious jelly imaginable. We collected large quantities of walnuts, butternuts, hickory nuts, and hazelnuts in the fall. We got our year's supply of horseradish from a patch growing in the woods near an abandoned log cabin once occupied by an early settler. I knew all the wild strawberry patches along the railroad. There were several different varieties. Some were quite small and grew together on a stem, resembling the delicious *fraises du bois* that I was to know years later in France. Others were larger and softer, but they were all sweeter and more delicately flavored than cultivated berries. There were never enough to can, but sometimes we got enough for a wonderful shortcake made from biscuit dough, which my mother was so good at making.

On Thanksgiving Day we went along with the national fiction that all American families had a turkey for dinner. I do not believe that in fact more than one or two families in Berwick out of some forty ate turkey on Thanksgiving. It was much too expensive. This situation was not, of course, peculiar to Berwick. At the turn of the century and for a considerable time thereafter, certainly not 10 per cent of the population did eat turkey or could have afforded to do so. I never tasted turkey until I was in my teens, but it would have been an unthinkable breach of folk-ways for any of us to have admitted it. In our schoolbooks and in the newspapers, everyone ate turkey on Thanksgiving, and we children all tacitly pretended that this was indeed so.

We had a home vegetable garden with radishes, lettuce, onions, peas, and beans. Besides this, there was a patch of about four acres of surplus land which belonged to the railroad company near the stockyards where cattle and hogs were loaded to be sent to the packing plants in Chicago. The manure from these stockyards was cleaned out every five years or so and dumped on this land, on which my father exercised squatter's rights. He had another garden of about an acre on this land on which he worked after his ten-hour day on the railroad. I also worked on it rather sullenly after school hours. In this garden we raised sweet corn, potatoes, cabbage, and pumpkins. On the remaining three acres my father raised oats and corn by giving half the crop to some farmer who would plow the land and cultivate the corn a time or two. My father had somewhere managed to get hold of an ancient "cradle" which he used with a beautiful, though even then obsolescent, skill to mow the oats and lay the stems in geometrically perfect straight lines. He tied the oats with skilful speed into bundles, using the oats themselves for the ties by means of another out-of-date skill. He also sometimes sowed turnip seed in bare patches in corn fields where the corn planted had not come up.

In the winter our main source of meat was rabbits, with which my father, my older brother, who was a fabulous rifle shot, and I supplied the family. All this makes it appear that we lived an easy life, at least as far as food was concerned. But remember, we had no land on which to pasture the cow, so my father had to pay two dollars per month to a neighboring farmer for this. The sugar which had to be used in canning the blackberries, peaches, and grapes had to be bought. The pig, which became a hog at slaughter time, had to be paid for. Indeed, some supplementary feed had to be bought for the cow and hog and later for the horse which my father purchased so that my sisters could get to the rural schools in which they taught. We could not afford a fully sound horse. The first one we had suffered from a fistula. After this horse died, we bought a blind mare which I used to "graze" along the road to save feed. We raised a couple of fine colts from this mare.

We owned our own small house of six rooms which my father had built with the minimum of help from hired carpenters and other expensive skilled labor. Our barn and other outbuildings he built himself. My father had borrowed $600 from "the Building and Loan" when the house was built, and he was slowly paying this off during all the time I was living at home. Poll taxes and property taxes had to be paid. "Lodge dues," which also covered a small life insurance policy, had to be paid. We got part of our fuel by picking up coal which had fallen off railway cars along the right-of-way, but we had to buy some. We also burned old railway ties, but these were so impregnated with gravel that it was hard to work them into stove lengths without ruining our axe and saw. My father had a cobbler's kit and repaired our shoes by nailing on leather soles which he bought at the store.

Thus, in spite of all this "do it yourself" and raising as much of our food as we could, we were far from self-sufficient. There were two stores at which we bought groceries and paid for them monthly. Each grocer gave a sack of candy when the bill was paid. I cannot describe the joy of our getting two sacks of candy a month. My father bought nothing for himself except for the absolute minimum of clothing and a ten-cent plug of tobacco twice per week. I can remember his remarking once in later years, "This is the first whole orange I ever ate." When we took our dinner along with us to work, my father would often refuse to eat one of our two hard-boiled eggs, insisting that I eat it, because he was "not hungry." We would sometimes supplement what we had in the "dinner bucket" by stewing in a tin can a young rabbit we had killed when mowing weeds, or a chicken which a passing train had killed.

My father suffered from an abdominal rupture, but he never took any time off. He simply knew that he could not afford to be sick, since, of course, there was no sick leave. There was no labor union to protect my father's interests against those of the railroad company. There was no Social Security. There were no paid vacations except for Christmas and the Fourth of July.

Struggling to raise and educate his large family, having to boss an uneducated, often shiftless and unruly section gang, always inadequate in size for the work he was responsible for its doing, I never knew my father to show fear, to be unkind, or to complain. His devotion to duty never faltered. Other parents in Berwick whipped their children "to make them behave." My father never laid a hand on one of his children. Yet he was not in the least indulgent about our behavior. We were judged by a strict moral code. I often envied the other boys who simply got a sound thrashing as the sovereign remedy for the varieties of juvenile delinquency of that day and place. He never scolded. It was the almost unbearable sense of guilt at having broken the code of conduct of a stern but loving father who never broke his that I dreaded.

Like my father, I have always found it hard to be tough

enough to deal with mean or irresponsible men. However, my father's experience as foreman of the railway section gang taught me the unforgettable lesson that in dealing with evil men or with nations led by evil men, a policy of limitless "giving in" is impossible. I resolved at this time that at whatever cost, I would never allow myself to be "walked upon." This resolve was to serve me well.

These recollections of the economy, the attitudes, and indeed, the whole way of life of a family and a village in rural Illinois at the turn of the century furnish only limited support for the romantic nostalgia which one often feels when confronted by the problems and evils of contemporary urban civilization. Life in Berwick was certainly simpler. The struggle for a living was, however, far harsher then than now. I have pointed out that vegetable gardens and family cows did not constitute economic self-sufficiency or an adequate substitute for Social Security.

The injustice inherent in the institution of private property. reflected in the ownership of land by some families and not by others to which I have referred was simply recognized by the community as a fact of life. There was no sentiment, much less any agitation, in favor of any alternative economic system nor even for any governmental aid for the propertyless since there was hardly any knowledge of such alternatives.

Neighbors did indeed know each other in a way which is impossible for urban dwellers in apartment houses. There was some neighborly feeling and some sense of community. The village Baptist church had a yearly Sunday school picnic, in which the meats, pies, cakes, and other food brought by all the families of the church were pooled. I always felt that our family of eight came out much ahead by this arrangement. There were sack races, potato races, and other typically rural games.

On Christmas Eve there was a Christmas tree at the church with "exercises." Everybody brought their presents to the tree for distribution, with the names of the recipients called out by an announcer. The unequal number of gifts received was one of the first evidences of the difference in incomes attendant upon the institution of private property and inheritance which came to my attention. However, the practice of the church of providing a bag of mixed candy for each girl and boy seemed a kindly means for the scriptural "tempering the wind to the shorn lamb." Since there were six of us "shorn lambs" in our family, this primitive form of "transfer payment" with which I became acquainted at this time, and which later became explicit in our Social Security system, seemed quite generous.

There was also bitter personal envy and even hatred in the village, in spite of much good neighborliness. One Christmas Eve when I was eleven years old, my older sister put a "Henty book" on the church Christmas tree for me. I could not wait until I got home to unwrap it, and I saw that it had the title, *Among Malay Pirates*. I did not wait for the festivities to come to an end, but hastened home, lit the lamp on the table by the stove and began to read, with what enjoyment and absorption you will see in a moment.

When the rest of the family got home, they cried out in amazement. The room in which I was reading was full of smoke and the odor of kerosene. A large hole had been burned in the carpet, and the bottle in which the incendiary had brought the kerosene to burn down the house was lying on the floor. I had noticed none of these things. Fingerprint procedures were quite unknown, and no one thought of trying to find them on the kerosene bottle. My father and mother supposed that the incendiary was a man who had been passed over when my father was made section foreman on the railroad, but we never did really know whether this was so.

In spite of the woods, fields, and creeks and the hunting and fishing which they afforded, life in Berwick was very boring to me. Compared with urban youth who are now forbidden by child labor laws from working, and who are not able to hunt and fish or to carry on the other activities available to us, we were of course, in this respect, fortunate. The heavy physical labor which became my lot at a very early age did substitute fatigue and even exhaustion for boredom. If it were not for this, time would indeed have hung heavy on my hands.

My own reaction was a desperate hope to get away from Berwick into the world of which I read in books. I wanted to see far places and to have the adventures which both historians and novelists agreed had happened to men through the ages. It had apparently been my misfortune, however, to be born into an age in which nothing ever happened. The frontier had passed away. There were no longer wars, revolutions, or indeed, any opportunities for adventures at all. Capitalism, with its creed of hard work and respectability and its economic institutions which seemed to be widening the spread between those with and those without property had expanded over the whole world and could be presumed to be immortal. I never gave up my dreams of escape to a different world but always I had the gnawing fear that perhaps that other world was no longer there.

Never, of course, could anyone have been more mistaken. The society which seemed so unforgivably stable and dull has turned out to be characterized by successive convulsions and catastrophes. Yet living now in a world in which the survival of man is in gravest doubt, I confess my deep thankfulness that I escaped from the narrow and stable world into which I was born.

Chapter two. *Educational prelude to World War I: history begins to move again*

Since villages the size of Berwick did not have high schools, and since at that time there were no rural consolidated high schools with buses to provide transportation, getting a high-school education was as difficult as if I had been faced at once with paying for a college education. The only thing to do was to attend the high school in Monmouth, the county seat, distant some twelve miles from Berwick, even though non-residents had to pay tuition. It was, however, out of the question for my sister and me to pay cash for board and room and other living costs in addition to tuition. Hence, we resorted to numerous expedients. For some months we drove by horse and buggy six miles to an interurban car line and thence another six miles to Monmouth.

In the dead of an Illinois winter, this two stage round-trip of twenty-four miles per day was just not feasible. My sister got a job for the remainder of the school year, helping a family in Monmouth with housework for her board and room. A job in a boarding house paid for my board and a small windowless room, in which a cot was the only furniture. I got up at five o'clock and fired the furnace and then helped to serve breakfast to some thirty boarders. Afterwards the dishes had to be washed, the bedrooms cleaned, and the beds made. I helped serve dinner and supper and wash the dishes. I did these and other chores when I was not in high school. Fortunately, there were "study periods" during the school session in which I could prepare my work. My "contract" provided for one hour off per day in addition to the time when I was in school. The day ended for me at 10:30 P.M. when, under the supervisory eye of Mrs. Nash, the boarding-house keeper, I banked the furnace for the night.

The next year my sister and I rented one good sized room in a home a few blocks from the high school. We divided the room into two by means of a heavy curtain on a wire. We brought most of our food from home over the weekends. We had "cooking privileges" in the kitchen of our landlord. My sister graduated from high school that year, and this arrangement was then given up. Fortunately, for the next two years the M. & St. L. Railway, for which my father worked, provided me with a "pass" so that I could live at home, taking the passenger train back and forth every day.

I have gone into some detail in the matter of how it was possible at that time to get a high-school education, since viewed in the light of the current *mores* of our affluent society, our family income could not possibly have covered the expenses involved. Yet all six of us children did manage to get some education above the grade-school level. Even with the expedients to which we resorted, this was possible only by means of a sort of pooling of the family income. As soon as my sisters had graduated from high school, they began to teach in the rural schools of the country. Apart from one summer when I worked as a hired hand for a Swedish farmer near Berwick, I worked every summer as a laborer on my father's section gang.

Although Monmouth had a population of only some eight thousand, I nevertheless felt all the shyness and insecurity of a country boy in the city. This feeling was accentuated by our poverty. I can remember my embarrassment when one of my classmates noticed the pieces of harness strap which my father had tacked over the holes in the soles of my shoes. This feeling of insecurity produced a sense of personal identification with the underprivileged in society at the time and a continuing sympathy with them which was never to leave me even after I had become a member of what might be considered the privileged classes.

Full assimilation into the everyday juvenile world around me was also prevented by my persistent effort to identify current life with the world of which I avidly read in novels and histories. In the novels, at least, the heroes always bested the villains, whatever the odds. In the histories as written, the right also seemed eventually to triumph, and the right was always on *our* side. All this did nothing to cure the Don Quixote complex which had won me many a beating in Berwick.

In Monmouth there existed a sort of low-level "town and gown" feud between the boys in high school and the local pool-room denizens of about the same age who did not attend high school. As I was returning from lunch one day, I came upon two local toughs beating up a high-school boy who, like myself, came from the country. Both the hooligans were older and larger than the boy who was being taunted and beaten. I intervened, and totally unlike the way such affairs always turned out in the Horatio Alger juvenile books of the day, got the beating of my life. If the smaller boy had stayed to help me, I would not have fared so badly, but he at once took to flight.

The two toughs, who had at once slipped on brass "knucks," blacked and closed both my eyes, bloodied my nose, and severely slashed my face. I was blood from head to foot; a piece of my upper lip was cut loose and hung down over my lower lip. Although I was able to inflict little damage on my opponents, I hung on grimly until a crowd gathered and the two hooligans slipped away. Although a number of high-school students were in the crowd which gathered, prudently enough, they did not intervene in the fight.

The high-school boys in the crowd did lead me to the chemistry laboratory at the high school where one of the instructors sponged me off with alcohol. When the instructor could see what the damage was, he insisted that I be taken to a surgeon who sewed my upper lip back together again. I still carry the scar. Even this experience did not cure me of the Don Quixote complex, however. I shall describe later how I did get cured, or at least acquired some degree of immunity to it.

During the summer of 1914 I was able to find a job on the railroad which paid slightly better than that of a section hand. This was particularly desirable since I planned to enter Monmouth College in the fall. I became timekeeper on an "extra gang" of some eighty men. These extra gangs were composed of "Bums" (native Americans), "Dagoes" (Italians), "Greasers" (Mexicans), or Greeks (for some reason there was no nickname for the Greeks). Everyone lived in bunk cars, but the foreman and I did have a bunk car to ourselves.

This was the period when our annual immigration reached its peak at about a million a year, consisting largely of the new immigrants from Southeastern Europe. At the present time, with hard-core unemployment in the United States of several million men, it seems strange that a million immigrants a year could have been absorbed during the immediate pre-World War I period without causing a crisis. There were no labor unions among unskilled railway workers at that time, however, so the large supply of labor could keep the market price low enough to absorb it. Some railroads were indeed hard put to it to obtain the volume of workers which they wanted.

My earnings from a summer as timekeeper did enable me to enroll in Monmouth College that fall. A succession of jobs as waiter and dishwasher in various restaurants provided meals. I eventually received a small scholarship which paid for part of my tuition. The next summer I sold aluminum from door to door, and the next year I peddled maps. A small loan from a kindly member of the faculty saw me almost through my junior year, which I interrupted to enlist in the U. S. Army about a month after our entry into World War I.

During my three years at Monmouth College, I had begun to shed my feelings of insecurity and my feeling of being different. Here at last was a world of intellect in which to be interested in knowledge for its own sake was not to be thought queer. Monmouth was one of five United Presbyterian colleges, and the denominational ties were close. The fathers of the students, for the most part, were farmers, preachers, doctors, and small merchants. Nevertheless, social cleavage existed among the students, represented by those who belonged to fraternities and sororities and those who did not. Quite naturally, I belonged to the non-fraternity group. I continued during college years to think of myself as a socialist. I had no realization as yet of the connection between a statized economy and authoritarianism. It took the years in the army which were just ahead of me to bring about this realization and for me to develop a hearty dislike for arbitrary authority.

College life at Monmouth attempted to model itself upon the image of the Ivy League colleges of the Northeast. This meant, among other things, the customary emphasis upon football, in which, however, the necessity for earning a living did not permit me to participate. Monmouth was coeducational, and in the second year I met my future wife, who was to provide, in addition to inspiration, both the support for my self-confidence and the balance wheel which I so badly needed. We participated in the picnics, parties, and other college activities which made college life so pleasant in an age when academic standards were not so rigorous and when the educational pressure of competition with the Soviets in the field of the sciences was generations in the future.

Yet the strange thing is that the intellectual level at Monmouth was nevertheless high. The student body through some informal process had managed to select itself so that the average student was, I should think, decidedly superior to the average in the typical large university of the present day. The faculty was by no means so well trained as the faculty of a modern university. There was almost no published research by the faculty. Yet colleges like Monmouth did supply a much larger proportion of the graduate students who were to furnish the future faculties of the great American universities than did those universities themselves. The professor of chemistry at Monmouth had such a phenomenal record in stimulating students to continue their studies in graduate schools that he was eventually elected President of the American Chemistry Society in recognition of his achievement even though he had published very little.

Perhaps the main reason that so many undergraduates from small liberal arts colleges went on to graduate school and eventually became university professors was a negative one. Since these colleges had no professional schools, a student could become neither an engineer, a lawyer, nor other specialist. When he graduated, he had indeed no immediately marketable skills for which he could expect to be paid at the level appropriate to his years of study. Furthermore he was not likely to have the contacts which would give him entry even at the lower levels of the corporate hierarchy. In those days there were no recruiters such as swarm annually on every university campus seeking talent for the ever-growing bureaucracies of the great American corporations. By contrast, the student of the small liberal arts college could find out from his professors how to get into graduate school. Once he got an advanced degree, there were regular channels by which he could enter academic life.

Why was the educational process at small liberal arts colleges like Monmouth so effective in spite of quite modest physical facilities, and a relatively low pressure to spend the maximum number of hours on highly organized and formalized course work? First of all, the students wanted to learn and most of them took the courses which they thought were of value to them, not simply those which were the easiest. In later years when I became Dean of the Graduate School at Duke, I was to look over the transcripts of students applying for admission and to ask despairingly, "How could a man graduate from any college or university with so few courses of substance?" In such cases, the very minimum of work in the sciences, mathematics, history, and languages would have been taken. Obviously, courses chosen had been those which were considered the easiest or perhaps the "most interesting." At Monmouth this was not so, partially because only courses with "guts" were required and these made up a large part of the curriculum, partially because the college could not afford the proliferation of courses in each department which has become the curse of modern American higher education, but also partially because the typical student at Monmouth seemed to realize that he was investing four years of his life and he did not wish to waste those years on courses with a minimum of content.

Second, students had leisure in which to think. It was not assumed at Monmouth that the only way to get students to accomplish anything was to fill all their time with assigned readings and other prescribed chores so that they would not be able to waste their time. On the contrary, it was assumed that the student might think a bit on his own and read books which were not required in his courses. Consequently, even with the necessity for earning a living on the side, the three prewar years at Monmouth afforded me a really delightful opportunity to think, to read, and to discuss, even though we were left in no doubt about the necessity for doing a thoroughly respectable level of work in our courses.

Whether this sort of system—or lack of it—would work in today's colleges and universities, I doubt. A huge superstructure of extracurricular student activities, dances with "name bands," weekends in Florida, and the like, does seem to require a much more rigorous monitoring of students' lives and rigidly policed course work than exsited at Monmouth. If somehow we could get rid of the masses of students who do not really want to learn but only wish to have the prestige of a college or university education, perhaps we could restore an academic world in which students would have the responsibility and freedom of educating themselves.

In college I was able to make those warm friendships which have always meant so much to me. Hugh Williamson, a future corporation attorney in New York City; John French, who was to become a public school teacher; Bruce Gillis and John Lyons, who were to become ministers of the United Presbyterian church; George Story, later in civil service; Ellis Bell, later a business executive and a colonel in World War II, were my boon companions in college. In spite of having simultaneously to work for a living and to study, I talked, kidded, and loafed. College life with these wonderful fellows was for me a magnificent romp, as indeed it should be for everyone. Almost without exception they were to follow me into the army when the United States entered the war. We went through the war together, and we kept up our friendship through life.

I had been tremendously excited when I read of the assassination of the Archduke Ferdinand at Sarajevo in late June, 1914. In spite of the foreboding which I had of the tragic events which were to follow, to me it meant that history was under way again. From the beginning, I was a passionate adherent of the Allied cause. Looking backward, I realize that I swallowed whole the Allied propaganda line. To me as to most of the American public, it was indeed a war in defense of Western civilization against the militarism of the Kaiser. The fact that Tsarist Russia was one of the Allies was awkward but could be conveniently overlooked. From the opening moment of the war, I favored maximum aid by the United States to the Allies, and I quickly came to advocate our entrance into the war. I was completely disgusted with President Wilson when he talked about our being "too proud to fight."

We whistled "Tipperary" and believed the legend that the tiny British Expeditionary Force, after administering a rebuff to the German invaders, had carried out the heroic retreat from Mons and had then taken the major role in turning back the German army from the gates of Paris. To us the French armies, for all their dependence on the British, were always gallant and romantic, and we thrilled to *Madelon* and to a more sentimental song turned out by our Tin Pan Alley, which went, "Come lead your troops to victory, Joan of Arc, they are calling you!" I read every line of war news in newspapers and magazines. I also read every obtainable account of personal experiences in the war zones, such as Sergeant Guy Empey's *Over the Top*!

Now, after living through and participating in two and a half wars, I reflect upon the catastrophes which followed World War I. On the eve of World War I, the lot of the common man had been growing continually better, and the political power of his duly elected representatives in the national legislatures ever greater. This despite the fact that capitalist society had attained a peak of prosperity and of arrogant ostentation in bourgeois living in all countries. In Russia the Tsar had been compelled by the Revolution of 1905 to set up the Duma. In Germany the political power of the Social Democrats was growing in spite of the social security legislation initiated as a kind of back fire by Bismarck. In Britain Lloyd George was pushing forward his program of social legislation. In the United States Wilson had been elected President to the dismay of businessmen and was enacting legislation designed to curb monopoly and to prevent financial panics.

If World War I could have been prevented, there would have been no Bolshevik Revolution, no World War II. Peaceful economic and social progress could have gone forward without major violence and without the establishment of totalitarian dictatorships. It is one thing to ask what would have happened had there been no World War I; it is quite another question to ask what would have happened had the United States stayed out of the war.

I have asked myself many times whether it would have been better if we had remained neutral. The Germans, of course, would have won. German world hegemony would have been established. The Bolshevik Revolution might not have happened, and if it had, the German government would never have permitted a Soviet regime to rule Russia. There would have been no Stalin, but there would not have been a Hitler either. Would not German hegemony have been a moderate price to have paid if the world could have been saved from these two men of blood?

Yet the thought of a world dominated by an imperial Germany is abhorrent. One cannot believe that the world would have peacefully endured such a rule. We would not only have had reaction, but we would almost certainly have had wars and revolutions as well. The conclusion is that we can never hope to win liberty in perpetuity by winning one final war, but we must always be prepared to resist the threat of the tyrant in each succeeding generation.

When President Wilson declared war on Germany on April 6, 1917, I at once felt the necessity for personal participation. It was not merely a matter of "doing some sort of war work." I felt that having argued on the campus for our active entry into the war, I had a moral obligation which could be fulfilled only by exposing myself to the hazard of wounds and death. I realize now that I was dramatizing myself and that in all probability no one would have taken much notice of what I did. I did consider entering the American Ambulance Service in France, but I came to the conclusion that it would be immoral for me, under the circumstances, to choose a non-combatant's role, even though I would be exposed to some personal risk.

My enthusiasm for the Allied cause had been immensely strengthened by the overthrow of the Tsarist government in March, 1917. I still considered myself a socialist. As events moved swiftly, and Alexander Kerensky, the Socialist Revolutionary, became Premier of the Provisional Government, proclaiming his determination to intensify the Russian war effort against the Germans, it seemed to me that now the issue was clear cut—on one side the forces seeking to advance the cause of democracy, to improve the lot of the common man and to banish war from the earth; on the other the forces of reaction.

By now, it had become impossible for us to settle down to our studies. I made application to enter the first officers' training camp at Fort Sheridan, Illinois. I knew that I was nine months below the minimum age at which I could be commissioned. Consequently, I put down my birth date on the application form as April 14, 1896, instead of 1897. When I came to sign it, however, I changed the date back to the correct one. Illogically enough, I decided that I would lie if necessary in order to get in the army but not in order to get a commission.

I sent the application form in anyway and received back a kindly letter from an officer of the regular Army who strongly advised me to wait nine months and to apply again at that time. However illogical and romantic my enlistment as a private instead of waiting and taking training for a commission may have been, it should be noted that six other college friends who could easily have won commissions by attending officers' training camps made the same decision and enlisted in the same outfit as did I on the same day. My decision was in accordance with the romantic and patriotic ethic of that day, however silly it might seem today.

My father, however, sorrowfully resisted my intention to enlist. "I remember the young men who enlisted in the Confederate Army when I was a boy in the Shenandoah Valley," he said. "They never came back. Some who waited to be conscripted did survive. If you will wait until you are drafted, I won't complain, but don't enlist." But I couldn't wait. Together with five or six classmates, I enlisted in the local company of the National Guard, Company H, 6th Illinois Infantry, already in federal service, then doing guard duty some sixty miles away at the Rock Island Arsenal.

Chapter three. *In the army: a passage to Britain*

Rock Island Arsenal, operated by the Federal Government, was located on an island in the Mississippi River, surrounded on the river banks by the "Tri-Cities"—Davenport, Iowa, and Moline and Rock Island, Illinois. The Second Battalion of the 6th Illinois Infantry, of which Company H was a part, had been assigned to guard the Arsenal immediately upon the declaration of war upon Germany by the United States. A company of "regulars" were in barracks on the island, but we had absolutely no contact with them. They were principally engaged in mowing the fairways of the golf course which the Officers' Club maintained on the island in co-operation with the Tri-Cities Country Club. During the three months we were stationed on the island, I never saw them engaged in any military activity whatever, not even guard mount or close-order drill. They were doubtless representative of what a professional army tends to become during a long peace.

The island had been used as a prison camp for captured Confederates during the Civil War. A well-kept military cemetery, with something over nineteen hundred neat identical headstones, carved with the prisoners' names and their regiments, was a monument to those who had died in a smallpox epidemic. I examined the headstones to see whether I could find the names of any of my relatives, but I did not. I used to ponder in this cemetery the old German justification for taking up the sword in defense of liberty, "*Der Gott der Eisen wachsen liess, Der wollte keine Knechte!*" It was all very well to say that God would not have created iron if he had wished men to be slaves. My relatives in the Confederate Army, however, would never have agreed that they had fought to maintain slavery, but would have argued that they had risked their lives to maintain Southern independence. Perhaps in this war, too, I meditated, German soldiers might think they were fighting in defense of their freedom.

We had to go on guard duty every other day, with the off day devoted to close-order drill, which meant unutterable boredom. Although we remained on Rock Island Arsenal only for a little over two months, it seemed forever. Was this going to be the way in which I was to fight the war to save the world for democracy? The news left no doubt how badly the Allies needed additional troops. The failure of the Neville offensive by the French, the ghastly losses of the British at Ypres and on the Somme, the failure of the Russian offensive which Kerensky had launched against the Germans, while never fully disclosed in our newspapers now that we were in the war on the side of the Allies, made it plain that there was sterner work to be done than guarding arsenals.

I rejoiced when we received orders to leave the island and proceed to Springfield, Illinois. After joining the other battalions of the regiment there, we were ordered to Camp Logan, Houston, Texas, where we were to become a part of the 33rd Division, made up entirely of National Guard regiments from Illinois. Camp Logan was located in a forest of scrub pines not far from Buffalo Bayou, some ten miles from Houston.

No cantonments had been constructed to house the troops, only wooden mess halls, warehouses, and the like. A number of these military training camps had been located in Texas in the belief that the mild climate would facilitate training and permit the use of tents as shelter for the troops. The idea was sound enough, but no veteran of that winter would subscribe to the phrase "mild climate." It was the coldest winter in Texas in twenty years. Some of the teenage natives of Houston had never before seen snow. Yet we had several substantial snowstorms that winter. In our tents we had only Sibley stoves, which were like small inverted funnels of thin sheet iron. There had been no provision for fuel, except for what we could pick up in the surrounding woods, the debris from previous construction activities. We were not provided with straw for our bed sacks, and since we slept on canvas cots, I found to my astonishment that one could get very cold on one's back. We did eventually get both fuel and straw for our bed sacks.

There was bad blood between Major-General Bell, the Commander of our 33rd Division, and General Pershing, alleged to be due to Pershing's having been elevated in rank over Bell, in spite of Bell's seniority. General Bell was fiercely determined that his division would be a credit to him, and he put his whole heart and mind into getting the division ready for service overseas. Alas, he worked under great handicaps. To begin with, there had been no artillery regiments in the Illinois National Guard. The cavalry regiment was converted into the 122nd Field Artillery, and an entirely new regiment, the 124th Field Artillery was created. Our regiment of infantry was converted into the 123rd Field Artillery. We were supposed to be armed with French 155 howitzers, the two other regiments with French 75's. My survival may have depended upon our conversion from infantry to artillery. The losses of our infantry regiments overseas were to be very heavy; the losses of our artillery relatively light.

No 75's or 155's whatever were available for training. Indeed, there were no instructors available who were acquainted with the system of fire used by the French army, even had the pieces been available. Our officers were given some instruction in firing the obsolete three-inch guns with which our peacetime army had been equipped. This instruction was all but useless. There were, I believe, four of these old three-inchers in the division, but I never saw them. Close-order drill, calisthenics, and long marches did harden us, and there was some small-arms practice on the target range.

I had been made a corporal soon after arrival in Camp Logan, and I began to accumulate experience about the way in which an authoritarian system worked. This was eventually to disillusion me completely with socialism as an economic and political system. I began to realize that an organization of society run by the state was likely to have a built-in tendency towards authoritarianism. Certainly in an army neither personal liberty nor democratic control was possible. For example, each officer responsible to higher authority for his unit practiced a kind of Gresham's Law in reverse. According to age-old army custom, he kept his good men and sent off the bad whenever any of his men were requisitioned for whatever purpose. Confronted by a requisition for man-power, every company commander, aided by his top sergeant, mentally lined his company up from best to worst and simply chopped off the worst end to fill the requisition. By contrast, in a capitalistic market economy, employers would have had to bid to see which one would secure the more able employees since they would have been free to seek the most attractive employment opportunity.

About this time two of my closest friends from Monmouth College, Hugh Williamson and John French, came to Houston and enlisted—Hugh in Headquarters Company of the 123rd Field Artillery to which I had been transferred from Battery D; John in the 58th Brigade Headquarters Company. John, who was almost blind in one eye, passed the army physical examination by memorizing the optical test chart.

By this time voluntary enlistment had just about dried up and the draft had been in operation for some time. It has eventually proved necessary in all of our major wars to resort to conscription, but World War I was the last war in which voluntary enlistment played even a preliminary role of any importance. There was some antagonism among the regular Army with its divisions numbered below ten, the National Guard with its divisions numbered from twenty through forty, and the national army with its divisions numbered above seventy. An old Civil War ditty was revived and produced an occasional brawl:

> They issue us soap and a wire brush,
> To scrub behind our ears;
> We ain't gonna fight, by a hell of a sight—
> We're the handcuff volunteers.

Gradually the regular Army divisions as well as the National Guard divisions, which originally had entirely consisted of volunteers, had to be brought to wartime strength with conscripts. Eventually almost all replacements were from the national army and the distinctions were largely forgotten.

In the early months of the war, there had been a number of former soldiers of our regular Army who could not resist the prospect of action. Most of these men had sworn they would never, never enlist again. There were usually two or three of these men in any battalion. I remember one old sergeant who said, "Any man can make a mistake once, and it shouldn't be held against him. But if you ever see a man who has *re-enlisted,* you can be sure he is no good." "But this is your fourth enlistment, isn't it?" I asked. "Yes," said he, "I am no damned good!" He went on to recall his participation in the Allied relief of the legations in Peking during the Boxer Uprising in 1900. He recalled with nostalgia the gorgeous loot after the Allied take-over of Peking. He told how soldiers concealed scores of yards of the finest silk around their bodies under their uniforms. He pulled a tiny lady's silk handerchief out of his pocket and crushed it in his fist. When he opened his hand, the confined silk leaped out, retaining its vitality after all the years. "That is what I have to show for four enlistments!"

I have never seen a more soldierly figure than our own old soldier—Sergeant Andy Gillespie. He also had participated in the relief of Peking and had fought in the Philippine Insurrection. We never tired of hearing him recount his experiences in the pacification of the Moros. An American Company of the 9th Infantry had been treacherously attacked and massacred in its mess shack by the Moros. One survivor, the cook, who had been carving an ebony baseball bat when the attack occurred and hence had been able to fight his way out, reached regimental headquarters to report the massacre. Andy was with the relieving column which reached the scene a few days later. Andy was not in the least a boaster, but he recalled with grim pride that, although the Americans of the massacred company had not been able to fire a shot, yet there were two or three bodies of natives for each of the American dead. He also related with satisfaction and to our horror how after an American relieving column had arrived, the natives had been invited into a parley and then had been mowed down by rifle fire from ambush. He justified this action by saying that when the attack came, all the natives pulled out arms which they had concealed under their clothing for use in another surprise attack.

In November, 1917, the success of the Bolshevik Revolution had completed the demoralization of the old Russian army as a fighting force against the Germans. On the one hand, this increased the urgency of moving American troops to France to bolster the Allied forces against an expected German offensive, reinforced by forces released from the now dormant Eastern Front. On the other hand, it began to cause concern for the discipline among Allied troops. This concern was accentuated by the refusal of the small

Russian troop contingents in France to continue to fight and still more by actual mutinies among French troops themselves. A program of tightening discipline was begun. All of us non-coms were marched down to an auditorium in Houston to hear a colonel from the British army give a lecture on the necessity for discipline. He referred to the demoralization of the Russian army and to its tragic aftermath in the defeat of the Kerensky offensive of early July, 1917.

I was recommended for officers' training camp about this time, but again was too young by a few days. I was to be similarly recommended on three other occasions in France, but by a curious series of events, I was not to be able to take training for a commission on these occasions either. Although not getting a commission meant the war was a far tougher experience for me than it otherwise would have been, I am now profoundly thankful that I did not. If I had been commissioned, I rather think this might have brought me over definitely to the side of the "haves" instead of the "have nots." I was left between the private soldier and the officer in the "in-between world" of the non-commissioned officer.

Psychologically this in-between world of the non-com was not a comfortable world for me. On the one hand, it was perfectly clear that, released from all the normal sanctions of home life and the discipline of earning a living on the farm, in industry, or in an office, the young men who made up the army must have firm and even stern discipline. The enforcement of this discipline depended, in the first instance, upon the non-coms. This was distasteful to me. In particular, I opposed every recourse to physical brutality which often is used to supplement other means of maintaining discipline.

I resented the doctrine, inherited from the British and other European armies, that officers were gentlemen and enlisted men were not. In Europe this military caste system of discipline had been inherited from feudalism. It even implied that there was an ethnic difference between the gentlemen officer and the non-gentle enlisted man. No doubt in England in medieval days, for example, it was assumed that the officer was from the gentry, and hence possessed of some Norman blood. Nevertheless, even armies of revolutionary origin have found it necessary to retain the concept of an officer caste. This was true of Cromwell's New Model Army which overthrew the Royalists of Charles I. The *sans culotte* armies which so successfully defended the French Revolution against the armies of the reactionary monarchs of Europe had also found it necessary to retain this special class status of the commissioned officer. The Russian Bolsheviks, after utterly destroying the discipline of the Imperial Russian Army, quickly created an even more ruthless discipline for their Red Army.

Leon Trotsky has expressed in *My Life* more succinctly than anyone else the final sanction upon which the discipline of armies rests: "So long as those malicious tailless apes . . . the animals we call men, will build armies and wage wars, the command will always be obliged to place the soldiers between possible death at the front and the inevitable one at the rear." He was to give evidence of his belief in this doctrine when, as Commissar of the Red Army, he ordered the execution of every tenth man in a regiment drawn from the working class which had retreated against orders during the Civil War in Russia. By the end of World War II when I was to come in contact again with Soviet troops, the privileged status of officers and the ruthlessness of discipline greatly exceeded that of our own army.

Even with this record of the universality of the privileged status of officers in all armies, I resented it and came to have a feeling of antagonism to officers as a class. This developing sense of antagonism to the officer class was, to some extent, in conflict with my patriotic feelings and with my sense of responsibility for keeping order and getting things done. This feeling on my part was not uncommon among non-coms.

The private soldier disliked both officers and non-coms, but with a difference. He disliked officers as belonging to a different caste. He disliked non-coms more intimately, because they exerted authority over him even though they were from the same class. The worst mistake possible was for either an officer or a non-com to attempt to court popularity among the men. It was easy to attain contempt in this way, but never liking or respect. This attitude was to undergo change when the front was reached; then those officers who proved themselves professionally competent did come to be respected while the incompetent were held in contempt.

On May 1, 1918, orders were issued for the 33rd Division to begin its movement overseas. In actual fact the movement of the entire divison to the port of embarkation at Hoboken, New Jersey, required about a month. On May 26 we embarked on the old Canadian-Pacific liner *Scotian,* manned by the British navy, for Liverpool.

We sailed in a convoy of about a dozen ships in which the speed was, of course, determined by the slowest ship. Consequently, the voyage lasted some twelve days. I can recall the odor of the *Scotian*'s bilges to this day. A ship of some six thousand tons burden, she carried our entire artillery brigade. The men were crammed into the hold of the ship where they slept in hammocks, slung so closely that they touched. Fortunately, as non-coms, we were berthed only six men to a cabin, but even in our cabin the air was more than a little ripe. Food was adequate in quantity but fearfully greasy. When we complained about the marmalade, which in accordance with British taste was made from bitter Seville oranges, our British mess boy was enraged. "Just wait until you get in the trenches and get nothing but that plum and turnip jam to put on your hard bread!" he cried. We kidded him by explaining solemnly that while in the course of combat we well knew we might sometimes be short of food, when our army did get food to us it was always the very finest—roast turkey, steaks, and the like. The Lord forgive us!

When we sailed into the harbor of Liverpool, the Mersey estuary was lined with ships which had been torpedoed but which it had been possible to beach. They were repaired as rapidly as possible, but sinkings had been high and repair facilities were strained far beyond capacity. We were consequently arriving at a time when food was very short, and we had good reason to realize it during the some ten days we spent in England. Small boys ran along our columns as we marched through the slums of Liverpool, offering to carry bits of our equipment. Although these offers were declined, the troops tried to converse with the boys and were baffled to hear them speaking a dialect which they could understand only with the greatest difficulty or even not at all. They asked the boys where we were going, and the boys replied "Knotty Ash," the name of the camp to which we were being marched. Since the boys rendered this as "Nutty Ass," the troops were baffled and wondered whether they were being kidded. Several soldiers even asked me whether this was not England after all, but perhaps France.

We stayed several days at "Knotty Ash," where to our dismay we were put on British garrison rations, which amounted to about 2,000 calories per day. To troops who had been consuming from 3,500 to 4,000 calories, this first experience with actual food shortage was something of a shock. While the American press had reported

German advances which had not yet been halted, Allied losses had been minimized and we were quite unprepared for the thought that we might be losing the war. This uneasy thought was brought home to us by a British veteran who had been discharged for severe wounds after service in the muddy horror of Flanders. "We can't win," he would cry, as he harangued a circle of American soldiers who gathered around him. "At the bloody front, it's just like shoving pigs into shit." We were glad to leave Knotty Ash. We proceeded to a camp to wait for embarkation to France from Southampton. The "rest camp" was at Wimbledon, which in honor of British garrison rations was christened "Camp Dwindle Down."

After the Armistice we were to hear tales of brawls that started when a British soldier would ask an American whether AEF stood for "After Everything's Finished," and the American would reply, "No, it stands for 'After England Failed.'" When we were passing through England, it was quite clear that everything was not finished. Our relations with British troops were excellent and continued to be so in France when our infantry trained and fought by the side of the British.

We embarked for France on a converted British destroyer, tightly packed with troops. We had had no dinner, but our mess sergeant was issued a few crackers and a small hunk of cheese to be divided among the some fifty men of our 2nd Battalion Headquarters detail. The piece of cheese was so small that after vainly trying to divide it, the sergeant, in frustration, cried out, "I can't divide this damned cheese into fifty pieces. Any one who has the nerve to cut himself a piece, go ahead." I don't know what eventually happened to that small lump of cheese. I did not see anyone who had the nerve to cut himself a chunk. So we left England and disembarked at Le Havre.

Chapter four. *Arcadian prelude to battle: the front*

When we landed in France in the early days of June and marched up the streets of Le Havre from the quay, we saw our first evidence of a different culture. A quite respectably dressed man was relieving himself against the wall which bordered the street, apparently totally without embarrassment to himself or to the passersby. The column broke its rhythm and nearly came to a halt, but recovered and marched on. We were to become more and more blasé about such cultural differences as time went on.

We knew that the German army was still going through the Allied lines "like stampeding horses through a row of pup tents," as an ex-cavalry sergeant put it. We did not have the satisfaction of knowing at that time that this was the last successful offensive of the German army. It was, however, reassuring to find that food was not as scarce in France as it had been in England. We marched under full pack to a temporary camp outside Le Havre. By this time we had been almost entirely without food for some thirty hours. Our mess sergeant was at last able to draw rations for us, and he dumped it all, meat, potatoes, some vegetables, everything except the bread, into a huge iron pot. About three o'clock we were finally fed and even given "seconds." I have never enjoyed food more.

Early next morning we entrained for our training area, which turned out to be clear across France in the Department of Doubs, near the Swiss frontier. With hundreds of thousands of American troops arriving in France every month, to the wartime traffic demands on the railways, there had now been added the disruption caused by the great German offensive. There was, in consequence, an acute shortage of rolling stock. Fifty men were assigned to each of the famous little 40 *hommes*, 8 *chevaux* box cars. This meant even more than a 25 per cent overload, for we were bigger than the average French soldier. In their acute discomfort, the troops "pulled" the hoary old one, "Thank God they left out the eight horses!" It took us three days, in the disrupted state of French transport, to travel to our training area.

There was not room enough in one of the cars for all of us to lie down at the same time. We discovered that when night came and we tried to get some sleep, we could best utilize the space by ringing the sides of the car with our torsos and piling our feet on top of one another in the middle. I thereby learned a lesson about the difference in points of view of the "haves" and of the "have-nots" in society which I was never to forget. If one were unfortunate enough to find oneself with one's feet on the bottom of the pile, one tried to go to sleep and forget the discomfort. But the weight of all those feet in hob-nailed army boots inevitably awakened one in a few minutes. The only thing to do was to drag one's feet out and put them on the top of the pile. What a blessed relief! One could doze off at once with the happy thought that at last everyone was comfortable. But, of course, the man whose feet were now on the bottom soon found it necessary to withdraw his feet and put them on top. When this happened, one always thought wearily and bitterly, "Why must there always be at least one soldier who can't hold still when we would otherwise all be comfortable?"

We detrained at Ornans, not far from Besançon in what had been, before France was unified, Franche-Comté. It was a mountainous, rural area of great beauty. Ornans lay in a valley surrounded by towering cliffs, on one of which a statue of the Virgin could be seen from all parts of the valley. Through the valley flowed the river Loue, which gushed out of the mountains a few miles away at a scenic cave called the Source of the Loue.[1]

The regiment was billeted in a number of villages some miles from Ornans, but I soon returned as one of a number of officers and non-coms selected to attend a communications school. We were

1. If anyone wishes to see what the area looked like, he may visit the Phillips Gallery in Washington, D. C. and see *Les Rochers d' Ornans* by the famous painter Gustave Courbet, himself a native of Ornans.

given instruction in coding messages, using the now long since obsolete Playfair system. We were also given instruction in carrying out *regulage* of artillery fire by liaison with Allied aviation. This system of observing and correcting battery fire by plane was unbelievably complicated and turned out to be wholly useless when the front began to move. Yet this was the system upon which the American artillery and the observation planes attached to it was to depend. I shall describe later its utter failure.

Since we were detached from Headquarters Company for this special school, we were assigned to mess with a battery of the 124th Artillery which was billeted in Ornans. After our food was dumped into our mess kits by the cooks and KP's, we had no place to eat except in the street. By now we did not look on this as any great hardship. As it turned out, it led to a really idyllic experience.

A French lady, Madame Victor Amiotte, happened to pass by and asked me if we would not like to bring our mess kits into her dining room and eat at her table. I cannot now remember how she knew I could speak French, but I told her at once that we would be delighted. Some six of us thereafter always ate at her table. Madame Amiotte asked me where I was billeted. I told her that I lived in one of the finest stables in the town. "Ah, that is terrible," she said. "You must come and stay with us." Whereupon, I moved in with the family, which consisted of a charming little girl of some eight years of age, Marie Jeanne, in addition to Madame and Monsieur Amiotte. I was treated in every way as a son.

In the tradition, I fear, of the camel in the Arab's tent, I soon stopped eating in the battery mess and ate with the family. This was my first acquaintance with French cuisine. Madame Amiotte cooked on a tiny stove fired by *fagots,* those bundles of dried brush French peasants use for fuel. In spite of wartime shortages, every meal, however modest the menu, was a triumph of culinary skill. They would have delighted the palate of a gourmet, a status which I had not then attained. We celebrated both the Fourth and the Fourteenth of July with flags, military parades, bands, and speeches in the little town square. We had champagne on the Fourth, and appropriately enough, vintage wine on the Fourteenth in lieu of the *vin ordinaire* which we usually had with our meals.

The home of the Amiotte family was located directly above the blacksmith shop of Monsieur Amiotte. He was a rugged and kindly soul who smoked black tobacco cigarettes which were sold at an exorbitant price by the tobacco monopoly of the French government. However, the smell of the red-hot horse shoes being fitted to the hooves of the horses brought in to be shod largely drowned out the odor of the cigarettes. He was grateful for the government issue Bull Durham tobacco which we gave him, saying that its flavor was "excellent but unfortunately totally unsatisfying."

While the relation I had with the Amiotte family was unusual, since we were the first Allied troops stationed in the area, relations were generally very good between our troops and the civilian inhabitants of the village. The intimate family relationship was in sharp contrast with its absence between American soldiers and the French population in World War II. I was generally included in the dinner invitations extended to the Amiottes. I remember dining with the mayor and his family. I went to church with Madame Amiotte (in the male French tradition, Monsieur Amiotte had little to do with the church). I accompanied Madame Amiotte when she called to condole with the mother of five small children whose father had just been killed at the front. The poor lady kept saying, *Cinq petits enfants, cinq petits enfants.* One of the five clutched her skirts and peering from behind them kept repeating what he had heard so often, *Cinq petits enfants, cinq petits enfants.* I could thus realize that the war which seemed to us to have been going on so long, had always new individual depths of anguish to be plumbed.

When we received orders to leave Ornans for Valdahon, we purchased a large silver spoon and fork set which was the only silverware to be had in the little jewelry shop. I had engraved on them, "To our French mother from her American sons." When I was to revisit Ornans with my wife and little girls in 1933, Madame Amiotte proudly showed the silver set to me. When I once more visited Madame Amiotte and Marie Jeanne in 1950, she put them on display again.

In early August we rejoined our own regiment of 155 howitzers in Valdahon, where, together with the two light regiments of our 58th Artillery Brigade, it was undergoing training in the French system of artillery fire. Since up to the time of the Armistice no American-made artillery was to be in use at the front, this was highly essential. For our part, we received practice in the use of

French radio material which was at last now issued to us. Just before we left for the front, I was recommended for officer's training at the old French artillery officers' training school at Saumur. General Todd of our 58th Artillery Brigade rescinded our orders on the grounds that he could not afford to lose his non-coms just when we were to go to the front. I have always been glad that I did not go to Saumur at this time. If I had done so, I would never have got to the front.

We entrained for the St. Mihiel front at Besançon and detrained at Foug, which involved for the unmounted men, who made up about half of an artillery regiment, long marches under full pack before and after detraining. We wore heavy woolen uniforms with woolen wrap puttees, woolen shirts, woolen underclothes and socks. Our packs contained a shelter-half and tent pegs, two blankets, mess kit, change of underwear and socks, and toilet articles. We carried a heavy overcoat and a rain coat. An extra pair of hob-nailed shoes was tied on the pack. Non-coms carried a pistol and two extra clips of ammunition. Other enlisted men carried a rifle and bayonet plus a belt of ammunition. A canteen of water and a first aid kit completed our equipment. To march with that weight under an August sun was tough for a man in good condition. Those who had been frequenting the wine shops and brothels of "Rainbow Alley" in Besançon really suffered.

After we had detrained at Foug, we moved to the Forêt de la Reine, which bordered on the little plain dominated by Mont Sec, which the German army had held since its capture of the St. Mihiel salient in 1914. The front-line trenches ran through this little plain, in which several ruined and abandoned villages had changed hands a number of times during the years. Even during the daytime it was perfectly safe, however, for one man to walk in full view out to the trenches which communicated with our front lines. Although the German artillerists had the plain under full observation and easy range, in their precise way they had calculated that the chances of killing one man did not justify shell fire. However, two men or even one mounted man would usually draw shelling, since the Germans had made so fine a marginal calculation.

On September 4 our brigade suffered its first casualties, two men were killed in our own battalion, both from Monmouth, by German counterbattery fire. Preparations were now pushed forward for the offensive which was about to open up. The night before the offensive opened on September 12, I moved my small radio detachment into a just evacuated machine-gun nest on the edge of the wood skirting the plain. I was very worried for I had received absolutely no instructions with respect to radio liaison with our own batteries and with the aero squadrons assigned to us for observation purposes. My nervousness increased as the massive preliminary bombardment began. Still no orders.

Next morning our battalion adjutant, a young captain, handed me a mimeographed memorandum of a dozen pages or so. It contained the whole plan for liaison and *regulage* of artillery fire by the assigned aerial squadrons, together with code signals and other details. "I guess I should have given you these before," he said airily, "but I just forgot." It really would have made little difference, however, for much more carefully implemented personal liaison than had been arranged would have been necessary to have carried the plan into effect.

The American attack, in which we supported the 1st Division, was a spectacular success. The German army was caught just as it had started to carry out the evacuation of the salient. Heavily fortified Mont Sec, which had cost the French army thousands of casualties when an attempt had been made to capture it in the early days of the war, was outflanked. The whole salient, which had been such an obstacle to Allied communications in the area, fell with losses to the Germans of thousands of prisoners dead and wounded and with very small losses to ourselves.

Even before the battle of St. Mihiel, the German advance on Paris had been stopped with fearful losses and an Allied counteroffensive had been successful. By the middle of August the German General Staff informed its civil government that the war had been lost and peace terms must be sought. Hence, after we reached the front, we were confronted by an already beaten German army. Our easy success at St. Mihiel did not prepare us for the bitter and sullen resistance which the German army was nevertheless still to offer in the approaching Meuse-Argonne offensive.

The success of this first American offensive did, however, greatly strengthen the hands of General Pershing, who had doggedly insisted on the establishment of a separate American army. Particularly after the crisis created by the successful German offensives in the spring of 1918, both the French and British general staffs, backed by their governments, demanded that American troops be incorporated into their armies in units of battalion size. Pershing had resisted the utmost pressure, sometimes without adequate support from his own government. No doubt he was motivated partially by personal ambition to command an independent army of his own. But he realized as others did not that it would have been absolutely disastrous to American morale to have used our soldiers simply as replacements for Allied casualties. To have done so might indeed have lost us the war.

This is illustrated in a very small way by the incident of the French lieutenant who was assigned to be an aide to Lieutenant Colonel Holabird, who had temporarily replaced our Colonel Davis while he was away at some school of command. Colonel Holabird was enormously proud of his perfumed and pomaded *ambusqué*, with his perfectly tailored uniform, his highly polished boots, his silver spurs, and his effeminate manner. The lieutenant persuaded the colonel to adopt what was alleged to be the French system for grooming horses. This involved a highly formalized grooming, almost like guard mount. It also involved currying the horse so energetically against the grain of the hide and so often that the horses developed sore hides.

The men who naturally had gravitated into the position of horse drivers of our gun and caisson teams in our artillery regiments had tended horses all their lives on Mid-West farms. This "French system" of grooming our horses really enraged them. Only half humorously, they argued about who was going to have the privilege of shooting the lieutenant when we got to the front. This fate was always talked about by the men for every very unpopular officer. It would have been a most unrewarding technique for undetected assassination in an artillery regiment, of course. But we had been an infantry regiment originally, and this hoary old consolation of the harrassed infantryman who dreams of shooting his hated officer under circumstances such that death could be made to appear to have occurred by enemy action was now revived. Doubtless this sort of assassination in revenge rarely happens, if for no other reason because in combat soldiers are so busy trying to preserve their own hides that previous grievances are forgotten. In any event, our French lieutenant left us before we ever came under fire. The men pretended great disappointment. This small semi-comic incident reveals, however, the endless opportunities for bad blood which would inevitably have happened had we been incorporated into British or French units of tactical size.

After the victory at St. Mihiel, we began our march to the Argonne Forest, where another offensive had been planned. We passed behind Verdun on through Pierrefitte to the Forêt de Hesse, where our guns were emplaced for the offensive which was to begin September 26. We marched at night to avoid observation and bombing by enemy aviation. We usually began our march at about 5:00 P.M. and marched behind our guns, caissons, *chariots de parc*, and *fourgons* until about 9:00 A.M. I found employment a good part of the night pulling men out of the *fourgons* in which our radio equipment was hauled. We simply did not have the horsepower to allow these men to ride. We usually felt too tired to eat when we halted in the morning, but a cup of the black lye which our cooks called coffee and which they had boiled on our rolling kitchen restored appetite enough to eat the corned beef and hardtack which we got twice a day. We marched at night, and the French roads, of crushed limestone, white in the moonlight and lined by tall poplar trees, were eerily beautiful. I thought of the song so popular at that time, "There's a Long, Long Trail A-Winding into the Land of My Dreams," but, of course, no one ever sang it, for to do so would have raised doubt both as to one's sanity and one's sex.

One night when our convoy halted for a few minutes at a crossroads I got into conversation with a rather elderly French officer apparently in charge of some rear installations. As I noted flashes of artillery fire in the near distance, I asked in some surprise, "Is Verdun still an active front?" He replied grimly, "My boy, Verdun is always active!"

A few days later, the infantry of our division, taking off from the ill-famed Le Mort Homme ridge, was to capture the hitherto impregnable German positions across the Forges swamp and, co-operating with other American divisions, was to bring the siege of Verdun to an end.

Our artillery brigade passed on into an area near Vauquois in which the characters of Jules Romains' novel *Verdun* had soldiered three years before us. I was to read Romains' novel almost twenty years later and then to experience in Paris in 1939 a curious sidelight on his personality. Of this, more later.

Until the offensive opened, I occupied, with my radio detachment, a small, shallow, neatly constructed dugout which had been previously occupied by a similar French detachment. The area in the Argonne in which our dugout was located had been fought over with the greatest fierceness in 1915. There were only skeletons of shell-shattered trees, and there was scarcely a foot of soil which had not been churned up. It was now a morass of mud.

During the few days until the Argonne offensive began, I sometimes talked with French soldiers who used to come to a nearby spring. In order to make conversation, I asked the orderly of a French battery commander who had come for a bucket of water from what part of France he came. His face lit up as he replied, "I come from the Côte d'Azur. There the sun always shines and there is never any mud." He then launched into a glowing description of the Riviera which surpassed, at least in spontaneity and depth of feeling, anything I have seen in travel brochures since. I hope he made it back to the "Azure Coast." He almost certainly did, for although neither of us realized it, the war was even then in its last two months.

A few days before the offensive began, I was much relieved to receive two radio operators sent from the Signal Corps. They were fine fellows, much more skilled at sending and receiving Morse code than were we. We sat in the dugout one night, and someone raised the question of the statistical probability of surviving the coming battle. One of the Signal Corps operators, Jack Cowden, then voiced the saying common among soldiers, "If a bullet has your name on it, it will curve around a tree to get you." The night before the offensive began, in the inscrutable way of the army, the two radio operators were withdrawn, and I never saw them again. Months later in an inn in Luxembourg I heard a soldier talking and from the conversation I could tell that he was from the detachment of the Signal Corps to which these men had belonged. "Did you know Bob Smith and Jack Cowden?" I asked him. He looked at me rather queerly and said, "Didn't you know that Cowden was killed in the Argonne?" I asked him to tell me about it. He said that the two men had been sent as radio operators to the headquarters of the 91st Division. Headquarters was in a deep dugout which had been constructed and occupied by the German army. The entrance had been dug with a sharp angle in it to prevent penetration by a shell. "Yet," he said, "somehow a German shell did score a direct hit on the dugout entrance, enter the shelter, and explode. Jack was killed. Bob had the radio receivers blown off his ears and was wounded but recovered."

The Meuse-Argonne offensive began in the early morning of September 26. In the expectation of the kind of success we had had at St. Mihiel, we were ordered to be ready to move by noon. I evacuated my neat little dugout, got my radio equipment packed on the *fourgon*, and awaited orders to move. They did not come. When night fell, a friend and I stretched out on the ground to sleep. But everybody who passed stopped and asked in horror, "You don't intend to sleep like that without any protection at all, do you?" The first half dozen enquirers we assured that that was exactly what we intended to do. After the seventh inquiry, we got up and went back to our neat little dugout. We found it crammed with French soldiers. We were finally compelled to find shelter in a huge old dugout, half ruined by shell fire. It appeared to contain the better part of a battalion of French soldiers and only the wrecked part had any unoccupied space. But it was that or nothing, so we spent the night as guests of the French army.

The next morning, we found we had lice, but we did not hold it seriously against the French army since by then everybody had them. I was not able to get rid of lice until we finally left the front. Actually it is not difficult to avoid getting lice or to get rid of them even after one has them if only he does not have to sleep in his clothes. Lice will not stay on a man who bathes and does not sleep in his clothes, because the eggs cannot hatch. It is as simple as that. But we slept in our clothes for weeks.

We moved up to new gun positions the next day, stopping while held up by the ill-famed Avocourt traffic jam long enough to engage in a little extracurricular activity by firing some captured German 77's. The Germans had had to abandon both guns and ammunition in their hurried retreat, but had removed the sighting mechanism from the guns. We simply cranked up the guns as high as they would go so that we were sure they would clear the new front lines and fired in the general direction of Germany.

At the close of the day, we took up new gun positions alongside a splendidly constructed two-way road of heavy planks which the Germans had built between Very and Epinonville. We were to hold these gun positions for the next two weeks and during that period were to come under close fire for the first time. A small creek flowed alongside the road some fifty yards away. Our gun positions were between this creek and the road. My radio detail in a small foxhole under a shelter tent was located some thirty yards from the road on the side of a hill sloping upward in the direction of the German lines. This put us in front of our own guns, which fired over us.

From this vantage point we could see everything which happened on the plank road which was one of the main arteries of communication with our front lines. Troops marched up the road, ammunition trains rolled over it, ambulances loaded with wounded came back. Sometimes when the road was blocked by shell fire, the ambulances would have to wait for a half hour or so and the moans of the wounded would be heard. Sometimes a mounted courier trotted down the road, his horse's hooves making a great clopping on the planks of the road. The troops would poke their heads out of their foxholes and jeer at the rider, "Here comes Paul Revere!" On one such occasion a German shell exploded right smack on the road. The horse reared and plunged, the courier fell off, everyone dived for his foxhole. To this day, I sometimes uneasily wonder what happened to Paul Revere. Was he killed or wounded or had he just fallen off his horse? One often was left without the sequel to these incidents.

One day a battalion of French 75's moved up the road. The Germans started an intensive bombardment. Apparently a gun or caisson farther ahead was hit, and the column was stopped for some time just abreast of our position. Under the rain of fire, the French drivers and the gunners sat on their horses or on the limbers of their guns without panic, but ducking their heads into their collars, "trying to make themselves small," just as men will do in an ordinary rain. I thought, "Some of those artillerymen have been in this war for four years. I am sure my nerves would never hold out that long."

Shortly after our arrival at our gun positions along the plank road, one of the battalions of the 5th Artillery of the First Division began to set up their headquarters about a hundred yards away. I got into conversation with two of their veteran non-coms as we were setting up our radio aerial. I had learned that falling on the ground was the best protection against shell fire if underground shelter were not available. When some German shells passed overhead with their characteristic howl, I threw myself on the ground. To my acute embarrassment, the old timers of the First Division did not. I came to the conclusion that I must imitate these fearless paladins and with a great effort remained erect thereafter. I quickly discovered the answer to the puzzle when shells began to land nearby. When a shell "begins to look for you," it ceases to howl and begins to hiss. When the German shells began to hiss, I discovered that these veterans could beat me to the ground every time. It was astonishing, however, how quickly one learned to distinguish between the howl and the hiss.

As the bombardment continued, I took temporary refuge in a foxhole which an infantry man had dug in the side of the hill a few hours before. It was only big enough to get one's head and shoulders into. However, I ordered "St. Peter" McCormick, one of my radio operators, to lie down beside me for what protection we could get. He had lied about his age in order to enlist when he was only sixteen. "St. Peter" was a devout Catholic. Queerly enough, although he was afraid of gas attacks, he was totally unafraid of shell fire. He sat down beside me and would call out cheerfully, "Here comes one, Hoover!" and I would press my head and shoulders harder into the dirt. I cursed him and ordered him to lie down. He grinned and refused. Just then we heard that tell-tale hiss. Out of the corner of my eye, I saw "St. Peter" go flying through the air, end over end. A layer of dirt some three or four inches deep folded itself over me. We discovered later that a German 105 millimeter shell had made a direct hit on the foxhole but had not exploded. If "St. Peter" had been lying down as I had ordered him to do, his head and shoulders would have been obliterated. As it was, the shell went under his buttocks and threw him out of the foxhole as if he had been on a giant scoop shovel. I called out to find if he had been hurt. He had not been scratched, nor had I!

I moved away a few yards and was telling a tough young lieutenant who had been sent to us from the First Division what had happened. We were sitting with our backs to the slope of the hill over which the German shells were coming. Just then we heard a shell hiss. To our fevered imaginations we could feel the hot breath of the shell as it passed over as we bent over and pressed our heads hard against our knees. The shell, a "whiz-bang," lit some twenty feet away. This time the shell exploded, sending fragments whistling in all directions. Some claim that an exploding shell produces an "umbrella effect" which sometimes protects anyone near enough to be under the arc described by the exploding fragments. Perhaps this saved our lives. Once more neither of us was scratched. The lieutenant ran in one direction and I ran for about thirty feet in the opposite direction. Then the same question seemed to strike us both—"Where am I going?" We both stopped running and went about our duties. After a couple of hours, I found that I had acquired an involuntary quiver of my lower jaw. It lasted for some twelve hours. I guess it was not noticeable to anyone else, but I felt most embarrassed. "St. Peter" suffered no such symptoms of shell shock.

The number of these German "dud" shells at this time reflected the new materials and other production difficulties which German industry was now encountering. The Allies took advantage of the situation to concoct a propaganda yarn. According to this yarn, Allied ordnance examined a number of these "duds" to determine their cause. (True.) Inside one of the defective fuses was found a tiny piece of paper on which was written "We are doing our part; are you doing yours?" Supposedly this message was placed in the fuse by Allied war prisoners whom the German authorities had compelled to work in munition factories. (False.) A corny yarn, but counted upon to boost the morale of the Allied soldiery.

I had always prided myself on having no fear of death as such. I had worried while we were an infantry regiment about the possibility of having to bayonet other men. Now I was humiliated to find that I simply did not want to die. I warmly wanted to live. I rationalized this feeling by saying to myself what a pity it would be to die without having really lived, without having married and had children, without having had a career. While the primitive instinct to live was no doubt the heart of the matter at this time, in later years the thought that I *had* indeed lived restored once more my tolerance for death.

I have described the failure of liaison between the artillery and aviation at St. Mihiel, and it was to fail in the Argonne as well. An artillery observer in a plane was supposed to send messages by Morse code on a small radio to the battery commander whose fire was to be regulated. This was done through a battalion radio detachment such as the one of which I was in charge. The battery commander could communicate with the plane only by means of white cloth panels (black when snow covered the ground) laid on the ground in particular patterns.[1] The non-com in charge of the radio receiving set for a battalion also was in charge of the men who laid out the panels. Unbelievably, the plane was supposed to fly over the target, correct deflection right or left of the battery's fire, fly back over the target, observe and send back by radio the results of bracketing fire, then after a "bracket" had been placed, count and report by radio the number of "shorts" and "overs" in a pattern of twelve shots. The battery commander then corrected his range upon the basis of the percentage of shorts and overs in the pattern and was only then supposed to be "on target."

Remember that there were no helicopters; the plane had to keep moving all the time. The chances of having a crew of panel men and radio operators, a pilot and an observer and a battery commander well enough trained to carry out this kind of operation was so small as to be negligible. It could work only on an absolutely stationary front, in cases where all the participants had worked together for months. Furthermore, it depended upon at least temporary absolute control of the air, since an observation plane under such circumstances would be a sitting duck for a fighter pilot.

Soon after our arrival, I noticed at a distance of a mile or so a huge tent hangar of a squadron of aviation in course of erection. Remembering the failure of the liaison with our aerial observation at St. Mihiel and with the terrible itch of responsibility which has always afflicted me, I set off across the fields for the hangar. I walked up to an officer and asked, "Who is in command here?" He answered, "I am Major Brown in command of the ——th Aerial Squadron." I told the major of our fiasco at St. Mihiel and asked whether he knew how this kind of thing could be prevented for the offensive which was just about to get under way. "You may be

1. This complicated and cumbersome panel system of communication was necessary since radio reception by observation planes was not feasible with the old style crystal receiving sets.

interested to know, Corporal," he said, "that my squadron was assigned to carry out artillery *regulage* at St. Mihiel. We were in the air all that day desperately trying to send map co-ordinates of targets to the radio details of the artillery battalion and regimental command posts. We received no radio or panel replies whatever. We might just as well have been back on Kelly Field in Texas for all we were doing to get the war along. Now it's a hell of a note when a corporal of artillery has to try to make arrangements for artillery-aviation liaison." We tried to work out together a simpler and more flexible system and agreed on one. It turned out to be hopeless to try to implement it in this unofficial way.

I heard only one attempt at *regulage* by the old system while we were in the Argonne. The poor devil of an artillery observer who was trying to observe the shots of the battery at first could not locate them at all. He then reported "deflection 1000 meters right," which was preposterous, since a typical early deflection error might be expected to be of the order of 50 meters. He then radioed, "Visibility very poor. Going to land." That was the end of the old system of *regulage*. This experience, however, was to be the prototype of much of my life's work, which, thank God, has been somewhat less frustrating. My specialty both as an economic theorist and as an economic advisor to government has been cutting through preposterously complicated and processed masses of largely irrelevant mathematical and statistical data and reducing them to meaningful concepts with which men could deal.

It was a great shock to us to find German planes not only carrying out reconnaissance over our lines but even dropping bombs on us. These bombs caused few if any casualties, but the German action was annoying. We simply could not understand it. What about the huge plane-building program we had read so much about in our newspapers before coming to France? How about our friends who had joined up with scores of thousands of others as aviators? Where were they? The facts were that not one American plane ever flew at the front. The highly touted Liberty engine turned out to be so slow that it had to be mounted in a de Haviland British plane and used as an artillery observation plane. Somehow, too, there was a great shortage of American aviators as well.

I received every day at the front a mimeographed sheet prepared by our Intelligence. The first day the comment was "Enemy aviation active." The next day, "Enemy aviation very active." The third day the sheet reported in evident disgust, "Control of the air entirely in enemy hands." When the American army tried to send up observation balloons, German aviators shot them down as fast as they were sent up. Since these balloons could be seen over great distances, I must have seen as many as six shot down. As the last was shot down, a lone American plane finally appeared and chased the German plane away. Just as the German plane reached its own lines, the American aviator (it was probably the American lone wolf, Luke) shot it down. First one blazing figure and then a second fell out of the burning plane and went spinning to earth. All up and down the little valley men jumped out of their foxholes and cheered to see those two poor devils die. I cheered too, but then I was ashamed of myself and shut up.

Since the system of *regulage* of artillery fire by aerial observation had turned out to be a complete flop, the principal function of our radio detail came to be the receipt of "corrections of the moment" from meteorological stations in the rear for transmission to our battery commanders. These "corrections of the moment" came to us by radio every four hours in the form of a series of code numbers, giving the direction and velocity of the wind at successive 500 meter levels. Since our 155 millimeter howitzers had a high angle of fire and hence traversed a number of 500 meter levels in their arc of fire, accuracy depended heavily upon these corrections of the moment. Once having received them, the battery commander turned to his firing tables and incorporated them by formula into his firing data. How many battery commanders in the U. S. Army knew enough mathematics to make effective use of these corrections of the moment, I do not know. A battery instrument sergeant of the 149th Field Artillery told me later that when his captain received these corrections, he would tap his teeth with his pencil, pretending to do the impossible by doing the computations in his head. He would then invariably give the order, "Increase the range fifty meters!"

When we were not receiving corrections of the moment, I would often listen in on our propaganda broadcasts to the German soldiers. Although by now the Germans could not take the trouble to do counterpropaganda, radio operators on both sides of the line were strictly forbidden to listen to either side. However, all radio operators on both sides tried to pick up anything of interest quite regardless of these orders. Except for copies of the *Stars and Stripes* occasionally dropped by plane, we had no other source of news. Consequently, officers and men alike waited while I translated our propaganda out of German for our own use. In this way we got such choice bits as "On the average one American soldier lands in France every six seconds" and "Following the surrender of the Turkish forces to the Allies, the Bulgarian army has now asked for an armistice."

At other times we assisted in unloading powder and projectiles for our guns. The powder came in large silk bags with eight smaller silk bags inside. Major changes in range were affected by removing one or more of the small bags before charging the howitzer. Since this type of powder would burn but not explode unless confined and since fuses were not screwed into the projectiles until just before firing, there was little danger in handling either powder or projectiles. However, if a German plane spotted a convoy delivering ammunition to us, we could usually count on getting shelled. Even so, I was always amazed at how many shells on the average it took to kill a man. After a lively fifteen minutes of shelling, we might have one or two casualties. We often had none at all if it were possible for the men to take to their slit trenches which gave protection against anything but a direct hit.

One day a plane dropped a number of copies of *The Stars and Stripes* over our area. In those early days of October, the press had already begun to talk of an Armistice. Now here was a statement by former President Taft declaring sternly that there must be no compromise and that we must fight on to Berlin. I still remember the rage I felt. I fear my rage was totally illogically associated with Taft's corpulence. "Yes, you fat old so and so," I thought, "I wish you were here for the march on Berlin."

In every war there are those who believe that peace is to be found only in unconditional surrender and the absolute crushing of the enemy. I did not feel so then, and I have never felt so since. I do not believe that we would have had a more durable peace if we had marched to Berlin. On the contrary, I favored a peace without annexations of countries inhabited by enemy populations and without indemnities. I had taken our propaganda of "the war to end wars" seriously. I hoped that we were now going to have a peace without revenge and a world without war, once the German army could be brought to capitulate. I, of course, had no slightest premonition that there would be a second World War and that I would one day be in a position to help in preventing a completely Carthaginian settlement of that war.

During the weeks we had our gun positions along the wooden plank road, our horses with their drivers and other men not needed to operate the guns and communications were left in a wood a couple of miles away in the "rear echelon." Horses were far more vulnerable to shell fire than men. They could not crawl into dugouts or slit trenches. They could not even lie down. If they were even slightly wounded, particularly in the legs, they usually had to be shot. I visited our rear echelon once and came upon our old color sergeant, Andy Gillespie, boiling coffee in a can over a small hobo-style fire. He was visibly shaken. One German shell had fallen on the picket line the previous night and had killed the picket guard and nineteen horses. After Andy had greeted me, he remarked, "You know those wars I was always telling you recruits about, the Boxer Uprising, the Philippine Insurrection and so on? Well, I have to admit now those were not really wars. *This is* a war!"

When on one occasion an ammunition train was delayed, one of our battalion commanders, who had been quite a hard-boiled disciplinarian, came up to our gun positions. Our German counterparts chose this occasion to shell us. The major ran up and down shouting and then hastily departed to a deep dugout some two miles in the rear which had formerly been occupied by the Germans. Our telephone men had to lay a wire back to his dugout, and he did not appear again. Thereafter he was always called "Dugout" by the troops. After we left the front when we were at "route march" and the major happened to ride by, a soft chorus of "Dugout! Dugout!" would begin and rise to a crescendo, the men being careful not to move their lips in the process. The only way to stop them was to call them to attention, when, of course, all talking was forbidden.

We had supported successively the 91st and the 32nd Infantry Divisions in their advance against stubborn German resistance. Both divisions suffered heavy casualties. After the 32nd Division pierced the second German defense position, the *Kriemhild Stellung*, our artillery brigade was withdrawn from the front for refitting. Our casualties in men had been relatively light, but our losses in horses had been very large. In part this was due to shell fire, but even more to our horses simply wearing out, partially due to shortage of forage. One of our captains who happened to be from Alabama endeared himself at this time by exhorting his men to groom the horses more vigorously, "For," said he, "we can get mo' men but we cain't get mo' hosses." We had to use the mounts of officers and non-coms in order to pull our guns away from the front.

As we left the active front and marched through the old no man's land and the old front support areas, I did not know that I was leaving the front for good. I did recall the eagerness with which I had advocated our entrance into the war against Germany. I had not wavered in my belief, but I saw matters in a different perspective now. I had completely accepted Allied propaganda about German *Schrecklichkeit*, and I had assumed scrupulous observance of the rules of war by the Allies. As we marched away from the front, I was to see another bit of evidence that neither frightfulness nor knightly regard for the rules of warfare was a monopoly of either side. As we marched, we came to a French railhead where supplies were brought up from the rear and stored. We could see in the moonlight several low buildings with large Red Cross insignia on their roofs, presumably hospitals. We could also see interspersed among the buildings large piles of artillery shells, covered with camouflage nets. These piles of shells were not marked with red crosses, but it would have been almost impossible to have bombed them without hitting the hospital buildings.

I recalled, too, a walk in the woods back of some captured German trenches. I came upon a grass-grown grave of a French soldier. Over the grave was a cross with a date early in 1914 with an inscription, *Hier liegt in ewiger Ruhe ein tapferer französischer Krieger.* "Here lies in eternal rest a brave French warrior." I found several other scattered graves with similar inscriptions. I recalled with remorse the callous handling which the bodies of German soldiers usually received from our side.

We marched to Ville-sur-Cousances in a rain which soaked through the miserable raincoats which profiteering manufacturers had foisted on the American army. (It was to be a great satisfaction to note in World War II the enormous improvement in the quality of army issue raincoats). Ville-sur-Cousances had been a French advanced base in which there were a number of wooden barracks. Unfortunately, there was not room for all the troops; so "St. Peter" McCormick and I found ourselves confronted by the prospect of pitching our pup tent in about an inch of water. I had felt a cold coming on, and I was sure I would catch pneumonia if I ever bedded down under such conditions. I looked about until I found one of our covered supply wagons; and, ignoring the feeble protests of the sentry guarding the wagons, we climbed in. The wagon was loaded with saddles which had been piled in hit or miss. Of all beds which I would not recommend is one made up on saddles, which have the maximum number of irregular projections which can be got in a given space. When we got up in the morning, I had a well developed case of "flu." My nose began to bleed and I ran a fever.

Just at this moment our brigade commander decided to send a three months' quota of candidates for commissions to the artillery training school for officers at Saumur. I was once more recommended, but the higher echelons informed our general that he could not thus fill up previously unused quotas and once more I did not go to Saumur. I was in no condition to go in any event. I might well have died on the road had I been sent. Our battalion medical officer strongly recommended that I be sent to a base hospital. I as strongly demurred. I knew the hospitals were full of wounded, and besides I hated the thought of getting separated from the regiment. When that happened, one never knew to what outlandish organization one might be sent after convalescence. Our medical officer reluctantly agreed to my staying with the outfit.

A roof over my head was found in a small three-room hut which had been built by the French army and which was now occupied by about half a dozen men of our regiment. There was no floor in the hut and no "official" means of heating it. Since it was now the middle of October, it was a bit chilly. French troops who had previously occupied the hut had nailed a piece of bent tin in the corner of one room so that a small fire could be built without burning down the hut. Someone had then poked a hole in the ceiling and a little of the smoke could escape in this way. Presumably the French soldiery had somehow been able to get hold of *fagots* to burn in this primitive fire-place. We had no means of getting *fagots*, but American troops are ingenious and adaptable. We simply restricted ourselves to two rooms of the hut and burned the third in the fireplace. I have often wondered what happened after the second room was burned for fuel. I had been bedded down in my two blankets spread over my shelter-half on the dirt floor in front of the fire. Another one of those lads who had lied to get into the army at sixteen brought me all my meals from the regular mess. Bless his kindly heart!

When the regiment moved, I simply got out of bed and moved with it. As a result I suffered for a couple of months from severe shortness of breath, an aftermath of the "flu."

Chapter five. *Post Armistice:* Madelon de la Victoire: *Epilogue in Luxembourg*

We detrained after our trip from Ville-sur-Cousances and began a march over a mountainous area to Saucourt, in the Department of Haute Marne, where we were to receive tractors in place of horses to pull our guns. We had turned over what was left of our horses to the light artillery regiments of the brigade as replacements for losses they had suffered at the front.

While at Saucourt, my Second Battalion Headquarters Detail of about twenty-five men was billeted in, oddly enough, a former fish hatchery. Until this period at Saucourt, I had fortunately never had to live for any substantial period in a room with any more than eight men, who made up a squad tent. Now I was to experience for two months what to me was one of the most repugnant aspects of an army private's life, total lack of privacy. The status of non-com in charge of quarters gave me less rather than more privacy.

While we were still at Saucourt, the Armistice of November 11 was announced. Someone immediately wrote a successor song to *Madelon* called *Madelon de la Victoire,* which was sung everywhere:

Après quatre ans d'espérance
Tous les peuples alliés
Avec les poilus de France
Font des moisson de lauriers
Et qui préside la fête

C'est la joyeuse Madelon
Madelon ah! verse à boire
Et surtout n'y mets pas d'eau
C'est pour fêter la victoire
Joffre, Foch et Clemenceau.

All France, after four long years of hoping, did indeed rejoice with the Allies. Certainly Madelon strictly observed the admonition against putting any water in the glasses which were raised in toast that day. There was no premonition of the discord to come over the terms of the peace treaty and the years of frustration to follow.

We left Saucourt and began moving up to join our army of occupation at the beginning of January. Our first stop was to be at Stenay, an old French garrison town which had been the headquarters of the German army during the years of the fighting around Verdun.

When we arrived in Stenay, we found it a sea of mud, with the inherited filth of the French, German, and American armies during four years of war. There was, nevertheless, a residual civilian population which had somehow learned to survive. A number of warehouses were stuffed with live ammunition, some of it left over from the time of the capture of the town by the German army from the French. French children in the eight to fourteen years bracket had developed a rather unusual sort of amusement for themselves. They had somehow learned to set the fuse on a shell so that it gave them time to run before it exploded. How they got the shell to explode, I was never able to learn. This game was somewhat destructive, but since it was usually played in an area where the houses were already considerably battered, this was no great matter. I was to be reminded again of this adaptability of children to the most terrible and bizarre conditions when, in Berlin after World War II, I was to see German boys of about the same age playing soldier around a wrecked Soviet tank within a few months after the capture and sack of Berlin by the Russians.

As a result of conditions in Stenay, I picked up an acute case of dysentery. Fortunately, after about a week, we moved into the Grand Duchy of Luxembourg as part of the American Army of Occupation in Germany. Here we rejoined the two infantry brigades of the 33rd Division from which we had been separated since our arrival in France. Our infantry had trained and fought first with the British and Australians, and then had taken a major part on the right flank of the Meuse-Argonne offensive. They had fought over a good part of the old Verdun battlefield with noteworthy success. The division had been included in the five which the German General Staff rated as "first-class." It ranked fourth in the AEF in the number of German prisoners taken, twelfth in the number of its wounded, and twentieth in numbers killed in action.

The Grand Duchy of Luxembourg, in spite of its situation in the geographical heart of Western Europe and the existence of a substantial steel industry, still retained in its country districts many of the quaint characteristics of Graustark. Soon after our troops moved in, a mutiny-strike of the Luxembourg army of two hundred men combined with a popular uprising in the city of Luxembourg, overthrew the government of the reigning Grand Duchess, Charlotte. The revolution against the Grand Duchess was based upon the claim that she had been unduly friendly with the Kaiser and the German occupational authorities. The revolutionists, backed by the striking army, demanded the abdication of the Grand Duchess and the establishment of a republic. They also demanded an increase in the pay of army privates to the dollar per day of the American army. As an earnest *bourgeois* Luxembourger described the scene to me, "We assembled in front of the Grand Ducal Palace and proclaimed a republic. Then the French troops arrived and we had to go home."

The general commanding the French occupational forces was a monarchist in his own domestic politics. He detested all "radical movements" and, consequently, had forcefully intervened in the *opéra bouffe* revolution. The upshot of the matter was that the reigning Grand Duchess went into exile in Germany and was succeeded by her sister, Marie Adelaide. The French government recalled the general, and the Allied governments agreed among themselves that the future government of the Grand Duchy should be determined by a plebiscite. The Luxembourg army was disbanded, except for four officers.

About this time, I became acquainted with a dapper, cheerful and completely cynical little Walloon who rejoiced in the title of Secretary to the Grand Marshal of the Court. He described to me how one went about rigging a plebiscite. "If we had a vote simply on whether or not the present dynasty should continue, we should certainly lose. But we shall see to it that that is not the issue on which the people will get to vote. We shall see to it that *four* alternatives are presented, (1) a custom's union with France; (2) a custom's union with Belgium; (3) the establishment of a republican form of government; (4) continued independence and the retention of the present form of government. Independence and the retention of the present form of government means, of course, the continuation of the present dynasty, the court, and my job. We shall campaign under the slogan which is the title of our national anthem, '*Wir wolle bleibe wass wir sei!*' You know that in our Luxembourger *patois* that means 'We will remain what we are!' We can't lose." They didn't lose.

Our battalion was billeted in the adjoining villages of Differdingen and Bofferdingen (in French, Differdange and Bofferdange). We found that the Luxembourg peasants spoke their own peculiar dialect of German, but most also spoke either German or French. The people in the larger towns often spoke both languages. I found that the vestigial Low German which had remained in our family after two hundred years in America, added to one year of college German, afforded me easy communication with the Luxembourgers.

I found life in an army of occupation unutterably boring. This boredom was slightly mitigated by a series of schools which were set up, partly to keep the troops occupied, partly because our generals felt that this opportunity to improve the military training of the couple of million Americans in the AEF should not be wasted. To attend one such school, about a hundred officers and non-coms were sent back to Saizerais in France, Headquarters of the 7th Division, for a School of Liaison of Infantry, Artillery, and Aviation. The school was a solemn farce, in which everybody, now thoroughly acclimated to the inscrutable vagaries of an authoritarian system, co-operated without resistance. Our instructors were young lieutenants from the Air Corps who had never been at the front. Their students were, without exception, officers and non-coms from infantry and artillery who *had* carried on liaison with our aviation in combat. The young aviators were horribly embarrassed and apologetic about the whole thing; but precisely because this was apparent, none of us gave them a hard time.

Only once, a tough young infantry captain during the question period asked, "Lieutenant, if you were flying ahead of an advancing wave of our infantry, and you spotted a German machine-gun nest, what would you do?" The lieutenant thought a moment and hesitantly replied, "I would fly back over brigade headquarters and drop a message." "Well, Lieutenant," said the leg-pulling captain, "You might be interested to know that statistics show that the average time required to deliver a message from brigade headquarters to an advancing wave of infantry was just slightly in excess of thirty-six hours."

In the boredom of an occupying army, it became easy to believe that (1) we had been entirely forgotten by our government; or (2) our generals were reluctant to go home and be reduced to their peacetime rank at some army post left over from the days of the Indian wars in the West. This feeling was widespread. A Marine wrote a poem in the *Stars and Stripes* which contained this couplet: "Silver threads among the black, Darling I am coming back. Now that peace in Europe nears, I'll be home in seven years." One of our boys wrote a longer poem which told how in 1939 a convoy of battered ships sailed into New York Harbor, and a regiment of elderly soldiers disembarked. Clad in their patched O.D. uniforms with their tattered battle flags, but with band playing martial airs, they marched smartly if somewhat stiffly up Broadway. When people asked in wonderment who they were, they replied only "Ich kann kein Englische sprechen" or "Je ne parle pas l'anglais." Finally, they asked a bearded old colonel (recognizable from the description as Colonel Sanborn of the 131st Infantry). "I speak a little English," he said, with much precision. "This is the first contingent of the 33rd Division."

It was a more serious matter when rumors began to spread that instead of going home we were to be sent to join the American contingent of the Allied Expeditionary Forces at Murmansk in Northern Russia to fight the Bolsheviks. British and Canadian troops who had been ordered aboard ship to go to Archangel and Murmansk had promptly mutinied. Now I had no illusions about the Bolsheviks. I knew they were a bloody dictatorship which had overthrown by force the democratic government of Kerensky. Yet I believed it was not at all good policy for the Allies to try to destroy the Soviet regime with foreign bayonets. Besides, I felt strongly that I had enlisted to fight the Germans, not the Bolsheviks. (I realize now that when one becomes a soldier, one cannot limit one's liability to getting shot in any particular war. There is no "war of limited liability" for soldiers even though there may be such for generals.)

At this time there appeared a speaker at an evening lecture sponsored by the YMCA. He discussed the peace terms which were then being negotiated in Paris. During the informal question period following the lecture, I asked, "Why is Germany to be allowed to have an army of one hundred thousand men? The Allies have just beaten the German army at the cost of several million casualties. Why do we want to let them build up an army at all? Why not limit them to a *gendarmerie*?" Before the lecturer could answer, the regular Army lieutenant colonel who had temporarily replaced our Colonel Davis in command of the regiment and who happened to be present spoke up, "The answer to that is simple. A German army is needed to prevent Germany going Bolshevik." "But," said I, "is that the way to prevent Germany going Bolshevik? Is not the popular hatred of militarism the chief source of what Communist sentiment there is in Germany?" The colonel flushed with rage. To have an enlisted man "talk back to him" was a new and intolerable experience. I would not, of course, have addressed the colonel directly, but he had intervened in a conversation I was having with the YMCA lecturer. The colonel burst out, "I have served my country from the festering swamps of the Philippines to the burning sands of Mexico, and you are the first disloyal American soldier I have ever met!" I learned later that the colonel had had my service record examined the next day to see whether I were indeed a dangerous subversive. In point of fact, the colonel was probably right about the role of the new *Reichswehr* in preventing Germany from going Communist; but, of course, his attitude was inexcusable.

At the end of April the 33rd Division began its withdrawal from Luxembourg towards Brest, which was to be the port of embarkation for New York. I felt some concern when I was left behind with a lieutenant to settle any claims which the Luxembourgers might have against our occupying forces. Since the lieutenant knew no German, dealing with the natives became my responsibility. The claims were all minor—here a window in a billet had been broken; there some credulous innkeeper had cashed a check for an American officer, and the check had bounced. One claim was a little unusual. A villager claimed that his hens had been laying a dozen eggs per day before we moved in. Then we parked our guns in front of his house and every day we held gun drill. Thereafter the hens never laid another egg. All he wanted was the market price of the aborted eggs, a Luxembourger mark (about 18 cents) per egg per day for the period of the occupation.

The lieutenant and I settled the claims in jigtime. Instead of the week or so that we probably had been expected to take, we settled the claims in about six hours. Neither of us had an intention of getting left behind as detached casuals while the division went on home. We caught up with the train carrying the regiment before it got to Verdun. I remember this because I was very much impressed to note that although the war had been over only about five months, the reserve trenches back of Verdun had been filled in and a green crop of wheat was growing over them. Probably down through the ages mankind has been able to survive wars largely because it is necessary at once to turn to civil pursuits to make a living, and with work, memories of unspeakable horrors soon begin mercifully to fade.

We sailed for home on the *America.* "St. Peter" McCormick, who had been in the foxhole with me when the shell hit, suffered a final small indignity. Some officer had discovered a half dozen extra rifles, of which there was no record. One was issued to "St. Peter," who as a radio operator was supposed to be armed only with a pistol. "St. Peter" had by now become an old soldier. The rifle was not charged to him or to anybody else. As soon as we had sailed and it got dark, he simply dropped it over the side.

After a few days at Camp Mills on Long Island, we entrained for Chicago and then to Camp Grant at Rockford, Illinois, where we were discharged. The official history of the 33rd Division states, "Notwithstanding every effort on the part of Governor Lowden and other Illinois officials, the War Department refused permission for a review of the entire Division." I recalled how at the grand review of the division in Luxembourg by General Pershing at which Secretary of War, Newton D. Baker, had been present, the Secretary had suddenly leaned forward and asked the men of a regiment assembled before him, "Do you want a divisional parade when you get home?" With one voice the regiment had roared, "Hell, no!"

I had feared that when we were discharged I would permanently lose contact with my friends. Fortunately this did not happen. Our "band of brothers" stayed in communication through the years. I was never to see George Story again, but we stayed in touch through letters. "St. Peter" McCormick and I exchange letters every Armistice Day. George Story, John French, and Ellis Bell are dead, but our friendship was lifelong. The few who are left still are close friends.

In retrospect, I can see that my army experience conditioned my whole life. It greatly toughened me. Above all, it taught me how to exercise responsibility even with the minimum support of rank and authority. I had always been far too sensitive and even timid. After my two years in the army, I was never thereafter to be confronted by a situation that could not be faced even if I could not master it.

The life of a non-com at the front and in the rear had given me an experience which was not common for men in the profession and at the level of life in which I was to find myself for most of the rest of my life. It permanently established my opposition to caste and privilege. On the other hand, it confirmed the experience I had had working on the railroad. Consequently, I have never idealized or romanticized "the common man." To imagine some special kind of humble virtue which is embodied in a man just because he is in a lower income class is as silly as the unreal "noble redskin" about which romantic authors used to write. I had come to realize that in the very nature of man and things a minority must always carry out the actual task of ruling. I knew now after two years in the army that the power of that ruling minority needed always to be circumscribed and never allowed to escape from the final sanction of control by the majority of the electorate. My army experience cured me of being a socialist. It did not cure me of being an egalitarian to the extent equality of income could be attained without intolerable sacrifices of either individual liberty or social productivity. I came to the conclusion that a completely socialized society would mean an authoritarian society. Authority and discipline are necessary in war, but for peace give me a society of freedom and contract instead of one characterized primarily by authority and status.

The net effect of my army experiences in World War I was to produce for me a sort of social extra-territorality in which I served as an academic, as a social analyst, as an advisor to our government, and as an administrator without allegiance to any one economic or social class.

Chapter six. *Return to civil life: the farm; tent on a Wisconsin lake*

Very shortly after my discharge in June, 1919, from the army, I was married to Faith Sprole of Garner, Iowa. We had been college mates and had been engaged all during my army service. My plans for the future were still dominated by my intense desire to get away from swarms of other human beings, particularly regimented swarms. Since modern urban society was inevitably regimented in some degree, the only escape seemed to me to be found on the farm. The picture of farm life in my mind was one with a large degree of self-sufficiency in food production with some free time for hunting and fishing. This idealized image which has even yet not wholly disappeared from the American folk-mind had already become obsolete except for limited areas of low standard of living in the Southern Appalachians. Nevertheless, this archaic fantasy largely determined the course which the next few years of my life were to take.

Since it was not feasible to start farming at the time of the year of my discharge from the army, it was necessary to make a living until I could. Consequently, I got a job as principal of a village elementary school in Youngstown, Illinois. There was one other teacher besides myself. I taught the three upper grades. I received $115 per month for nine months. Since the rent we paid for our house was very low, we managed to save about a third of this. Until school began, I worked as a hired hand for a neighboring farmer during the harvest. This was heavy physical labor at which one worked for about ten to eleven hours a day during the hottest season of the year. However, one could allow the sweat to run without inhibition and the sheer physical expenditure of energy was very satisfying. Since I worked for a farmer who was a member of a threshing ring, the food was superb. Each farmer's wife vied with the other in the amount and variety of the food, and the ladies were magnificent cooks. Moreover, I had no chores to do and I lived at home. I could read in the evening; so it was physically and emotionally a very satisfactory life. It was a quite deceptive foretaste of what farming was really like when I was on my own.

In the late spring of 1920 we moved on to our farm near Goldfield, Iowa. My father-in-law, an Iowa banker, had purchased the farm of some 220 acres for us, and I rented it from him. I farmed only about 120 acres. The rest was rented out to another tenant. It had been necessary to make this arrangement in order to have a farm of a size which could be handled without hired labor. I had insisted on doing all the work myself as an essential part of my image of the self-sufficient farmer. In reality, this meant that I had deliberately chosen what as an economist I would later call an inefficient combination of land, labor, and capital. If I had bought a tractor—tractors were then just coming into use—and had employed a hired man, I would have had a more profitable, much less onerous operation.

In addition to my inefficiently sized farming unit, I had had only limited experience with farming. As a consequence, I had to work an even longer day than did my neighbors in order to get the work done. I customarily worked from 5:30 A.M. to about 10:30 P.M. The really onerous part of the work was the "chores," which involved the feeding and watering, harnessing and unharnessing of my four work horses, the milking twice a day of my four cows, and the separating of the cream, plus the care of some fifty hogs and some one hundred chickens. Added to this was the cleaning out and spreading on the fields of the manure, the repair of buildings and fences, and so on. This was in addition to the plowing, planting, cultivating, and harvesting of the crops.

Middle Western farmers of that day were quite well-to-do. Since the turn of the century they had benefited from good and stable prices for grain, hogs, cattle, and dairy products. During the war they had received very high prices for farm products, and the prices of land had skyrocketed. Consequently, farmers had forgotten the agrarian agitation of the eighties and nineties and had become thoroughly capitalistic and generally anti-labor in their point of view. The typical Iowa farmer had to be and was a businessman with a substantial investment to be managed. Yet the Midwestern farmer continued to labor long hours which no urban laborer would have tolerated. The educational level was relatively high. There was no illiteracy. Good elementary and high schools were attended by the children. A considerable percentage of farmers' sons went to the state universities even though they did not usually return to the farm after they graduated.

But during the great decline in farm prices of 1921, only partially to be mitigated by the industrial recovery which followed the recession of 1921, Midwestern farmers began to lose their faith in the free market system of capitalism and began to demand governmental intervention in their behalf. By the time of the Great Depression of the thirties, this was to have epochal effect upon the politico-economic balance of forces in the United States.

I found farmers in Iowa harder working, more business-minded, and better acquainted with the latest methods of farming recommended by the agricultural colleges than had been true in the area in Illinois in which I had lived. The business-mindedness of Iowa farmers should have made for greater profitability. Doubtless it did, but it also led to greater speculation in land, which eventually was to prove ruinous.

There was no time for relaxation. Although the Iowa River, well populated with fish, ran at the edge of our farm, and although rabbits, squirrels, and pheasants were fairly plentiful, I never had time to fish or hunt. Neither did my neighbors. We had almost no time for reading or other cultural activities. I could not even find the time to take proper care of a vegetable, much less a flower garden. In part, this was due to a Protestant ethic which dominated Middle Western rural life and in which work was admirable, leisure or sport suspect.

I soon realized that I had somehow managed to tie myself to a way of life in which there was neither adventure, intellectual activity, nor leisure. Sometimes when I allowed the horses to rest for a moment at the end of a furrow, I used to ask myself in gloomy wonderment, "Is this then the end of my dreams of an interesting and exciting life?" I fear that I was rescued from this situation not by a considered decision of my own but only by financial disaster. If I had been able to make a living on the farm, I might be a farmer today.

The first phase of financial disaster took the form of a steep fall in farm prices in 1921. The price of farm land collapsed. Many farmers who had placed mortgages on their farms, often in order to buy additional land, now lost their farms. These mortgage foreclosures went on for years, often dragging down the small country banks in the process. Sometimes all the banks in an entire county would be closed. This phase, however, came some years later. In my own case, I had stored a thousand bushels of corn in the local co-operative elevator in the expectation that prices would improve later. I got a loan on the stored corn. Instead of improving, prices kept on falling. While I was gone from the area for a week or so, the price of corn fell below the amount of the loan which I had received. Not only did I receive nothing more from the stored corn, I had to pay storage charges plus the deficiency in the value of the stored corn.

The second phase of financial disaster came when hog cholera struck, and almost all my hogs died. The law required that hogs which died of cholera must not be buried but burned. For days I used up all the down timber in our wood lot constructing funeral pyres for hogs. I had supposed that fat hogs would burn rather like Roman candles. In fact, the carcasses resisted the fire as though they had been coated with asbestos. I was to recall these non-inflammable hogs in Berlin some twenty-five years later when I saw the fire-blackened spot just outside the underground bunker in the courtyard of the Chancellery where the body of Hitler was alleged to have been burned by two Nazi SS men who poured gasoline on it after he had committed suicide. After my macabre experience with the hogs, I just did not believe it.

At this moment of financial need, the principal of the Goldfield high school fell ill, and the school board asked me to serve as a replacement. After about six weeks, the regular principal recovered and came back. Whereupon the local school board asked me whether I would be willing to become superintendent of schools for the following year. Here then was an opportunity to escape not only from my current financial plight, but to escape from farming.

I did not accept the informal offer, since I had found the superintendent a friendly and co-operative soul, and I would not have been a party to taking his job from him. However, it did set me thinking about the possibility of return to the educational world.

If I were to return to the academic world, it would obviously be essential that I should resume my long interrupted study for an undergraduate degree. I regretted now the messy state in which I had left my college career. I had enlisted just before the end of my junior year without even taking the final examinations for the semester. It looked as though it might require more than a year of college work to get a degree.

My daughter, Carol, who has been such a joy to us throughout our life, had been born the previous year. Now more than ever I felt my family responsibilities. How could I support a wife and child for a year after I had lost almost all my savings in this unfortunate farming venture? I simply did not have the nerve to try it. Fortunately my wife supplied the courage which I lacked. "How do I know I could support you and Carol?" I cried. "I know very well that you can," said my wife.

The question then arose about what I should prepare myself to teach. As an undergraduate I had majored in romance languages and I had assumed that I would be a teacher of languages. I had really never had much enthusiasm at this prospect even though I was much interested in languages. The prospect of drilling students in grammar and of correcting innumerable papers had always chilled me. I know now that I would indeed have been a poor stick as a teacher of languages. I have studied and made great use of five languages in my lifetime. However, it has always been difficult for me to perfect myself in the use of a language. As soon as I know a language basically well enough to speak and read it, the complexities of grammar bore me. In particular, highly inflected languages annoy me, primarily because so much of the complexity is unnecessary or at least highly inefficient.

My wife realized this and asked, "What are you really interested in? What would you like to study if you were free to start from scratch? We might as well make a clean break and a new start if we are going to undertake this venture." I blurted out that what I was really interested in was economics. Above all I wanted to understand why farm prices had fallen and how it was that we could suddenly be so much worse off as a nation simply because we were producing too much. "Well, why not become an economist?" asked my wife. Only then did I realize that in a subconscious puritanical way I had felt that it would be too good to be true to be able to earn a living working at something in which one was so interested and which would cost so little pain to learn. My wife had given me the courage to choose the primrose path, and I now decided to become an economist.

I sold my horses, cows, farm equipment, grain, and hay. I would never be able to cite my farming career as evidence of my natural astuteness as an economist. I had bought everything at the peak of the price level. I now sold out at the bottom. Consequently, after I had paid my debts, I found my savings gone. I borrowed a thousand dollars to be used only for temporary emergencies and determined to earn our living while I worked for my degree.

I shall always be grateful to Monmouth College that I was permitted to earn my degree with only an additional semester of work. The fact that I had not taken my final examinations in my junior year was overlooked. A special "veteran's semester of credit" for war service was allowed me. I became an A.B. of the class of 1922 instead of 1918, as I would have been had not the war intervened.

I had decided to go to Wisconsin for graduate study because at that time, according to one of my professors at Monmouth, the economics department of the university was probably the best known in the United States. This was due in large part to the presence there of Professor Richard T. Ely. He had been one of the handful of bright young men who had studied economics in Germany and who had given a new impetus to the subject in the United States at the turn of the century. He had been one of the founders and an early president of the American Economic Association. His *Principles of Economics*, which went through many editions and revisions at the hands of associates, was the most widely used textbook in the field. Professor John R. Commons was also widely known for his monumental two-volume work on the history of the labor movement in the United States. Professor William Kiekhofer gave the lectures in what was the largest, most popular, and widely known course in principles of economics in any American university.

It was possible for us to meet the expense of attending summer school because the University of Wisconsin provided, without charge, wooden platforms for tents in the woods on the shores of beautiful Lake Mendota about two miles from the campus. Tents could be rented from local firms. When we arrived at Madison, we found that all tent platforms had been occupied by previous arrivals. For the next ten days we lived in my army pup tent, which we pitched along the road which bordered the "Tent Colony." We slept on new-mown hay which I collected from a field on the university agriculture research farm nearby. We cooked on a camp fire. Fortunately, the university authorities decided to build additional tent platforms. After we moved down into the Tent Colony proper, I bought a tent and built some rustic furniture. I built a porch overlooking the lake, and enclosed it in mosquito net. Almost every morning before breakfast, we took a swim and every day we hiked in the surrounding woods. Our expenses were at rock bottom. It was one of the finest times of my life. We were to spend four summers in the Tent Colony while I was working for my Ph.D. Tent and furniture were stored from one season to another in a small storeroom belonging to the university.

I majored in labor in the economics department at Wisconsin under Professor Commons. His manner of teaching helped to convince me that methods of teaching by the best professors may vary widely; one might even say wildly. Indeed, by now I am convinced that it is very desirable that students should have the experience of being taught by widely divergent methods. Commons' lectures seemed to have no organization at all. There was little evidence of advance preparation. He sat sideways with his legs hanging over the arm of his chair, seeming to say whatever happened to come in his mind.

Yet Commons was not only a great research scholar, as his writings testify. He was the leader in the whole field of institutional economics. He somehow stimulated his students to do research themselves. Up till now, I had thought of graduate study as learning as much of the accumulated knowledge in my field as possible. I have since known some graduate schools which have functioned primarily to delimit the horizon of knowledge and to fill their students with the pride of detailed acquaintance with the works of the great masters who have worked within this horizon. Commons made us realize that there were vast reaches of knowledge not yet explored and above all that we could do exploration ourselves.

It was Commons who aroused my interest in economic history. At his famous "Friday Nights," his graduate students gathered with him for dinner at the Faculty Club. There one night Professor Eugene Byrne of the history department gave us a talk on the work he had been doing in the archives of the city of Genoa. He had brought back thousands of photostats of the notarial records of the thirteenth century. Commons had stimulated my curiosity in the origins of modern capitalism and now here were records of its very beginnings. Commons agreed that I might do my doctoral dissertation on the subject of "Capital and Contract in Genoa in the Twelfth and Thirteenth Centuries." The records of the twelfth century had been previously published in *Monumenta Patriae*, but the even more interesting records of the thirteenth century existed only in the medieval Latin script of the notaries, who wrote in what was almost a kind of shorthand. At first it looked as though it would be impossible to decipher this script. I found, however, that it was mainly a matter of getting used to the handwriting of a particular notary. I was to spend three months of each of the next three summers working on this material. Eventually I was to publish two articles based on these documents of which the most basic was "The Sea Loan in Genoa in the 12th and 13th Centuries," published in the *Quarterly Journal of Economics* in 1926. I found this research was to be of the greatest value as background for the work in economic systems, which was to become my field of special interest.

Professor Selig Perlman, who had been a graduate student of Commons and who had assisted him in the research for his labor history, had by this time taken over the regular courses in labor in the economics department. His courses in both the American labor movement and foreign labor movements were to be invaluable to me. Professor Perlman had been born and had grown up in Russia, and his knowledge of the field of Russian labor and radical movements and doctrines was encyclopedic and brilliantly analytic. Without this background, I would not have been at all adequately prepared for the studies of the Soviet economic system which I was later to carry out.

My work at Wisconsin greatly strengthened my interest in and sympathy for the labor union movement in the United States. A number of Wisconsin graduate students were to work in the labor movement in the years to come. This was the period of the "Open

Shop Movement," of the "Yellow Dog Contract," and of professional strike breakers, in which the labor unions were not only failing to make progress but were in a weak defensive position. The Republican administration of President Harding, who had been elected on the slogan of a "Return to Normalcy," represented the recrudescence of a self-confident American capitalism. Capitalism, which had been momentarily shaken by World War I and by the Russian Revolution, now once more felt secure, and with security, arrogance returned. With my invariable instinct to favor the underdog, the Wisconsin idealization of the labor union as a social institution struck a responsive chord. Dave Beck and Jimmy Hoffa and their likes were still in the future. I had not yet seen the Soviet system at work. Consequently, I had not learned the lesson that the seeds of arrogance reside in most human beings who have the urge to power. These seeds tend to germinate and grow when such individuals attain positions of power under all forms of political, economic, and social organization. Consequently, society, to protect itself, must always strive to limit and mitigate arrogance not only by controlling the forms which political and economic organization take, but by constantly restraining the leaders of such organizations in their wielding of power and by insuring the rotation of leadership.

The balance between liberty and order is most complex and delicate. Leadership must have a minimum of authority to be able to administer the affairs of society. Yet both incipient tyranny and incipient anarchy lurk behind all organizational forms. Revolution cannot be depended upon to overthrow tyrants, for while all revolutions do not produce tyrannies, almost all tyrants have been produced by revolutions. Only an organically developed set of political, economic, and social institutions can make possible both liberty and order. But all this, I was to learn only over many years of observing society in great travail.

I had expected to stay on at Wisconsin for the following year. I was to have a teaching assistantship, but how we would have managed to live I do not know. Fortunately, just at this time I was offered an instructorship at the School of Business at the University of Minnesota with the opportunity to do half-time graduate work. It paid $2200 for nine months, and it seemed a fortune. I gladly accepted.

Chapter seven. *University life, North and South*

In the School of Business at the University of Minnesota, I taught sections in principles of economics, economic history, and production economics. My graduate work at Minnesota under Professors Garver and Hansen went a long way in compensating for the deficiencies in my training in economic theory up to this time. The opportunity to teach principles of economics while I was studying theory was an invaluable experience. Young men are better instructors than older men in elementary courses even though, or perhaps because, they know less about their subject. Young men naturally find it easier to present basic principles in terms simple enough so that they can be understood and mastered. The sophomore finds undue complexity revolting. He is inclined to say to himself, "Make up your mind, Professor; is it this way or that way?" Perhaps it is unallowable to purport to present reality in terms which are unreally simple. Yet I think this is permissible in the early stages of learning. A young man has the energy needed to dominate thirty or forty students while explaining basic theoretical material in such a way that it becomes an integral part of their minds. I know of no other profession which places such demands on mind and energy if the job is to be adequately done. Fortunately, it is only as one grows older that one fully realizes this.

A large majority of the faculties of American colleges and universities have for many years been Democratic by sympathy and vote, unless there happens to be a third party somewhat more leftist in program participating in an election. While I was at Minnesota,

LaFollette was the third-party candidate in 1924. A number of us young instructors signed a statement in favor of LaFollette. Reporters of the leading newspaper called us to ask whether each of us had signed the statement. I now believe it was merely an effort to verify the signatures, but at the time we interpreted it as an effort to intimidate us.

One night a number of us attended a meeting of the AF of L City Central which we had heard had been arranged in order to expel the Communists from the City Central. At the meeting a representative of the AF of L served a blunt and detailed ultimatum on the City Central. This representative of the national leadership had been sent to observe the effort of Communists to infiltrate and dominate the City Central. Unbelievably enough, he had spent two whole years at his observational task. He had concluded that the City Central had been infiltrated and then dominated by the Communists. He presented a long list of demands, all of which had to be accepted under penalty of withdrawal of the charter, i.e., wiping out the City Central. Not only must all Communists be expelled; no member of the Central could be elected from any union which permitted Communists among its own members. The Central was also required to promise that Communism or anything related to it should not be discussed or even mentioned in meetings.

The AF of L representative was a paunchy man who looked just like the cartoons of capitalists which appeared in socialist newspapers. He was not very gifted in mind or speech, and the Communist sympathizers in the Central literally skated around him throwing verbal darts into him the while. To this he only replied, "Have your fun tonight, but this will be the last night. I won't even discuss our demands with you, but you will accept them exactly as presented, or there will be no City Central Labor Union in Minneapolis." In spite of bitter recriminations, the demands were agreed to.

We did have some understanding of what Communists were like, and I think all of us favored their expulsion. Some of the AF of L demands, however, seemed quite outrageous to us in their denial of free speech. It was only in after years when I had had experience in Soviet Russia of the absolute repression of personal freedom and I had also come to understand the completely unscrupulous methods used by Communists to infiltrate and seize control of labor unions with the most callous disregard of the wishes of the majority of the members that I came to sympathize with the inept AF of L representative.

I left Minnesota with regret after two years still a strong sympathizer with labor unions. I went to Duke University into an area in which labor was still the underdog and was to remain so for many years to come. We had stopped in Madison long enough for me to pass my final examination for the Ph.D. and to teach in the summer session at Wisconsin. I shall always be grateful that I was permitted to get the degree in three calendar years, during two years of which I taught full time. I had been careful to fulfil the letter of the regulations of the Graduate School at Wisconsin. It would have been easy, however, to have so interpreted the regulations that I would have had to spend at least another year. But nobody did.

We were so happy when our second daughter, Sylvia, joined our tightly knit family circle just before we left Minneapolis for Duke University where I had been appointed Assistant Professor of Economics. Duke University had come into existence in December, 1924, through the establishment of the Duke Endowment by James B. Duke, which provided funds for the transformation of Trinity College into Duke University. Trinity College had been a small college closely connected with the Southern Methodist church. When we arrived at Duke, it was still in its physical form entirely unchanged from Trinity College, and its intellectual modification was just barely beginning. Trinity was indeed a Southern college, but neither the college itself nor Durham, the town in which it was located, had much connection with the stereotype of the plantation South—Southern colonels, faithful colored servants, moonlight and roses, etc. Such a South had, of course, been largely fictitious anyhow, but it had even less relevancy to Trinity College and Durham, North Carolina, than almost anywhere else in the South.

Durham had barely existed before the Civil War. At the census of 1870, it had had 256 inhabitants. It was an industrial town of some 40,000 inhabitants when we arrived. It owed its existence first to the tobacco factories which the Duke family had been largely instrumental in establishing, and secondly to the textile mills, in which there had also been a Duke investment. Trinity College had been moved to Durham some years before from its original location farther west in the state with the prospect of financial support from

Washington Duke, the father of J. B. Duke. This financial support had been forthcoming and had been largely responsible for the survival of the college.

From the first I thought of myself as much more radical in my social and economic outlook than was true of the trustees of Duke University, the trustees of the Duke Endowment, the university administration, the city of Durham, and the state of North Carolina in general. I realize now that I carried a chip on my shoulder for many years.

Shortly after my arrival, Paul Blanshard, a reporter for the *Nation*, appeared on the campus and suggested that he might talk to one of my classes. I willingly agreed. In the course of his talk he made the statement that Southern textile workers were the lowest paid industrial workers in the United States. It happened that one of the students in the class provided the Associated Press with occasional items about events at the university. The statement about the lower wages of Southern textile workers was published widely. One of the Duke trustees was outraged. He wrote a letter to President Few saying that he was "shocked that anything of the sort could have happened within the sacred portals of Duke University." I was shown the letter but was not reprimanded. As I thought the matter over, I felt that the trustee perhaps had a right to be irritated. I had been hired to teach classes in economics. Did I have a right to turn my class, a captive audience, over as a forum for an outsider to present his point of view? It is not easy to give a categoric answer.

I have always felt that an instructor should not be a protagonist of policies in the economic, political, or social fields. I would be ashamed to give a course which glorified capitalism, and I would frown on its being done by an instructor for whom I had some responsibility. Certainly I should feel the same way about being a protagonist for socialism. Protagonism for Soviet Communism would be ruled out on more positive grounds since the system denies all freedom. Yet, perhaps, I am naïve in disclaiming protagonism for capitalism. A student who took my courses could not fail to know that I found our present system of modified capitalism in the United States preferable to alternative economic and political systems. Yet I think the comparison could be presented in no other way. It would be quite intolerable intellectually to present the advantages and disadvantages of alternative economic systems so that they exactly balanced, when in fact, in my judgment, they do not. Indeed, I have never favored the method of presenting the good and the evil of alternative economic systems as a method of teaching. On the contrary, it is much better simply to analyze their structure and functioning and allow the student to decide about their goodness and badness.

What Blanshard had said about low wages in Southern textile mills was quite true. The workers not only were unorganized, their political power was almost nil. Consequently, they were unable to improve their lot either through collective bargaining or labor legislation. Yet the development of the textile industry had given employment to men and women who would otherwise have been unemployed or living at a still lower standard of living in the back country. The South had been an underdeveloped area up to this time. In this stage it had *needed* low wages, in the first instance, to enable its yarn and cloth to be sold in competition with those of the established mills of New England. Further, the Southern textile industry could not obtain economic aid in the form of grants or low-interest loans from abroad as do India and other underdeveloped countries from the United States today. Contrary to what is commonly believed, the textile industry did *not* move down to the South bodily from New England. Much the greater number of Southern mills were indigenous, built up by Southern entrepreneurs with Southern capital. The Southern mill owners had had more sense than to invest their scarce capital in secondhand machinery from New England. They bought new machinery with capital built up out of the profits attainable from paying wages which were low in comparison with the North but high in comparison with other employment opportunities available in the South.

All this is changed now. If Southern organized labor does not have the quasi-monopoly of economic and political power which it wields in the industrial areas outside the South, its economic and political power is already great. Ironically enough, however, the competition which the Southern textile industry now has to try to meet comes not from the dead textile industry of New England, but from low-wage countries of the world favored until very recently by cheap subsidized American raw cotton.

Since I have been at Duke, the issue of academic freedom has occasionally arisen again. Many years later one of our wealthy alumni wrote a letter and sent us an article which had been written denouncing as radical and subversive Lorie Tarshis' *Principles of Economics*, which we were using as the text in our course in principles. I had, in fact, adopted the text on the recommendation of the committee of instructors who were teaching the course, but as chairman of the department, I assumed general responsibility for all texts used. Professor William H. Wannamaker, then Vice President and Dean of the University, showed me the letter and article, and we then both individually examined the text. While I naturally would not have agreed with everything in the book, I could find nothing in it which would have made its use as a text inappropriate. Dean Wannamaker made exactly the same finding. We courteously so informed the alumnus. I do not think he was happy with our reply, and perhaps we lost a potential million dollars in endowment thereby. I know of no instance since I have been at Duke of repression of academic freedom. Certainly I know of no other institution at which I could have been freer to study, to teach, to write, and to talk about anything I liked.

Professors sometimes would restrict the freedom of others to criticize us. I have heard professors denounce any criticism of themselves as though it were a crime or at least should be made a crime. It is charged that professors of economics generally advocate "creeping socialism." I do not believe it, but I think that this is an expression of opinion which anyone should be free to make. I do not believe that professors should be exempt from criticism. I have been referred to orally, although not in my presence, as a Red and as probably a Communist. This is on a par with being called a Fascist or a Nazi. Some left-leaning professors seem to think, however, that they should be permitted to refer to persons by these terms without any inhibitions. I have been referred to in print as "the celebrated reactionary, Calvin Hoover." I did, indeed, resent the use of these epithets. Yet if a man speaks, writes, and takes part in the formulation of public policy, he must expect to be denounced sometimes. As former President Truman has put it, "If you can't stand the heat, you had better get out of the kitchen."

Since I was impressed on my arrival in Durham by the low level of both economic and political power of labor in North Carolina, I was eager to do whatever I could to improve its situation.

At that time, North Carolina had no Workmen's Compensation Act to provide compensation for injuries suffered in employment. Consequently, if a laborer was injured on the job, he was dependent upon the good will of his employer or he had to bring a court action. In the latter case, he might have to pay half of anything the court awarded in lawyer's fees. Wisconsin had had one of the first and best of the Workmen's Compensation Acts, and it had been drawn in such a way that the courts had held it to be constitutional, and I was familiar with it. A committee was formed which included Frank Graham, later President of the University of North Carolina, T. U. Wilson, representing the AF of L, as well as a number of professors from neighboring institutions. We got the American Association for Labor Legislation, headed by a Wisconsin friend, to draw up a model bill.

Fortunately, the representative of the manufacturers of North Carolina in dealing with these matters before the committee of the legislature was a most able and forward-looking attorney, Melville Broughton, later governor and senator. He fully recognized the merits of the proposed bill and supported it before the legislature. In consequence, one of the most liberal Workmen's Compensation Acts in the nation was adopted. Almost the only opposition was from a handful of "ambulance-chasing" lawyers.

After a few years my contacts with political, economic, and educational personalities and movements were greatly facilitated by my membership in the Watauga Club. This club consisted of some twenty members, made up of several of the leading newspaper men, educators, and holders of state offices. It usually included the governor, a former governor or two, a senator or former senator, the President of the University of North Carolina, the Chancellor of State College, and others. Dr. Clarence Poe, editor of the *Progressive Farmer*, was the moving spirit of the club. Membership was for life, except that for reasons of health or absence from the state one might go on inactive status. We had dinners twice a month, originally at the home of a member, but eventually, as the servant situation changed, at a hotel or club. The club was the means of informal contact by which new and old ideas and projects could be informally discussed and often developed and put into effect without political or class acrimony. Contacts of this sort among influential people in the state have played a role in preventing the rise of the political demagogue or the corrupt politician which have plagued some other Southern states as well as others outside the South. The club became my main source of political lore and of acquaintance with North Carolinian personalities.

From the Watauga Club I also absorbed a wealth of information on North Carolinian folkways, together with a choice collection of tales of events, full of local color. Some of the best of these tales dealt with the accommodation made by whites and Negroes to local mores. According to one tale, a large landowner who also operated a general store sued one of his tenants for a sum which he claimed was due him. The facts in the case as stated by the white landlord were apparently incontrovertible. The Negro offered only one defense. "I know Mr. Johnson is a fine, educated man, and he wouldn't lie. But Mr. Johnson's got five farms and twenty-two share croppers. Besides that, he got that big store. He got to keep track of all them things, and any man is just bound to forget some things. Me, I only got this little share crop piece of land to remember about, and I can remember one thing and that's like I told you all." The all white jury found for the Negro. The judge set aside the verdict as patently contrary to the facts. The case was tried again with the same result. On the third trial, the landlord asked to be heard and said, "This case has been heard twice before, and the jury found for the defendant. I would like to ask that the case against the defendant be dismissed." Needless to say, it was dismissed.

Another yarn had to do with a "mean white" who had made a good deal of money running a general store and loaning money to Negroes at high rates of interest on chattel mortgages. Hearing of a state highway which was to be constructed to run through a small farm owned by a Negro farmer, he encouraged the Negro to borrow money on a note secured by a chattel mortgage on a hog. He knew that the owner of the farm would get a handsome payment for the land required by the highway. After a while the Negro sold the hog, doubtless intending to pay the holder of the mortgage eventually. But to sell mortgaged property without the consent of the mortgage holder constituted a criminal offense. The "mean white" threatened the Negro with jail if he did not sell his farm to him for a pitifully low price.

The Negro went at once to a local white lawyer with a reputation for looking after poor men in trouble and told his story. The lawyer went to the white man and said, "Here is your money due you on your note secured by your chattel mortgage. I know this man acted illegally when he sold the hog without your permission. I can assure you, however, that regardless of the law, no jury in North Carolina before which I will try this case will convict this man." "O.K.," was the reply; "you can't blame me for trying."

When the lawyer reported the happy result to his Negro client, the Negro said, "Mr. Eaton, I surely do thank you. I know you've got a white skin, but you've surely got a mighty black heart." [1]

Soon after my move to Duke I wrote an article based upon my doctoral dissertation which was published in the *Quarterly Journal of Economics*, "The Sea Loan in Genoa in the Twelfth and Thirteenth Centuries." Since I had learned how important so-called scholarly publication was for advancement in the profession, I had been delighted when the article was accepted. I even received fifty dollars for it, which was a small additional delight, for I did not know that anything at all was paid for such articles. Soon thereafter I published an article in the *Nation* entitled "The South is Still Solid."

The favorable reception of both articles was, I think, largely determinative of my life as a writer. If both these articles had been rejected, I doubt whether I would have had enough self-confidence to continue research and writing. It is sometimes charged that too much emphasis is placed in the academic world on publication of research. This is true in many instances. Academic advancement does indeed depend much more upon research and publication than upon the quality of one's teaching. It is often erroneously assumed, however, that a good research man is almost never a good teacher and vice versa. This is simply not so. Still less true is the crass form of this which runs, "He does no research and consequently he is bound to be a good teacher."

During the next forty years I was to write eight books and some hundred articles. Most of the articles were in so-called learned journals such as the *American Economic Review*, *The Economic Journal*, *The Journal of Political Economy*, the *Quarterly Journal*

1. The late William T. Polk, genial correspondent of the *Greensboro Daily News* and a member of Watauga used to tell the story. It can also be found in his *Southern Accent* (New York: William Morrow & Co., 1953).

of Economics, The Southern Economic Journal, and the like. But I also wrote for a wider public in the *Virginia Quarterly Review, The Yale Review, Foreign Affairs*, the *Economist, Current History, Die Neue Rundschau* and others. I even wrote articles for the Sunday *New York Times* and, after my friend Russell Wiggins became editor, an article for the *Washington Post*.

I do not believe that this research and writing was at all detrimental to my service as a professor except in the sense that I could not be teaching during the years when I had leaves to carry out major research projects. For twenty years I was also Chairman of the Department of Economics, and for ten of those years I was Dean of the Graduate School. Through the years I have also participated actively in the various committees and councils of the university.

Much the same could be said of my service as an economic and strategic Intelligence adviser to government. This began in 1933 with the emergency engendered by the Great Depression and has continued substantially to the present time. I recognize, however, that there is always a potential conflict of interest between the claims of one's own university on one's time and the needs of government. Except in dire emergency, universities cannot be expected to release members of their faculties for governmental service at any moment and for periods of indefinite length. It has come to be a routine ploy for my friends whom I may meet at a conference in Washington, New York, London, Paris, or Berlin to exclaim, "Don't you ever stay home?" My answer is that actually I stay home most of the time, but I naturally meet them when I am away from Duke. In fact, much of the time that I have been away from Duke has been during the summer, on weekends, or on regular sabbatical leaves. The exceptions have been the emergencies of two wars and the Great Depression.

It would assuredly not have been possible for me to have served for twenty years as Chairman of the Department of Economics while carrying on so many other activities if it had not been for Dr. Frank de Vyver, who for many years took so much of the management of the department off my shoulders. Rarely have any two people worked so closely and amicably together. We continued to do so after he became my successor as chairman.

That the department has been rated in recent years among the top ten in the nation has been due in significant degree to the insistence of Dr. Joseph Spengler, who for some years has been Director of Graduate Studies in the department, on the maintenance of the highest standards in graduate work. His own scholarly articles have also constituted a major element in the very substantial publication list of the department.

I had taught principles of economics at Duke from the first, and as the department grew in size, I had general direction of all our sections in addition to my two graduate courses, the one in economic theory, the other in economic systems. At first I had just two graduate students, Dick Harvill and Ben Ratchford. The one is President of the University of Arizona, and the other is now Vice President in charge of Research at the Federal Reserve Bank of Richmond. For years the latter was a colleague professor at Duke, and I sent for him whenever I had a difficult assignment whether in Washington, Berlin, or Paris. He always came and performed with the efficiency which characterizes all that he does. Another of my early graduate students, Dr. Robert S. Smith, has been and still is an esteemed colleague at Duke and is now chairman of the department.

Like all university professors, I have through the years had thousands of students. I have learned an enormous amount in the process of teaching them. I keep meeting my former students pretty much all over the world. It is a pleasure since students almost always look back on their college days and even on their professors through rose tinted glasses, however critical of them they may have felt in their student days. I recall walking down the Rue de la Paix in Paris on my way back from our Army of Occupation in Germany in the late summer of 1945. An army jeep rolled by. A head stuck itself out of the jeep and yelled, "Hi, Doc Hoover!" I am sure the student had never before seen me in uniform. I do not know to this day who he was, but it gave me a small thrill.

One of the finest things about the academic profession is the almost four months that one has off in the summer. Perhaps 20 per cent of the profession take these months simply as a vacation. Personally, I do not see how anyone could do it. Most of the profession, however, teach in the summer session, do research at home or abroad, work as consultants for the government or for industry, or perhaps just work up their courses for the next year. The opportunity to do something quite different from what I do during the regular year, which for me has usually meant research abroad or acting as economic advisor to our government, has been a privilege beyond price.

During the summer of 1927 I taught in the summer session at Cornell University. After the six weeks' summer session was over, I worked on a research article based on material from the medieval Genoese archives. Almost every afternoon our family went on picnics along the lovely Finger Lakes or in the glens. I have never seen anything more lovely in the world than Enfield Glen, and we enjoyed these picnics immensely.

What was really noteworthy about the summer in Ithaca was an incident which finally dampened the Don Quixote complex which has always afflicted me. While I was walking along University Avenue one day with my daughter Carol, then about six years old, I became aware of an altercation going on in the yard of a house a few yards ahead of us. The ground sloped steeply down from the sidewalk here and one looked down almost on the roofs of the houses. It was as though I had suddenly walked into the middle of a movie. I saw a burly man in painter's overalls pick up a board and strike a rather slight, well-dressed man over the head. The board split in two, apparently because of the violence of the blow (actually because of the rottenness of the board), the man fell to the ground, and his assailant began to kick him in the head. I was overcome with horror. I assumed that the attacker must have suddenly gone insane. I felt that I should at once defend the man on the ground against his brutal assailant.

However, I feared for the safety of my small daughter. Hastily I grabbed her hand and ran back with her about a block and planted her behind a rose bush, enjoining her not to move until I got back. I then returned to the scene of the incident. The painter was standing beside his ladder, which leaned against the house, saying not a word. The wife of the man on the ground, who was bleeding slightly from the nose, had come out of the house and was wringing her hands. It no longer seemed appropriate to try to restrain the assailant, since he was momentarily not moving. I picked the man up off the ground and carried him into the house and laid him on a sofa. I then started to phone the police. To my surprise the woman tried to dissuade me. I nevertheless did call the police, and as soon as I was sure that they were on the way, I went back and collected my daughter and took her home. I worried over the memory of that brutal attack for several days with the feeling that I should have intervened more rapidly and violently than I had been able to do.

I later heard what had happened just prior to my arrival on the scene, and it was like seeing the first half of a movie which one had missed by coming in late. The painter had been on the ladder painting the house. The owner of the house, who got knocked down, had been drunk and had tried to pull the ladder out from under the painter. When the painter had tumbled down the ladder and protested, the man had drawn a knife on him. At this point I had come in, and from there on out the incident had taken on an utterly deceptive appearance. I never forgot it, and it was to prevent me from going off half-cocked in a good many situations thereafter.

I spent a good part of the summer of 1928 doing research at the Federal Reserve Bank of New York. I wrote a couple of articles dealing with the volume and velocity of bank deposits in relation to broker's loans, the one published in the *Annalist*, the other in the *Journal of Political Economy*. My interest in money and bank credit, investment and speculation has continued to the present day, and I still write in this field occasionally.

My observation of capitalism viewed from Wall Street at the height of the boom which preceded the crash of 1929 was to serve as a useful point of reference when I was to study the economic system of Soviet Russia in the following year. I had applied for a fellowship from the Social Science Research Council for the previous year but had not been successful. I applied for a grant to study the Soviet banking and monetary system. I really wanted to study the entire economic system, but I had feared to say so lest such a project would seen too ambitious. I was most grateful when on my second try my application was successful, and I was informed that I could study anything I wanted to.

I had already begun to study the Russian language, and now I intensified my efforts. My teacher was a student at the School of Commerce of the University of North Carolina. He was the finest type of White Russian, handsome, reserved, with an erect military bearing and beautiful manners, speaking well-nigh perfect English, deeply patriotic, hating the Bolsheviks and all their works with passion. He had been an ensign in the Tsarist navy just before the Revolution broke out. He had fought against the Bolsheviks first under Yudenitch, then under Denikin, and finally under Wrangel. He had had to go into exile when Wrangel was driven out of the Crimea. From Constantinople he had gone to Paris and had finally reached the United States. He was an excellent teacher, and as a by-product of studying with him, I got a personal account of the Revolution and Civil War in Russia which was to add much to the many published volumes on the subject I had been reading and was to read in the future. I heard many other such accounts during the coming year while I was living in Moscow.

If in succeeding chapters little space is given to academic life, this does not reflect a lack of either respect or affection for it. It is simply that for the task of describing economic, political, and social change in my lifetime, the events of my life outside the academic world when I began to analyze the major types of economic systems, and later when I began to participate in the formulation and administration of our national policies, serve the purpose better.

Chapter eight. *The economic life of Soviet Russia during the First Five Year Plan*

I had received notice of my appointment as a Social Science Research Council Fellow for research on the Soviet economic system in the spring of 1929. Although I did not know it at the time, this was just on the eve of drastic events in both the capitalistic economic system in the United States and in the Soviet economic system in Russia. In the United States we were just approaching the crest of the great wave of prosperity which was to crash in the stock market in October, 1929. In Russia in October, 1929, there had just begun the second year of the *Piatiletka*, the first five year plan, which coincided with the end of NEP, the so-called New Economic Policy.

Following the period of War Communism, Lenin had inaugurated NEP in 1921, some three years before his death. Since the New Economic Policy was inaugurated at the time of the great famine of 1921, it was generally assumed outside Russia that this retreat to capitalism "had been caused by the famine." The record is quite clear, however, that Lenin had ordered the change in economic policy before the famine, because he could see that unless action was taken, the production of grain was bound to be inadequate to feed the Russian people. According to the New Economic Policy, all grain above that necessary for subsistence was no longer to be requisitioned from the peasants. Instead, after the payment of a definite tax, the peasants were to be free to sell their surplus grain on the free market for as much as they could get for it. The rather feeble attempt which had been made to collectivize the peasant farms was abandoned. Retail trade, which had been absolutely prohibited, was once more permitted. As a result, a small class of get-rich-quick merchants called "Nepmen" had come into existence. These Nepmen and their families, however, were not allowed to have even those vestigial civil rights which were allowed the urban workers and peasants. Rationing was gradually abolished, although later it had to be restored. Equality in compensation was abandoned, and a hierarchy of seventeen stages in the wage structure depending upon skill, training, and responsibility was set up. Concessions were granted to foreign capitalists to invest capital and "know-how" in Russia. Permission, later withdrawn, to remit profits abroad was also given. The currency was temporarily partially stabilized.

Lenin himself referred to NEP as "a step back, the better to leap forward," and it was inevitable that this temporary retreat to some of the practices of capitalism should have been widely interpreted as incontrovertible evidence that a collectivist economic system had failed, as it was bound to have failed. Among liberals in the West, it was hoped that the Soviet system would now develop democratic and parliamentary political institutions together with some form of "industrial democracy."

The triumph of Stalin over Trotsky had also been widely interpreted as a further movement of the Russian revolutionary movement to the right and towards stability. Trotsky had advocated the doctrine of "Permanent Revolution" on both the domestic and international fronts. He had insisted that the capital for the industrialization of Russia should be squeezed out of the peasants by means of high prices for goods produced by industry and low prices for grain. He had advocated pressure against the kulaks, the so-called rich peasants, and the eventual absorption of the squeezed out peasantry into the working class. He had advocated the militarization of labor. All these Stalin had opposed. Since Trotsky was first stripped of his offices, then expelled from the Communist party, and finally exiled from Russia, it looked like a clear victory for the conservative Right.

When I arrived in Russia in August, 1929, NEP was already in decline. While I lived in Moscow from that time until May, 1930, all of NEP which represented a movement towards capitalistic conservatism and stability was to be swept away. The relaxation of the

Terror under NEP came to an end, and the GPU, the secret police, began to resume the dread role which the *Cheka* had exercised during the Revolution and Civil War. I was consequently to be the observer of a radical shift in Soviet policy which I would not have been on the scene to observe if I had got my appointment as a fellow of the Social Science Research Council for the previous year as I had originally requested.

Living conditions in Soviet Russia in 1929 had made it very inadvisable for me to take my family with me to Moscow. Consequently, we had traveled first to Dresden, where I made arrangements for my family to stay in a *pension*. It had turned out that a number of White Russian refugees lived at this *pension*, and when I subsequently visited my family, the stories which these people had to tell were an additional source of information, even if one-sided information, about the Revolution and Civil War in Russia.

I had a letter of introduction to Miss Doris White, an Irish lady who presided over the remains of the Quaker Center in Soviet Russia which had originally been set up to carry on relief activities during the great famine of 1921. This Center at 15 Borisoglebsky Pereulok was in the old quarter of Moscow known as the Arbat. The Arbat was actually a main street running out of the Arbatsky Ploshad, a square in which the well known old church of "St. Nicholas-on-the-Chicken-Legs" was situated. A number of alleys extended off the Arbat with names like "Tablecloth Street," "Fork Street," "Overshoe Street." According to legend, these alleys were so named from the serf artisans who used to live on them and supplied the tsarist court with such articles of use.

The Quaker Center was established in an old but very solidly built house, occupied in tsarist times by a well-to-do merchant. The living arrangements were a little complicated. Downstairs was the Greek consulate, except that one large room was occupied by the infant daughter of William Henry Chamberlin, the newspaper correspondent, and her Russian nurse. Upstairs, an additional room was occupied by Chamberlin and his wife. Bill White, an American graduate student, and his Russian wife occupied another room upstairs. Miss White had a room, and Marafusha, the Russian peasant servant girl, slept in the kitchen. These complicated and crowded living arrangements were due to the fearful shortage of housing in

Moscow and to the fact that only a very few special buildings had been allocated for foreigners to live in. One of the very few Americans living in Moscow at this time remarked that he had never seen a room in a house or apartment in Moscow without someone's bed in it.

I soon made arrangements to get dinner daily at the Quaker Center, but for some months I had a room with a Russian Jewish family on Kalashin Pereulok. I had determined that I would live with a Russian family if it were at all possible. This family had one of the very few "privately owned" houses in Moscow. The family had rebuilt an old carriage house attached to a former mansion and had in return received a lease on the house from the Moscow Housing Trust for twenty years. Consequently, this family could legally rent me a room.

The maid of all work brought my breakfast and evening tea. Since I had to make arrangements for her to buy me tea, eggs, bread, butter, and the like, this arrangement insured that I would get to practice my Russian. Incidentally, I also learned Yiddish without being conscious that I did so. I had found that the lady of the house understood German, and since I was much more fluent in German than in Russian, I fell into the habit of speaking German with her. One day she asked whether I knew why her German was different from mine. I replied that German was a foreign language to me, but that I knew that she spoke German like a native. She answered, "Oh, no! That is not the reason. You see, I don't speak German at all; I speak Yiddish."

I had come to Russia to study the Soviet economy, but I also wanted to get to know all that I could about the whole way of life of the people under the "Soviet power." [1] Consequently, I worked out every device I could think of in order to acquire familiarity with the structure and functioning of the Soviet economy and with Soviet life. There existed at this time a state organization, the Society for Cultural Relations with Foreign Countries, known by its Russian initials as VOKS. The services of this organization were invaluable to me in arranging interviews and conferences and in providing interpreter-guides. The director of VOKS, Serge Trevas, who was

1. This commonly used and very apt term, *Sovietski Vlast*, might also be translated as "Soviet regime."

very helpful to me, was to be executed during the purges of the thirties.

The knowledge of Russian which I had and which I worked diligently at increasing was immensely helpful to me. Nevertheless, my Russian was not good enough to enable me to conduct efficiently a long interview on detailed and complicated matters. Besides, in a totalitarian society like that of the Soviet, a guide is almost a necessity just as a door-opener and explainer of one's status with the Soviet government.

I spent some three to four hours a night, five nights a week, with a Russian teacher who was also my close friend. I felt that it was even more important to learn to read Russian than to speak it. I had had the experience of learning a kind of basic German which had enabled me to communicate easily enough with the peasants of Luxembourg when I had been in our army of occupation. I had later been shocked to find that I was unable to read economic literature in German, and I had had to correct that deficiency by the expenditure of much time and effort. I did not intend to make this mistake with Russian.

During the day time I conducted a series of interviews with Soviet officials at all levels, in industry, in trade, in banks, in producer's and consumer's "co-operatives," in the commissariats, in peasant villages, and on collective farms. I had hoped that I would find some book or books in Russian which would describe comprehensively the structure and operation of the Soviet economic system since there was virtually nothing in other languages. I found there was almost nothing in Russian either. I had, consequently, to start almost from scratch. In the case of industry, I started with *Gosplan*, the top planning organization. I had an interview with some of its officials at which Professor Strumilin was present. He looked to be an old man then, but unbelievably enough he is still working and writing to this day. I then had a similar conference with the officials of *Vesenkha*, the so-called Supreme Economic Council for industry.

I then chose the textile industry for particular inquiry since I had some acquaintance with it at home. I talked with the heads of the *Obedinenie*,[2] with the directors of one of the five cotton textile

2. I translated this as "Combination," and this term will hereafter generally be used.

trusts, and finally I visited several cotton textile mills. I followed a similar procedure for the other elements of the Soviet economy.[3]

In doing research on the structure of Soviet industry, I sometimes got unexpected insights into other aspects of Soviet society such as labor discipline. In late 1929 I attended a conference on productivity held for worker representatives by the management of the First Cotton Textile Trust at Serpukov, a textile town not far from Moscow. At one stage of the conference, workers were allowed to hand in written questions to the "praesidium" of the meeting, of which I had been appointed an honorary member, seated on a platform. The Director of the Trust was explaining why the last year's increase in production had not been greater. The principal cause, he said, was the activity of saboteurs. Then he unfolded one of the notes which had been handed in and declared dramatically: "We have such a saboteur in our midst at this moment!"

He then read aloud the question which one of the workers had handed in. "Just before the October Revolution, when the Kerensky government was in power, the Mensheviks urged us to work hard and produce as much as possible. The Bolsheviks, however, denounced the Mensheviks and urged us to go on strike and to do everything we could to hinder production. Now you Bolsheviks are saying just what the Mensheviks did, to work hard and produce much. What is the sense of this?" The Director then declared: "This shameless saboteur knows full well the answer to his question. The Mensheviks were urging the workers to produce for the capitalist exploiters. We Communists naturally demand the utmost productivity from all workers now that industry is in the hands of the toiling masses." The anonymous "saboteur" naturally did not rise from his seat and ask, as he might logically have done, just how the toiling masses had decided that the man who denounced him was to be the Director of the First Cotton Textile Trust. The Director, in fact, as in all such cases, was no more elected by the workers of the plants in the Trust than would be the president of any corporation in the capitalistic United States. The disciplinary powers of Soviet management were obviously far greater than are those of management in any unionized plant in the United States.

There was never any hesitancy evidenced in taking whatever

3. For a full account of the results of my study of the Soviet economy, see my *Economic Life of Soviet Russia* (New York: The Macmillan Company, 1931).

measures were necessary in order to maintain discipline. In Sverdlovsk, four workers were accused of *vreditelstvo*, which took the form of general hooliganism and wilful spoilage of machinery and materials. One of the workers was sentenced to from two to three years' "deprivation of freedom," another to five years imprisonment with strict isolation, and still another "to the highest measure of social defense, to be shot." [4]

I visited numbers of factories, and I sometimes visited the nurseries attached to these factories to care for the children of the women employed in them. These nurseries were relied upon to develop future members of a Communist society. It was considered the polite thing to ask the name of the factory, and I always asked the name of the nursery as well. The Soviet expression went, "This is the factory (or nursery or collective farm) in the name of the Hammer and Sickle or in the name of Red October (the Bolshevik Revolution) or in the name of Stalin." I once asked the name of a nursery attached to a chemical plant and was told proudly by the head nurse, "This is 'The Nursery in the name of The Second Loan for Industrialization and Strengthening the Peasant Economy.'" (Such a state loan was at the moment being forcefully pushed.) This custom of patriotic naming was sometimes carried over to persons. One Soviet father christened his daughter Ninel (Lenin spelled backward). The story was that another was christened Diamata for the Marxist doctrine of dialectic materialism. I always doubted this yarn. However, a factory worker who made the trip to Turkestan with us about which I will tell later always referred to himself as "Worker-Peasant" and insisted that this was his name.

I had an interview with the well-known Professor Kondratiev, who was an expert on business cycles and on agricultural production, prices, and policies. Most regrettably the fact that I merely mentioned this interview to another Soviet economist was unfortunate for Kondratiev. It was used against him in his subsequent trial, which resulted in his imprisonment.

I had a letter of introduction to the distinguished economist Yurovsky, who was head of the *Valuta* section of the Peoples Commissariat of Finance. I had a most useful interview with him. He introduced me to the librarian of the Commissariat and invited me to make use of the resources of the library. The librarian proudly

4. *Za Industrializatsiiu*, Jan. 28, 1930.

showed me a small room in which were kept recent issues of foreign periodicals and newspapers available nowhere else in Moscow.

The next day I was reading the *New York Times* when a rather sinister looking individual entered the room and asked who had given me permission to use the library. I replied that Yurovsky had given me permission. "What do I care for Yurovsky?" he cried. "You must leave at once!" I did leave, but very disgruntled. I wrote a note of protest to Yurovsky. I shall regret writing that note to my dying day, for it was most unfortunate in its results both for Yurovsky and for the librarian. I got a note of apology from the official who had thrown me out of the library together with a printed formal pass permitting me to use the library. I never did use the pass, but unfortunately this was not the end of the matter.

Within a week I read an account in *Pravda* of the *chistka* or "cleaning" to which the librarian had been subjected. One of the major charges against him was that he spent most of his time reading the foreign periodicals in the library. With a heavy heart, I realized that this really referred to his connection with me. He was "cleaned out in the third category," or in the current phrase, he was given a "wolf's passport." This meant that he could not vote (this was, of course, unimportant), he could hold no state job (there were almost no others), he would not be given a ration card, his children, if any, could not attend school beyond the elementary grades, and he lost his right to housing.

It was an added horror that Yurovsky was later a prominent figure in the purge trials and was sentenced to a long term of imprisonment. I never have heard whether he survived until the rather general freeing of political prisoners after de-Stalinization in 1956.[5]

As I walked along the streets of Moscow, I would read the signs on the buildings. For example, I saw a sign over a building designating it as the office of *Mosselprom.* I found that this was the headquarters of an organization which marketed the products of the local industries of the Moscow *oblast.* When I spotted the office of

5. At Yurovsky's trial he "confessed" to having conspired against the Soviet regime while abroad. Among those with whom he confessed plotting the overthrow of the Soviet government was Waldemar Hoeffding, a Russian emigré whom I later came to know well while he was assisting in the office of our commercial attaché in Berlin in 1932–33 and with whom I was to be in touch for many years thereafter. He assured me that not only had he not talked with Yurovsky at the time alleged, but that he had never seen him since they were graduate students together many years before. Since Yurovsky had to confess to the plot, he undoubtedly sought to implicate someone who would not be endangered by his "confession."

an economic organization of this sort of which I had not previously heard, I made a note of it and then made arrangements for an interview with the official of the organization and worked out its place in the structure of the Soviet economy.

As a further source of information, I usually bought from three to five newspapers a day, usually *Pravda, Isvestia, Za Industrializatsiiu, Ekonomicheskaya Zhizn* and possibly *Vechernaya Moskva.* About once a week I stayed up into the small hours while I clipped out and filed the significant articles from the week's accumulation. A substantial number of economic reports were published in those days, such as the "First Five Year Plan" and the annual "Control Figures," and I bought all I could find. I also bought such periodicals as *Vestnik Finansov* and *Planovoe Khoziaistvo.*

I went to the theater, ballet, or opera whenever I could, taking my Russian teacher with me in lieu of an evening spent with him pounding away at the Russian language. I was particularly moved by the plays based on events of the Civil War, such as *Days of the Turbines* and *Armored Train.* I saw the classic operas *Boris Godunov, Prince Igor*, and *Bride of the Tsar*, the classic ballet *Swan Lake* and the revolutionary *Red Poppy*, as well as others. I took occasion to go to the more experimental theaters such as Meyergold's and the Stanislavsky as well as to the Bolshoi, the Moscow Art Theater, and others. I did this not merely because of a lively interest in drama, opera, and ballet, but because it gave me an opportunity to see masses of Russians and observe what types and what classes went to what theaters. I could also note their clothes, their mannerisms, and their facial expressions as they circled in the foyers of the theaters between acts. Reputedly, the Russian theater, opera, and ballet had been very good under the tsars. There was certainly no sign of deterioration.

The non-proletarian elements in the cities thought with the bitterness of despair of the days which were gone. This was shown in a striking manner by the way in which the audiences at the opera and the theater sometimes took occasion to applaud whenever there was some reference to the "old days." This sometimes necessitated the removal or the alteration of plays or operas in order to remove the opportunity for such demonstrations.

I would have liked to have extended my personal friendships among Russians. This proved possible in only the case of the barest handful. The risk of contact with foreigners was simply too great.

A few American tourists visited Russia in the summer at that time. During the winter months the American colony was very small indeed. Since the United States did not recognize Soviet Russia at this time, there were no Embassy personnel. There was a handful of Americans hired as industrial experts, and a little later their number was to be greatly increased. The resident American colony was made up in major part of the newspaper correspondents assigned to Moscow.

Walter Duranty, who was a British national, was the correspondent of the *New York Times*. He was the dean of the corps by virtue of seniority in Russia, his knowledge of the Russian language, and his fame as a writer. By contrast with some of the other correspondents who had had socialist sympathies and consequently came to be extremely anti-Soviet in their sympathies, Duranty was sophisticated and blasé. When the other correspondents were horrified at the multitude of arrests and executions, at the enforced collectivization of the peasantry, and at the liquidation of the kulaks as a class, Duranty used to say, "You can't make an omelet without breaking some eggs."

William Henry Chamberlin was the correspondent of the *Observer*, the *Manchester Guardian*, and the *Christian Science Monitor*. His wife had been born in Russia, and he also managed to speak Russian. He read Russian with ease. In addition to a number of other books, he wrote his monumental two-volume work, *The Russian Revolution*. I have always been glad that I called the attention of my publisher, the Macmillan Company, to the manuscript. It was published after Chamberlin left Russia. Chamberlin had had strong socialist sympathies when he came to Russia. He became a hostile critic of the Soviet regime and came to appreciate some of the virtues of capitalism. Later he was simultaneously a staff writer on the *Wall Street Journal* and a contributing editor to the *New Leader*, a leftist anti-Communist weekly.

During the period of my first stay in Moscow, Eugene Lyons was the correspondent of the United Press. We all regarded Lyons as very pro-Soviet, as indeed in those days he certainly was. He had been secretary of the Committee for the Defense of Sacco-Vanizetti and had played a prominent role in collecting funds for their defense. I remember one night at a small party we had just received news of the shooting of some half-dozen old tsarist generals who had continued to serve the government after the Bolshevik seizure of power. These pathetic old men were probably innocent of anything except their tsarist past, and everyone except Lyons commented bitterly on the execution. Lyons rather ostentatiously remarked, "I just want to say that I am for these people" (meaning the Soviet government).

During the thirties when the arrest, torture, and execution of those Russians who were his personal friends began, he could no longer argue to himself that these things happened only to former capitalists and tsarist officials. He became greatly depressed and condemned himself for not having the courage to give the true facts to the world. Aware that Lyons had turned against them, the Soviet government set up a journalistic booby trap for him and expelled him from Russia. Thereafter Lyons wrote one of the best accounts of the terror and atrocities of the period in a masterpiece entitled *Assignment in Utopia*.

Jim Mills was correspondent for the Associated Press. A veteran newspaper man who had served all over the world, he had a wonderful series of yarns about his experiences. Carroll Binder was for a few months the correspondent of the *Chicago Daily News*. He had been stationed in Italy and furnished us with interesting comparisons of the two totalitarian regimes. Then there was Ed Deuss of the International News Service, who later was to cover with me the rise of another tyrant as brutal as Stalin when Hitler came to power in Germany in 1933.

Louis Fischer was correspondent of the *Nation* and was regarded almost as a Soviet official. He was later to break with the Communist party at the time of the Nazi Soviet Pact in 1939. Anna Louise Strong was a rather silly old girl who was an enthusiastic admirer of all things Soviet. She was to write *Red Star Over Samarcand* and other similar books. Absurdly enough, she was to be denounced by the Soviet government as an American spy shortly after World War II. Nothing could have been more ridiculous, and after Stalin's death, the charge was withdrawn.

Besides these Americans, there was the witty and whimsical Cholerton, British correspondent of the *Sunday Times*, long resident in Moscow. Before he "went on the wagon," Cholerton used to quote apocryphally St. Cyril as having first remarked, "No one can be blamed for getting drunk in Russia." When I last saw him in London in 1943 during World War II, he claimed that as the result of the constant purges of the party leaders, army officers, and economic administrators, the hair line of the typical Soviet official had been lowered by fully half an inch. He solemnly insisted that in any of the more expensive restaurants and hotels in Moscow the lower brows of these rougher types who had taken over from those displaced by the purges could be compared with one's recollection of those displaced.

Finally, there was Alexander Wicksteed, who had come to Russia with the Quakers during the great famine of 1921 and had stayed on. He taught English conversation at Moscow University. He had "gone native" as none of the other foreigners had, living on the same rations as Russians and in one room in an apartment house inhabited entirely by Russians. Paradoxically enough, he got along with a minimum knowledge of the Russian language. He wrote a book, *Life under the Soviets,* which remains one of the best descriptions of life in Moscow under NEP which has ever been written. Because there were so few of us, we were all the more closely associated, and we interchanged ideas and information fully. I profited greatly from this circumstance.

Writing more than thirty years after that year in Moscow, I am appalled at how frequently I have had to note the arrest and execution at a later time of Russians with whom I was associated. I do not think their association with me was the major factor in their fates. I never repeated any remark which one of these men made to me which could be interpreted by anyone to their disadvantage. Yet I could never deny that the mere fact of their connection with me weighed against them.

I came into contact with the suspicious nature of the Soviet state immediately upon my arrival in Moscow. I had directed that my mail be forwarded to me in care of the State Bank. It was never admitted that mail was censored. When my mail was handed me, I found among the letters one addressed to "The Greater Durham Building and Loan Association, Durham, N. C." I surmised at once what had happened, and I found inside this envelope, which had been intended as a return envelope, the outside envelope addressed to me. The censor had just got a little confused.

After a few weeks, we learned that our maid, Marafusha, had

been ordered to turn over the contents of our wastebaskets weekly to the GPU. It seemed rather silly to us, but we did not mind. Many years later, I was somewhat wryly to recall this surveillance of the wastebaskets when I found that, as a counter-intelligence measure against the Nazi *Sicherheitsdienst* and the *Abwehr*, my OSS people in Stockholm had instituted a similar check of the wastebaskets in the Grand Hotel during World War II.

It was more serious when a friendly minor official of the Commissariat of Foreign Affairs who used frequently to visit us for tea and a hand of bridge, and who we assumed had been delegated to the task of keeping an eye on us, was arrested. Even though he was a member of the Party and had apparently been carrying out assigned duties, we never saw him again. We did hear that he came under suspicion because an uncle of his had tried to escape to Latvia. We used to send him parcels of food and clothing in prison, something it was probably inadvisable for us to do. We never heard from him after his arrest. According to rumor, he was eventually executed.

The most serious danger to a Soviet citizen who has any connection with foreigners was and is the utter inability of people from a free society to realize the dangers therein to Soviet citizens. At its worst, this inability to understand the nature of the police state sometimes reflects a grotesque and disastrous naïveté. During this early period, an American connected with a religious organization used to make periodic visits to Russia. As he was about to leave after one of these visits, he told some of my correspondent friends how he had unmasked the Soviet claim that there was no persecution of religion. "I asked a Soviet official point-blank whether he denied that religious persecution existed. He replied that of course he denied it, whereupon I gave him the names and addresses of a number of persons who had told me that they had been the victims of such persecution." The indignation with which the American newspaper men told me of this can be imagined.

I tried hard never to endanger anyone with whom I came in contact. During my residence in Moscow in 1929–30, I never visited the home of my closest Russian friend; we always parted company some blocks away. My friend had reason to know the risks he ran, and he hoped that our association might not become known and that he might at least avoid involving his family in the risk.

This same friend told me how he had once been asked by a Soviet official to serve as interpreter for an American Communist who was visiting Moscow. He was most reluctant to undertake the assignment and tried to beg off on the grounds of his insufficient command of English. The official insisted that his English was good enough. However, he said, "Do you recall the case of———? [naming a man who was known to have been executed for alleged crimes.] Do you know the real reason he was executed?" "No," said my friend. "The reason was simple," said the Soviet official. "He chattered." The Soviet official mentioned the name of another man who had been executed. Once more he repeated his question, "Do you know why he was executed?" "No," replied my friend. "He chattered," said the Soviet official. A third name was mentioned with the same question and answer. My friend was as frightened as it was intended that he should be. In serving as interpreter for the American Communist, he used all his ingenuity to explain away any critical observations about the Soviet system.

I never saw or communicated with my Russian friend after the day I left him in May, 1930. I was always tempted to look him up when I returned to Russia through the years since I had a warm affection for him, but I never did. The risk to him and his family would have been too great. Only during my last trip in 1958 did I learn that he had been killed during the war.

I left Moscow in late December, 1929, to join my wife and children in Dresden for Christmas. I spent some three weeks in Germany before returning to Moscow. I had previously spent some ten days with my family in Germany before going on to Moscow. After I completed my stay in Russia, I was to spend another month in Germany. These periods were to be of great value in building up my background on German affairs for my forthcoming year in Germany in 1932–33.

I had left Moscow with serious misgivings lest I might be denied a visa when I wished to return. Consequently, I had applied for a return visa even before I left Russia. After leaving Dresden, I went to the Soviet Embassy in Berlin and asked for the visa which I explained was waiting for me. The rather sullen clerk went away and then came back to announce that there was no visa. I really had little hope, but I told him sternly that there was a visa there for me and to please get it at once. He went away and came back with the visa. A curious example of unpredictable Soviet bureaucracy.

On the train from Berlin to Moscow, I met an Austrian textile manufacturer who had one of the few concessions which had been granted to foreign businessmen under the NEP. He was a useful source of information with his experiences of day-to-day contact with the Soviet economic bureaucracy. He said that he was making a good profit but already saw the handwriting on the wall since he now found all sorts of barriers placed against remitting his profits outside Russia.

Finally he remarked, "Even if I had to liquidate my business now, I would have made some money. I regard myself, however, as a traitor to my class since I have been helping these Communists to learn industrial techniques. They are rather quiescent now, but some day they will try to overthrow capitalism throughout the world, but I had no choice. I came back to Vienna from the war to find the Austro-Hungarian Empire destroyed and my former business with it. This Soviet concession which I obtained was the gamble of a desperate man." As he spoke, we were passing through the area in which some of the most severe fighting of the German and Austrian armies against the Russian army had taken place. "Ah," he said, "I recognize that grove of trees. I recall a day when a Czech deserter from the Austrian army hung from each tree. We hanged those poor devils as traitors then. I suppose I am as much a traitor as ever they were."

I said, "Perhaps I am a traitor, too, since I am studying the Soviet economic system and will write a book about it." "No," said he, "Professors have extra-territoriality in such matters. They do not represent any class." I was much struck by what he said, and I have indeed tried always to maintain that extra-territoriality of which he spoke.

Chapter nine. *The Soviet totalitarian state*

The tremendous increase in tension and terror which had begun almost at the moment of my arrival in Russia in August, 1929, had its source in the decision of Stalin to give up his attempt at placating the peasants and to embark on a campaign for the collectivization of agriculture. The *Piatiletka*, the great Five Year Plan for the industrialization of Russia at forced draft, had depended upon the export of Russian grain to pay for the imports of heavy machinery needed to build up an industrial base. But the sown area was not expanding and hardly enough grain was being delivered to the state to feed the urban population.

The peasants were no longer allowed to sell their surplus grain on the free market. A ruthless program of compulsory delivery of grain was undertaken which often left the peasants with insufficient grain even for bare subsistence. Simultaneously, the program for the collectivization of agriculture was speeded up far beyond that provided in the Plan. The peasants resisted desperately, but in the long run to no avail.[1]

The tremendous social and economic upheaval in Russian agriculture caused by forced collectivization of the peasantry was to affect every aspect of Russian life. Since the peasants resisted collectivization by killing a large proportion of their livestock, the food supply was impaired for years to come. The much greater tempo of collectivization, added to the slaughter of their horses by the peas-

1. See my chapter on agriculture in *The Economic Life of Soviet Russia* for a detailed account of the resistance of the peasantry and the measures of force taken against them by the Soviet government.

antry, necessitated the importation of thousands of tractors. These could be paid for only by the export of grain which was really needed at home. Above all, the uprooting of millions of kulaks together with the general hatred of collectivization by the peasants led to the inauguration of the terror which was never to cease during Stalin's life.

When I returned to Moscow from Berlin in January, 1930, I found that terror and tension had greatly increased during the month of my absence. I made every effort to observe and record the terrible events of this period. I made trips to peasant villages and to collective farms. I never overlooked an opportunity to pick up information from even casual contacts. The peasant woman who delivered milk to us suddenly found her husband and herself declared to be kulaks. She poured out her tale of woe to me. I was able to document many of the cases of which I heard without referring to the individuals with whom I had talked, because many similar cases were reported in the Soviet press at a time when the official policy was temporarily reversed, and it was desired to print horrible examples of "mistakes" that had been made in order to justify the change in policy.

One of the main measures upon which the Communist party relied to overcome the opposition of the peasantry was the stimulation of class warfare in the village. In order to insure that class warfare should be brought into existence, every peasant found himself registered as a kulak, a *ceredniak*, or a *bedniak*. A kulak was theoretically a peasant who hired labor and was consequently an exploiter. A *bedniak* was a poor peasant, and a *ceredniak* was a "Middle" peasant. In many villages, however, there were practically no peasants who hired any labor, or who loaned money or seed grain or work animals, all of which things were supposedly done by the kulaks. The villagers in such cases might report that there were no kulaks in the village. But such a state of affairs was intolerable. If there were no kulaks, how could there be any class war in the village? And if there were no class war in the village, how was the growth of the petty bourgeois ideology to be prevented? So in most cases, the village would be ordered to designate some families as kulaks.

This task was shared by the village soviet and the Committee of the Poor of the village. So some poor wretches in the village were given the brand of Cain and from that time on were subjected to enormous taxes, deprived of electoral rights, and denied the right to send their children to any but the most primary schools,[2] even before the time of their final calamity, when their total "liquidation" was decreed. Of course, in many instances, the local authorities were willing enough to designate certain families as kulaks. It was the one way of working off old grudges.

One thing is certain. The average family which was designated as a kulak family was not the more or less legendary kulak in whose existence the Communists had at one time actually believed. Most of them were not usurers and exploiters, or, if they had been, they no longer were after the great misfortune of being designated as such had fallen upon them. No one in his senses would have willingly been classed as a kulak when he could have avoided it by giving up the practices which were supposed to characterize the kulak class. But so hard put to it to find families who might be classed as kulaks was many a village that anyone who had in times past, even before the Revolution, hired labor or loaned money or other goods, or who had been better off than the average peasant, was fastened upon by the village officials with relief as a means of satisfying the incomprehensible sadism of their Communist rulers.

I made a trip to a peasant village near Moscow with the particular purpose of finding out what determined whether a family was designated as kulaks. In this village the local Chairman of the Committee of the Poor, a kindly man, exhibited a family of kulaks quite in the manner of showing one a family of lepers on whom the judgment of God had fallen. He regarded them with hopeless pity and said that all the troubles in the village dated from the time when the villagers had been compelled to divide themselves into the three classes. When the query was put as to why the family was considered kulaks, he replied that someone had to be a kulak, and that this family had owned and operated a teahouse, or village inn, before the Revolution. He said they had not operated the inn for many

2. It was necessary to issue a decree of the Council of People's Commissars against the practice of excluding children of persons deprived of electoral rights from the first two stages of the educational system. It was considered undesirable to exclude children of this age, since it was possible, by proper educational methods to insure their development into supporters of the Soviet government. See *Pravada,* Feb. 2, 1930. This decree was not, however, to interfere with the policy of excluding the children of the "deprived" from the higher schools.

years and that the family was trying desperately to lose its status as a kulak family.

The family was present during the interview and confirmed all that the Chairman of the Committee of the Poor had said. They were deprived of electoral rights, the children of the family were not permitted to go to school, they paid 40 per cent of their meager income as taxes, and they were labeled as enemies of the Soviet State. When asked how long it would take for them to lose the status of a kulak, the family replied that it was said it might be done in five years. The Chairman of the Committee of the Poor interjected that he was not at all sure that it could ever be done. He no doubt wondered whom he could find to take their places as kulaks if they were to achieve emancipation.

In practice, since the number of people who might by any possible test have been exploiters was very much limited, anyone who had two cows and two horses, or who was somewhat less poor than the average peasant, might be considered a kulak. Actually there was no practicable way in which the line between the kulak and the *ceredniak* could be drawn. Nor indeed was the line between the *ceredniak* and the *bedniak* an easy one to draw. The poverty in the average Russian village was so great that had the task been carried out by a European or an American, all the villagers must have been labeled as *bedniki* without exception. The category into which a man was placed was mainly a matter of village politics. If there was a strong Communist group in the village, all those peasants who were hositle to Communism would be pretty sure to be labeled as kulaks.

In one case which came to my attention, a peasant who before the Revolution had employed twenty-five men as carters to drive his horses and wagons which he hired out in Kiev and who was as nearly the legendary type of kulak as ever existed, was labeled as a *ceredniak* because he had two sons who were Communists, one a general in the Red Army and the other a Young Communist. *Cerednìki* frequently complained bitterly that their neighbors, who had more horses or cows than they, were labeled as *bedniki* while they were registered as *ceredniki.* The status of *bedniki* was the most desirable of all since they were partially, and finally, wholly exempt from the payment of the agricultural tax.

The peasants also felt that they had a serious grievance in the great disparity between the prices which they received for their products and the prices which they were forced to pay for manufactured goods. A peasant said to me, "Before the war I received the same price in rubles for a sack of potatoes which I receive now. But I must sell more than twice as many potatoes now as I did then in order to buy a pair of boots, and such boots as they are! Look at these!" He stuck out a foot clad in a shapeless and disintegrating leather boot. "Boots which I bought before the war would outwear three pairs of these!" Consequently, in spite of the efforts of the party to light and fan the fires of class warfare in the village, the general tendency of the peasants was to preserve a united front against the urban proletariat.

Even among the urban workers there was a great deal of dissatisfaction and even of bitterness during the period of collectivization of agriculture. In Moscow, during the early part of March, 1930, I was returning home late at night accompanied by two other foreigners. We were all wearing fur coats and, consequently, were considerably better dressed than most Russians. A man in ragged clothes passed us in the street. He had evidently been drinking. As we passed, he hurled a bitter curse at us and said, "You Party people! Your time is coming! We will cut you to pieces!" This proletarian assumed that anyone who was warmly dressed must be one of the Party leaders. Two or three years earlier he would no doubt have cursed us as Nepmen, but now that the Nepmen were gone, his anger and bitterness turned toward the only class who were better off than he.

During the fall of 1929 began the great trek of the German colonists from all over Russia to Moscow with the hope that they might be permitted to leave Russia and go to some other country. Tens of thousands of German peasants came from Siberia, the Ukraine, the German Volga Republic, and the Crimea to Moscow and camped in the empty summer cottages on the outskirts of the city, while they waited for visas to leave the country. I made a trip to the outskirts of Moscow to talk with these people. These ethnic Germans had lived in Russia for generations. Since many spoke Russian and all spoke German, it was possible to communicate easily with them. In one tiny cottage of four rooms which I visited, forty men, women, and children were living. They declared that if necessary they would die in Moscow, but they would not return to Siberia.

It was customary to refer to these German colonists as Mennonites, and to imply that the cause of their desire to leave Russia was religious in nature. Actually these colonists included many faiths, among them Catholic, Baptist, and Evangelical. Although the impossibility of continuing religious worship if they joined the *kolkhoz* was an important factor in their determination to abandon their possessions and leave Russia, all the colonists with whom I talked emphasized the economic factors much more than the religious. They felt that they were like rats in a trap, with economic destruction certain. Some of them were permitted to leave Russia, but others were forcibly returned to Siberia, and all other German peasants were forbidden to come to Moscow or to attempt to leave the country.

The desperate resistance of the kulaks and their success in rallying the other peasants to a like resistance resulted in the determination of the party to exterminate these troublesome enemies. On December 27, 1929, Stalin announced the policy of the complete "liquidation of the kulaks as a class." [3] At least five million people were expected to be involved in this liquidation of a class, but because of the difficulty of distinguishing between the *ceredniak* and the kulak, eventually a much larger number were involved.

It is hard to say just what Stalin's intention was when he announced the policy of the "liquidation of the kulaks as a class." Of course, no one ever contemplated the outright massacre of millions of people. In the courses of the execution of the policy, some thousands of kulaks were shot. The severity of the treatment of the kulaks depended largely upon the district in which they lived. In some cases they were executed when the only charge against them was that of carrying on active propaganda against collectivization. Many kulaks and their families committed suicide. Nevertheless, the number who were actually executed or who committed suicide was small in comparison to the total number of kulaks, or of peasants who were included in that category.

The policy of the liquidation of the kulaks as a class was

3. *K Voprosam Agrarnoi Politiki V S.S.S.R.*, speech by Stalin at a conference of Agrarian Marxists.

seized upon as the opportunity to carry on wholesale expropriation and even unrestrained looting. The Moscow committee of the party declared for the policy of the "liquidation of the urban bourgeoisie as a class" and proceeded thoroughly to liquidate the remnants of the Nepmen.

The kulaks who were driven out or who themselves abandoned their farms were in an utterly hopeless position. They made desperate efforts to find work in factories, in construction work, or in the mines. I was to encounter kulaks from Tambov who were working on the Turkestan-Siberian Railway, near the Chinese frontier. Kulaks did not have the right to join labor unions, however, and wherever found were supposed to be rigorously "cleaned out." [4] The Chairman of the *okrug* Executive Committee of Serpukov told me that they were considering setting aside a *rayon* with the poorest land as a kulak *rayon*. This proposal was further developed in the North Caucasus where it was proposed to set aside the poorest land for the kulaks, give them one horse for every two families and one plough for every four families, draw up a program of production which they would be compelled to fulfil, and then to requisition all grain above a fixed ration.[5] Thousands of kulaks were deported to the lumber camps in the Northern Territories for compulsory labor. As late as May, 1930, on my way back to Moscow from Turkestan, I saw a train of box cars filled with kulaks and their families who were being deported from the Urals to Tashkent in Central Asia. What was to happen to them after their arrival there, they did not know. In some cases the more desperate kulaks turned to banditry.[6]

As further pressure was brought against the peasants, the food situation became steadily worse. In some instances peasants who had joined a collective were not permitted to have enough milk for their own use, even when they had turned one or more cows over to the collective. The disappearance of the peasants from the bazaars, since they were forbidden to sell their products, coincided with the closing of the private shops. Even the city proletariat became disaffected. Many of them had brothers or fathers who had been expropriated as kulaks. Some of the workers became so dis-

4. See *Pravda* of Feb. 20, and *Izvestia* of Feb. 16 and Feb. 20, 1930.
5. *Pravda*, Feb. 11, 1930.
6. See *Izvestia*, Feb. 8, 1930, for an account of the shooting of a group of men for taking part in an attack on a train near Vladikavkas.

tressed by reports from the villages that they returned to their native villages in the hope of protecting the interests of their families or relatives there. In meetings held in factories to work up enthusiastic support of the workers who were going out to manage *kolkhozi*, there were cases of the workmen themselves threatening with violence these future managers of the *kolkhozi*.[7]

Even the incredible capacity of the Russian peasant to bear oppression had reached a limit. Peasant insurrections flared up all over the union. In particular, there were risings in the Northern Caucasus, in the small republics making up the Caucasian Federation, in Turkestan, and even in the district around Riazan, which is only a few hours from Moscow. In general, these revolts occurred in districts inhabited by national minorities, where there still existed the tradition of freedom supported by the sword, and where the feeling of racial solidarity had prevented winning over even the *bedniki* to the cause of collectivization. But the revolts were not confined wholly to these districts. Isolated assassinations of the workers who had gone out to manage the collective farms were numerous. I was told of one Moscow factory which had sent out four of these worker-managers to the *kolkhoz*. Two of them had been murdered by the infuriated peasants. The most appalling stories of torture and mutilation of these workers by the peasants were spread by word of mouth, for the government rarely permitted news of these peasant assassinations to appear in the press.

One story was told of a woman who had attempted to smuggle some milk for her children out of the collective dairy barn. When her act was discovered by the manager of the *kolkhoz*, he ordered her to give up the milk. She refused, and he attempted to take it from her. The woman attacked the manager, who drew his revolver and shot her. The peasants, when they heard of his act, attacked the manager and killed him with pitchforks. The dead woman's husband then killed the brother of the manager, who was the bookkeeper of the *kolkhoz*. Many stories were told of instances in which the peasants at night had surrounded houses occupied by workers sent out from the city, had piled straw around them, and had burned the houses and their occupants.

Disaffection began to appear among the troops sent against the insurgent peasants. It was discovered that a very large propor-

7. *Rabochaia Gazeta*, Feb. 25, 1930.

tion of the officers of the Red Army were sons of kulaks. In one case it was said that the troops had refused to fire on the peasants and had been disarmed. For a moment panic almost took possession of the Stalin group in the party. It appeared that the party had been led into a cul-de-sac. To proceed further with collectivization and the "liquidation of the kulaks as a class" seemed madness, yet the loss of prestige which would be entailed by a complete retreat appeared to be an effective bar to such action. Yet Stalin succeeded in effecting this seemingly impossible maneuver. We foreign observers had not sufficiently grasped the fact that the Russian peasant was entirely helpless in any positive sense. All he required was for the pressure upon him to be slackened, and he ceased at once to resist the Soviet power. When the most flagrant abuses were halted, the peasant risings were quickly suppressed,[8] since the peasants were entirely unorganized and had no program of action.

The peasants were to try to carry out passive resistance against collectivized agriculture during the crop season of 1933. The Soviet government allowed some hundreds of thousands of them to starve during the following winter and thus finally broke their resistance. Agriculture has been completely collectivized in Russia now for many years, yet the problem of adequate production of foodstuffs has not been solved up to the present moment.

I had one of the most colorful experiences of my life during the last month of my stay in Russia. In late April and early May, 1930, I attended the opening of the Turkestan-Siberian Railway at the invitation of the Soviet government. However, the expenses of the trip were not paid for by the Soviet government but by myself. The trip was by special train and lasted just over three weeks. We traveled across the Volga, through Orenburg (Chkalov), on past the Aral Sea and along the great Tian Shan Mountains and finally on to Alma Ata in Kazakhstan. Our goal was a spot in the steppe called Aina Bulak, where the railroad construction crews from Siberia met those coming from Turkestan. At one point when the railroad began a long upgrade, an extra engine had to be attached to pull the train. It was explained proudly that this was a *subotnik* engine, i.e., that it had been constructed by workers without pay on

8. These peasant risings and their suppression by the military were, of course, never reported in the Soviet press. Almost everyone in Moscow knew about them, however.

their free time. The Pope had recently issued a statement condemning the persecution of religion in Soviet Russia. This had produced a momentary wave of papal popularity among the Russian peasants who were so bitterly disaffected over collectivization. The Soviet government had then issued a counterblast at the Pope. The name of the *subotnik* engine was lettered boldly on its side "Our Answer to the Pope of Rome." Since the engine made rather hard going on the upgrade, the newspaper correspondents amended its name to "Our Feeble Answer to the Pope of Rome."

While we were at Aina Bulak, we met Bill Shatov, a Russian-born American who had been at the head of the construction organization which had built the Turk-Sib Railway. Bill had belonged to the radical labor union, the IWW, in the United States before the Russian Revolution, and he used to claim an intimate acquaintance with what he called some of the best jails in the United States. He had played a role in the defense of Petrograd against Kornilov in the days between the February and the October Revolutions in 1917. It was said that for some reason he had not become a member of the Party, but at this time his prestige was high. He had great respect for United States industry. His chief engineer was a Pole who had also spent some years in American construction camps. When I asked Bill what the Pole had worked at in the American construction camps, he said the man had been a cook. But he insisted that just living in the American industrial setting was of first importance in making the Pole an effective construction engineer.

All the American correspondents, in addition to one Austrian newspaperman, as well as a number of Soviet journalists, besides two or three other foreigners, made the trip. The American correspondents were able for once to indulge their fondness for poker without stint. Sometimes a game would run for forty-eight hours with individuals rotating out for a few hours sleep. William Henry Chamberlin, who was the most scholarly type, was nevertheless considered to be the best poker player. He won enough money to buy a Bukhara rug. The one fly in the ointment was that the correspondents could only take money away from each other after a young secretary of the British Embassy, who had accompanied us thus far, left the train at Tashkent. The sleeping cars were used as dormitories even when we spent two or three days each at Tashkent, Samarcand, and Bukhara.

We attended the celebration of the joining of the rails, followed by a series of elaborate banquets. The culmination of the occasion was the driving of the spikes which joined the rails running from Siberia to those running from Turkestan. Engines from Siberia and Turkestan faced each other at the juncture of the rails. On the engine from Turkestan was a huge sign with the words *Daiosh Sibir!* I recognized the first word as some form of the verb "give," but I could not quite make sense out of it. I asked a Russian standing by, and he explained that it meant "Give Us Siberia!," a sort of Soviet version of "Siberia or Bust!" I was to recall this incident some twelve years later when we borrowed from an Allied intelligence agency a report on the railroads of Russia. In the article dealing with the Turk-Sib Railway, there was a photograph of this very same engine with the sign on it.

I watched a tremendous contest put on in honor of the occasion by thousands of native Kazakh horsemen in a kind of polo involving the use of a slaughtered sheep enclosed in its bloody pelt turned wrong side out as a ball. I cannot remember a more striking sight than these thousands of horsemen mounted on their tiny Kazakh horses, swooping like flights of swallows, as they pursued the horseman who happened for the moment to be carrying the bloody and slippery carcass.

Besides the newspaper men, there were a number of Soviet "shock workers" who were taking the trip as a reward for outstanding performance in industrial production. There were also several of the best known Soviet novelists on the train, including Boris Pilniak, later to become an "unperson" through liquidation for some reason never explained. On return trips to the Soviet Union in 1956 and 1958, I inquired about Pilniak from my Intourist guides. Both the well-educated young women stoutly maintained that they had never heard of any such writer. Ilya Ilf and Eugene Petrov were also on the train. They were already famous for their picaresque novel *The Embezzlers.* With so many writers on the train, it was little wonder that the Turk-Sib opening was one of the most extensively "written up" occasions on record.

After the official opening of the Turk-Sib, our train went back to Tashkent, Samarcand, and Bukhara. When we visited Samarcand, the Soviet government dug up a local amateur archaeologist to act as guide and lecturer on the local historical monuments. The guide was an old ex-colonel of engineers under the Tsar. He had been allowed to wear his starched white and gold uniform of other days, presumably because it was the only presentable suit which he possessed. We were shown the Registan, the tomb of Tamerlane, and finally the crumbling ruins of the Mosque of Bibi Khanum. The old colonel explained that Tamerlane had built the mosque in honor of his favorite wife, Bibi Khanum, and that at that time it was the largest building in Asia.

The old colonel went on to say that the architects whom Tamerlane engaged did not sufficiently understand the technique of constructing so large an arch as the ceiling of the mosque required. Consequently, they would get the vault of the ceiling just about finished when there would be a slight earthquake tremor or other disturbance, and the ceiling would come crashing down. Tamerlane would then have that set of architects executed and employ another set. The old colonel elaborated on and emphasized the tale at length. It quickly dawned on us that he wanted us to note the close parallel to the current hysteria over the crime of *vreditelsvo,* or sabotage, by which the Soviet government arrested and sometimes shot planning or engineering experts as scapegoats for what were fantastically imaginary crimes.[9] The colonel dared not actually make the comparison, and we did not, for his sake, dare to say that we had got the point long ago.

Among the official Soviet delegates on the train was an old Japanese named Katayama, a delegate of the Comintern. He had worked as a cook in restaurants and in the cook-shacks of construction gangs in the United States for many years. He spoke English, and it was reported that he was the American delegate to the Comintern at this time. He must have been eighty years old and was actually a simple, gentle old fellow.

Katayama was in the charge of another official of the Comintern named Kakhan who kept tabs on him and translated his speeches on public occasions. Kakhan had been born in Austria and had been an officer in the Austrian army in 1914. Shortly after the beginning of the war he was wounded and captured by the Russians. He was

9. For example, an engineer might be charged with *vreditelsvo* for having allowed cement to be poured too late in the fall so that it froze and construction was damaged, as actually happened in one case; or for ordering the pouring of cement stopped before it was necessary to prevent freezing and thereby delaying construction, as the engineer who was accused in the first case well knew might happen.

imprisoned in Siberia and then on the island of Sakhalin in the Far East until the Revolution broke out. He joined the Bolsheviks and fought on their side all during the savage Civil War in Siberia. He rose to be the equivalent of a brigadier general in the Red Army. He had married a Russian wife and had become a Soviet citizen. He had picked up some Japanese while on Sakhalin, and this was probably the reason that he had been put in charge of Katayama. Besides Russian and his native German, he spoke English and various of the native languages of Turkestan. He spent a good deal of time in my compartment of the train, and I found him one of the most engaging and unforgettable characters I have ever met.

He used to sing Austrian soldiers' songs, including one which went, "*Wir leben und sterben, wir sterben mit hurra,*" and another one which concerned Silesian wine which even the Devil found too sour to drink. He taught me the "match game," with rows of seven, six, and five matches, the perfect game for prisoners since it can be played not only with matches but even with clods of earth. Kakhan always won. He was the perfect type of the tough, dynamic, brilliant, able soldier of fortune. If he had lived in Italy in the fourteenth or fifteenth century, he would surely have been a famous *condottiere*.

After we got back from an elaborate official banquet given to us by the government of the Soviet Republic of Uzbekistan, Kakhan asked me, "What liquor did you bring back?" We had indeed been served the choicest of wines, brandies, and a perfumed liqueur in pottery bottles covered with gold leaf which must have been left over from the cellars of the tsars. I admitted that I had come back empty-handed. Kakhan opened his shirt and took out four bottles of cognac which he had somehow managed to pouch during the speeches. "And you claim to have been a soldier!" he cried in scorn.

I never saw Kakhan again after we returned to Moscow. Some seven or eight years later, however, during the Spanish Civil War, foreign newspaper men in Spain began to refer to the brilliant but mysterious General Kleber whom the Soviet government had sent to command the International Brigades fighting against Franco. Piecing together fragmentary references in these dispatches, I became pretty well convinced that General Kleber was in fact Kakhan. As I write these lines, I have looked up what Hugh Thomas has to say about General Kleber in *The Spanish Civil War*. "Kleber" was a pseudonym, taken from Marshal Kleber of French Revolutionary fame. Thomas says that Kleber was born in Austria-Hungary. He had been a captain in the Austro-Hungarian army. He was captured by the Russians, imprisoned in Siberia, escaped during the Revolution, joined the Red Army, and fought with it in the Russian Civil War. After the war he became an official of the Comintern. He was a good linguist, he was engaging, he was an able commander.[10] All these facts fit Kakhan as I knew him.

If General Kleber was Kakhan, he was almost certainly executed on Stalin's orders along with the Revolutionary hero Antonov-Ovseenko and practically all the other Soviet figures who participated in the Spanish Civil War. The liquidation of these men had long been a matter of common knowledge, but the fact was dredged up by Khrushchev as part of his attack on the dead Stalin in 1956. In Kakhan's case, at least, I feel sure that his connection with me had nothing to do with his execution.

The novelists Ilya Ilf and Ivan Petrov were to incorporate a good many of the events and personalities of this official train to the opening of the Turk-Sib when they published another picaresque novel in 1931, called *The Little Golden Calf:*

> Palmidov came up to the foreign professor of economics in quest of an interview. "I am enraptured," said the professor. "All the construction work I have seen in the U.S.S.R. is grandiose, I have no doubt the Five Year Plan will be fulfilled! I shall write about it!"
>
> A half year later he actually published a book about it in which he proved in the first two hundred pages that the Five Year Plan would be fulfilled by the time indicated, and that the U.S.S.R. would become one of the most powerful industrial nations. But on the 201st page the professor declared that precisely for that reason the land of the Soviets should be destroyed as soon as possible, because it would bring about the natural destruction of capitalistic society.[11]

I would like to quote first the actual statement I made when an interview was requested of me:

> This newly constructed railway, the Turk-Sib, joining the cotton-producing lands of an old civilization with the wide wheat-growing areas of the virgin lands of Siberia, constitutes a characteristic monument to Soviet Power.

10. See the references to General Kleber, pp. 302, 324, 327 and 621 in Hugh Thomas, *The Spanish Civil War* (New York: Harper, 1961).

11. Ilya Ilf and Eugene Petrov, *The Little Golden Calf* (New York: Farrar and Rinehart, 1932), p. 330.

Second, I quote the final paragraph of my book *The Economic Life of Soviet Russia,* published in 1931, of which the statement by Ilf and Petrov is a distortion:

> The significance to the capitalistic world of developments in the Soviet Union cannot be exaggerated. If the present crisis is passed, the Soviet Union, within a decade, will be in a position to offer a standard of living which will compare favourably with that of the more poorly paid manual workers in capitalistic countries. Unless in the meantime Capitalism has notably improved its technique of marketing and distribution, so that under-consumption and unemployment can be prevented, and unless the standard of living of such workers in the capitalistic world shall have been materially raised, the World Revolution will begin to make rapid strides.

A few pages previously I had written:

> The future of the Soviet régime depends upon whether or not the Communist party has miscalculated the breaking point of the Russian people. Only a people with the predominantly Asiatic character which the Russians have, would or could have borne the experiences of the last sixteen years. During all this period Russia has been on a war-time basis, with a slight respite during the years 1925 and 1926. Not only have material conditions of life been bad, but the psychological strain has been incredibly great. Everyone, whether a member of the Party or not, who rises a degree above the dead level of the masses lives under the shadow of the secret police. Agents of the police are found among all classes, so that no one dares trust anyone. No member of the old or new intelligentsia can expect to live a quiet and tranquil life. The key-note of life is struggle, and he who would stand aloof must suffer either suspicion or contempt. Life is so bitter and so oppressive that one feels as though passing from darkness to light when one crosses the Soviet frontier.[12]

These two quotations from my book, written in 1930, may serve to epitomize my feelings after a year in Soviet Russia in 1929-30.

12. See *The Economic Life of Soviet Russia,* pp. 343–344.

Chapter ten. *I observe Hitler come to power*

After I returned from Turkestan, I left Moscow for Dresden, where I rejoined my family. My concern now was to get out my book on the Soviet economy with all possible speed. I had already written several chapters, and I wrote several more before we left Germany. Indeed, my wife and I continued to work on the book, she editing and typing, I rewriting, as we spent some weeks touring Europe. It was rather hard on our two girls, since they had to amuse themselves as best they could in one hotel room while we worked in an adjoining one. We spent the morning on the book and took the girls sight-seeing in the afternoon.

An extraordinary stroke of good fortune enabled me to get the book published at least a year earlier than would otherwise have been possible. Some two months before I left for Turkestan, I had written to J. M. Keynes, editor of the *Royal Economic Journal*, suggesting that I write an article on current economic policy in the Soviet Union. I received a reply which I considered rather noncommittal. I then wrote him and said that the situation had changed a good deal, so I thought I would not write the article after all. I got an immediate reply in which Keynes expressed disappointment, saying that the editors had counted on the article for their next issue and giving its closing date. I was to leave on the special train for Turkestan in thirty-six hours, but I sat down and typed the article, taking time out for only a couple of brief snatches of sleep. I got the article off and barely caught the train.

When I got back from Turkestan, I found a letter from Keynes. He had been pleased with the article and asked me to come and see him when we passed through London. My wife and I had lunch with him and his wife, the charming and famous former ballet dancer, Lupokova. Since she had close relatives still living in Moscow, she was anxious to hear the latest from Russia. Keynes asked me whether I had another article for him. I told him that I did not, but that I had some chapters of the book I was writing. He kindly offered to take them with him for a weekend which he was planning to spend in the country.

After Keynes had read the chapters, he wrote me a most generous letter offering to arrange publication of the book with the Macmillan Company.[1] Keynes did make the arrangements so that the book was published simultaneously in the United Kingdom and in the United States. There thus began one of the most stimulating and gratifying relationships of my life. His was the most powerful and creative mind and the most dynamic personality which I was ever to encounter. It was my great good fortune that I was able to continue in contact with him both in person and by letter until his death.

Besides our discussion of the Soviet economy, we talked over the core of the ideas he was later to put forward in his *General Theory.* He was pleased to hear that I planned a theoretical work along somewhat similar lines. I regret to say that my involvement with the New Deal diverted me from this project. I continued to work in the area, but I never published a major work in this field. I was, however, to have a part in getting Keynesian policies adopted by the Roosevelt administration.

The first article on Soviet Russia after my return to the United States, which I published in *Harper's Magazine,* "The Soviet Challenge to Capitalism," afforded a test of the attitude of the Soviet régime toward my findings. I had expected a hostile reaction since I had taken a hostile attitude toward the Soviet economic and political system. The first reaction came in *Za Industrializatsiiu,* one of the leading economic newspapers, in a special article by a Communist economist named Pavlov with whom I had talked. He wrote that the reprehensible attitude shown in my article was no doubt attributable to my having talked to such disloyal Soviet economists as Kondratiev and Yurovsky. (I had only mentioned talking with these economists and had not said a word about what

1. Letter from Keynes, July 6, 1930.

they had said to me. Nevertheless, my conscience stabbed me again.)

In the rest of the article, Pavlov addressed me as though I could be dealt with just as Bukharin, Rykov, and Tomsky had been dealt with in the previous year. I was sternly directed to confess my *oshibki* (errors), the same word which had been used in the abject confessions of these Communist leaders now fallen from power. The eventual sanction for these three men, which they did not escape by their confessions, was to be death. In my own case, the sanction threatened was "to be considered no longer a friend of the Soviet Union." The special article was clipped and sent to me from two different Communist sources, one in the United States, the other in Russia, so that I would be sure not to miss it.

The sanction threatened was not at all serious to me, but in the case of a writer or newsman whose specialty was Soviet Russia it could be a very unpleasant one. Anyone familiar with Soviet practice would naturally conclude that the sanction would be at least the withholding of an entrance visa. If one had invested the time and effort to learn the Russian language and build up a background on Russia, this refusal of a visa could mean that all this became a rapidly wasting asset.

I never expected to be able to obtain a visa again. In actuality, I turned out to be wrong. I was granted return visas in 1933 and in 1939, 1956, and 1958. A possible explanation has been offered that the *Narcomindel* (the Foreign Office) had been purged so often that no one was any longer acquainted with my file. I think this an unlikely explanation. In Moscow in 1933 I happened to have dinner in private with an official of the *Narcomindel* who handled applications of American citizens for visas. Naturally I did not ask why I *had* been given a visa. He did volunteer the information as to why an acquaintance who had lived in Moscow when I did had never been able to get a return visa. One would never have suspected the reason given. The official said the American had written a prurient, untrue account of an alleged incident in connection with nude bathing in the Moscow River in a book which he had published. He also said that the American would never get a visa as long as he was on the job.

I had always insisted to Soviet officials that I was a "bourgeois economist" and had never pretended to have any connection with

Communist or socialist ideas or associations. Consequently, I was always considered to be quite plainly in the enemy camp and had never to suffer for the crime of being a renegade. I have never had the least complaint to make of my treatment by Soviet officials in Russia. There has been indeed at times special but usually unobstrusive surveillance. This I have never objected to nor do I think I would have any right to object. Furthermore, this occasional special surveillance primarily meant that I got a sort of V.I.P. treatment, since my attendants saw to it that I did. For some of them I even have quite a friendly feeling.

When I returned to the United States, I found the Great Depression under way and continually deepening. I became very much concerned about the ability of capitalism under conditions of economic depression to resist the spread of the Soviet political and economic system, the terrors of which I had so recently and intimately observed. It appeared to me that the first results of the effort of capitalists to resist Soviet Communism might be seen in Fascist Italy and in the Nazi movement in Germany. Fascism in Italy and National Socialism in Germany appeared to me to be the product of the fear of Communism on the part of capitalists. I assumed that Mussolini in Italy and Hitler in Germany were essentially the puppets of the great industrialists of those countries. Since Germany was a far more important country than Italy, and since I wished to study the nature of a Fascist movement before it came to power, I determined to go to Germany.

I was able to take advantage of a sabbatical leave partially to finance the trip. My book on Russia had been very successful and royalties added to receipts from articles and lectures enabled me to finance another year abroad. We arrived in Berlin in July, 1932, just in time to witness the series of elections, maneuvers, and intrigues which were to bring Hitler to power on January 30, 1933.

We were to live in Berlin until April and then to go to Munich before leaving for Italy in May. During this time my wife and I and our two daughters lived in a *pension* run by Fräulein Kadler in Dahlem, an upper-class district in Berlin. Since most of the time there was only one other person staying at the *pension,* Fräulein Kadler was more like our housekeeper than the owner of the *pension.* She was a strong personality of peasant stock who had for years been the housekeeper for a retired general of aristocratic family. She afforded me a continuous contact with the world of the German housewife. We had made this most useful connection through some German friends we had made in Dresden, who had now, most fortunately, moved to Berlin. The head of this family, Dr. Hans Mensching, had been a captain in World War I, had been severely wounded, and was presently a highly respected civil servant. This afforded another close contact on a different level.

I followed somewhat the same investigative procedure which I had followed in Soviet Russia. Here, however, it was possible to provide myself with a number of letters of introduction, and I was able to rely upon our Embassy for contacts as I could not in Moscow.

I arranged scores of interviews with industrialists, both from large-scale and small-scale industry, bankers, editors, labor leaders, economists, agricultural leaders, and governmental officials. I had interviews with leaders of almost all the political parties, both in and out of office. I talked with students and with shopkeepers.

I did not use an interpreter-guide as I had in Russia, both because I knew German better than I did Russian, and since a totalitarian régime was not yet in power, a "door opener" was not so essential. Nevertheless, I usually provided a dozen questions before each interview which I relied upon to get my man talking. I practiced these sentences on Fräulein Kadler, who never hesitated to make suggestions either in form or substance.

As had been true in Moscow, the correspondents of American newspapers were an able and courageous lot of men. Ed Deuss, who had been in Moscow when I was there, Herbert Knickerbocker of the International News Service, Louis Lochner of the Associated Press, Edgar Mowrer of the *Chicago Daily News*, and others afforded a most useful interchange of ideas and information.

I read four or five newspapers a day. Since most of the newspapers were in effect organs of the various political parties, I saw to it that I covered a considerable spectrum each week, through the *Morgenpost, Berliner Tageblatt, Vossische Zeitung*, and the Nazi newspapers *Der Angriff* and *Voelkischer Beobachter* to the German Nationalist papers, *Kreuz Zeitung, Lokal Anzeiger* and *Stahlhelm*, and occasionally the Communist *Rote Fahne*.

Among the political leaders of all the important political parties with whom I had interviews was Stegerwald, not only a leader of the Catholic Center party, but head of the big insurance company which was associated with the Catholic trade union organization. The last Republican Chancellor Brüning had been a protege of Stegerwald.[2] The Center party under the leadership of Brüning and Stegerwald had nearly succeeded in keeping Hitler out of power, but the deepening economic depression and the failure of von Hindenburg to support Brüning ruined their efforts.

The interviews I had with Breitscheidt, leader of the Social Democratic bloc in the Reichstag, and with Hilferding,[3] former finance minister in a previous Social Democratic government, made it completely clear that the Social Democrats had long ceased to be a socialistic party. They still clung to a formal Marxism which was without any reality. Breitscheidt stated quite calmly that the Social Democrats had had no intention of taking over the government at a time when capitalism was in a state of collapse. He even admitted that "our bills for dealing with the economic depression which we Social Democrats had introduced in the Reichstag were only for propaganda purposes." The Social Democratic program had become one of gradual economic reform measures to be pushed only during periods of economic prosperity. It is no wonder that the Social Democrats had little electoral appeal at a time of deep economic depression when the great majority of the German people were demanding drastic action "to prevent starvation in the midst of plenty."

Among my other interviews was one with the derelict politician, Treviranus. He had been an ambitious and brilliant young leader in the conservative German Nationalist party. He had tried to swing the support of a large part of his party for Chancellor Brüning but had failed and was left isolated. His political influence had dwindled to almost nothing, but he tried to convince himself that he was still a political leader with a rising star.

On the day that I had arranged an interview with him in the center of Berlin, I had also arranged for two Nazi students to see me in our apartment in Dahlem. As the students stayed on, the

2. In the election immediately following Hitler's coming to power, Stegerwald was badly beaten up by the Nazis. He was to be imprisoned by the Nazis during the war. By coincidence, I met him again in Bavaria in 1945 when I was with our army in Germany. He had been put in charge of one of the provincial governments by our occupational forces. His experiences had aged him greatly, and he died not long after.

3. Hilferding fled from Germany when Hitler came to power. He committed suicide to avoid falling into Nazi hands when France was occupied by the Germans.

time of the two appointments threatened to overlap, and I excused myself by saying that I had an appointment with Treviranus. "With that political corpse?" sneered one of the Nazi students. Nevertheless, the information I got from Treviranus with reference to the veto power of the Reichswehr on the German political scene prior to Hitler's take-over was both corroborative of what I had heard elsewhere and illustrative by particular occasions which he recounted. Thus, he told me of how Brüning's appointment as Chancellor by von Hindenburg had had to be cleared formally with the Reichswehr.

I do not know just why the Nazis hated Treviranus so fiercely, but during the Blood Purge of 1934 they were apparently determined to make him a real corpse. An SS squad was sent to Treviranus' home in the suburbs of Berlin to assassinate him. With unbelievable quickness of mind, Treviranus' father confused the assassins by insisting that he was Treviranus while the maid slipped out of the door to warn the younger Treviranus. He, with like quickness of mind, jumped in his car, and realizing that there would be road blocks to intercept him on the outskirts of Berlin, headed instead for the center. He decided as he drove that he would seek protection from General von Schleicher, now retired but formerly Commander of the Reichswehr. As he came near von Schleicher's house, he noticed a commotion, so he stopped and asked a bystander the cause. He got the reply, "The SS have just shot von Schleicher and his wife." Treviranus abandoned his car, walked away, and made contact with the British, who supplied him with a false passport and smuggled him out of the country.

I was next to see Treviranus in 1943 when General Donovan asked me to see him and an associate. He had been sent to Canada by the British authorities after the outbreak of the war, and he had now come to the United States with an alleged plan for an anti-Nazi movement in Germany to overthrow Hitler. I found his plan to be really no plan at all, utterly impractical and romantic, so that I did not continue contact with him. So far as I know, he never played any further role in German affairs.

The extent to which the political sympathies of the various quarters of Berlin were dominated by the economic interests and income levels of its population could be seen from the flags which were hung out and the political signs and slogans painted on the walls of buildings or on signboards as one went by train, bus, or subway from Dahlem, our quarter, to the center of Berlin. In our quarter the black, white, red banner of the Kaiser's reich was overwhelmingly predominant. As one came to Steglitz, the Nazi swastika took over. Then one began to see the red, white, gold of the Weimar Republic, and then in more proletarian East Berlin, Communist red flags and slogans, such as *Für Freiheit und Brot, Gegen Faschismus und Not*!

As I continued my study of the economic and political situation and watched events unfold, I became aware that many of my preconceived ideas about the Nazi movement were quite incorrect. It was perfectly true that the most reactionary class in Germany, the Junkers and their followers, did hope to make use of the Nazi movement to gain their ends. Furthermore, these Junkers shared with the Nazis an extreme nationalism and a particular hatred of the Treaty of Versailles which had humiliated Germany in defeat.

Some industrialists also hoped to make use of the Nazi movement for *their* purposes, which incidentally were *not* always the same as those of the Junkers. I was astonished, however, to find that neither Junkers nor industrialists had any great fear of Communism. Consequently, whenever either of these groups made temporary alliances with the Nazis, it was not fear of Communism which was the motivation. The ease with which the Communist attempt to take over power immediately after the collapse of the Kaiserdom in November, 1918, had been defeated by a handful of the newly re-created Reichswehr furnished the basis for the contempt which the conservative classes in Germany felt for the Communists. The repeated defeats of Communist-led strikes and riots through the year and the incredibly inept Communist leadership had confirmed this feeling of contempt. I found, too, that the conservatives of Germany uncomfortably realized that the Nazis were men of blood and violence, that they were psychologically not in the least capitalistically minded, and that they were indeed the enemies of an urban, respectable middle class civilization.[4] However much the Junkers might have wished to throw off the chains of the Treaty of Versailles and to re-establish their ancient privileges, they had little stomach for another war such as the policies of the Nazis

4. In this connection, see Hermann Rauschning, *The Revolution of Nihilism: Warning to the West* (New York: Alliance Book Corp., 1939).

would make probable. While rearmament had some appeal to the industrialists, the prospect of a war in which most of them were aware Germany would be defeated had even less appeal than in the case of the Junkers.

The psychopathic hatred of the Nazis for the Jews also set them apart from German conservatives. One was offered even by the most important of the National Socialist leaders the most extraordinary and diverse explanations of the racial antipathy which was felt for the Jews. The Protocols of the Elders of Zion were quite generally accepted as authentic, and in addition weird mixtures of distorted Biblical lore, pseudo-science, and folk tales were accepted without question.

This was illustrated by an interview which Louis Lochner, correspondent of the Associated Press, and I had with Wagener, the Chief of the Economic Bureau of the Nazi party. On the eve of the Jewish boycott, this high official of the party explained to me at great length why this aversion was so deep. In so far as his explanation dealt with economic causes, it was understandable, but he insisted that the economic cause was only secondary and that the racial difference was the deepest reason for the feeling toward the Jews. He said that the twelve tribes of Israel were originally pastoral and that since they were a pastoral people, they counted their increase in wealth by the increase in the number of calves in their herds. One tribe, however, began to engage in trade and finance, and they were responsible for setting up and worshiping the Golden Calf. Now the Golden Calf was actually only a symbol of usury, by means of which this one tribe of the twelve obtained its yearly increase in wealth. It harked back, however, to its pastoral origin in choosing the calf as a symbol. The Jews of today are descended from this one tribe and still worship the Golden Calf of usury.

The Jews were so hated by the Germans, he continued, because they possessed the peculiar ability of being able to dominate people of Germanic blood. This domination was of two sorts. First, the Jew could always get the better of a German in a commercial deal. The German was naturally unsuspicious, simple, and good-willed. With the Jew, he had simply no chance. Second, what was more important, if a Jew married a German wife, the children were Jews. As a consequence the Jews were not assimilated and never became Germans no matter how much intermarriage took place. It was quite different with other races. The Jew in Italy soon became an Italian, the Jew in France, a Frenchman, and even in England the Jew became an Englishman. Consequently, there was not the prejudice against Jews in other countries which existed in Germany.

Only the Jews possessed this peculiar ability to dominate the Germans. Not even other Semites possessed it. By contrast, the Germans were able easily to assimilate Slavic races, because here the Germanic blood always dominated. He remarked parenthetically that this assimilation of the Slavic strain in Germany was not always complete or successful unless the leadership of the Germanic strain was maintained. Thus, the districts in Germany where Communism had taken most firm root were largely of Slavic blood. Hamburg, for example, was not primarily German but Slavic, at least in the working-class districts. Communism itself was a Slavic concept and not a Germanic concept. In the case of the Jews, however, it was hopeless to think of assimilating them, and anyway such pollution of German blood was repugnant and unallowable.

I found, too, that the mass appeal of the Nazis had a decidedly anti-capitalistic basis. The evidence became quite clear to me that the Nazi movement had waxed and waned and waxed again with the worsening of economic conditions in Germany. Mass unemployment had been the major factor in the great upswing in the Nazi vote from 1928 to the election of July, 1932. Thus the fall of the Weimar Republic was basically due to the failure to deal with the mass unemployment of the Great Depression and not importantly due to a resurgence of nationalism in Germany.

In contrast, however, to either of the forms of Marxism in Germany, Communism and Social Democratism, the National Socialist movement did not derive its force from the masses of the urban proletariat. The masses which gave weight to the movement were the ruined aristocracy, the overburdened lower middle class, the discontented peasants, and the youth of the universities, inflamed against a world which offered them no future. The Nazi membership included only that fragment of the urban proletariat which saw no immediate hope in Communism.

The middle class, when under sufficient economic pressure, is as liable to infection by the mob psychosis as any other class. Under the circumstances which existed in Germany, it was possible to sweep this class into a movement as characterized by enthusiasm, passion, and hate, as was ever Communism.

I used to observe standing day after day in Potsdamer Platz a man wearing this sign: *"Ich nehme jede Arbeit an"* ("I will do any kind of work"). He wore an expression of pathetic dignity. He was dressed in neat but threadbare clothes, and he looked as though he might be an unemployed bookkeeper. It was millions like him who were unemployed or who feared unemployment or faced bankruptcy whose apostasy sapped the popular support for the Weimar Republic rather than the unemployed proletariat, who at least were usually eligible for unemployment insurance payments, as most of the lower middle class were not. I became convinced at this time that no government in the world could any longer wait for "natural forces" to overcome mass unemployment. This conclusion was to be determinative in my joining the New Deal in the United States late in 1933.

I observed von Papen and von Schleicher heading governments of the Right with narrower and narrower support in the Reichstag, ruling only by dint of decrees under the authority temporarily granted them by von Hindenburg but offering the last effective resistance to the Nazi take-over. The possibility that Hitler might be offered a deal by the conservatives in which he and some of his principal lieutenants might be given some decorative but unimportant posts in government was widely recognized, and this, indeed, was several times proposed to him. But none of the editors, bankers, industrialists, economists, and others whom I was interviewing at this time would consider the possibility of full power for Hitler. Such a catastrophe they simply refused to contemplate.

This inability to foresee social catastrophe is probably deeply imbedded in the human race. Catastrophe by its very nature cannot happen often. Not only, therefore, are the chances against its happening in any given situation very large, but the ability to foresee catastrophe is not a talent which is likely to be useful often enough to make it worthwhile to cultivate. It may even be that this inability to contemplate the possibility of catastrophe is a good thing. Perhaps humanity could not carry on the basic functions necessary to economic survival in the presence of constant worry about possible disaster.

Nothing so well illustrates the extent to which the possibility of Hitler's coming to full power was discounted as the split between the majority of the industrialists and the Junkers which was allowed to develop and which brought down first the government of von Papen and then the government of von Schleicher. Finally, the Junkers and a wing of the industrialists were even willing, in their vanity, to make the deal with Hitler which did bring him to full power. Incredibly enough, these men were to believe that they had brought Hitler into the government with his hands tied. They were to learn how wrong they were.

In spite of all the "secret" intrigues and maneuvering which went on, I was pretty well able to keep track of what was going on. Half the enjoyment of exercising great political influence is to be able to tell someone about it, and I was surprised at the risks men would take under this motivation. I never inhibited confidences by taking notes. Of course, I did not betray confidences, above all where harm to individuals might have resulted. One of the directors of the German Association of Manufacturers said to me after I had remarked that I supposed von Papen would be in office indefinitely, "Von Papen is an officer of Hussars—neither a politician nor an administrator. I think you can be sure he will not be Chancellor much longer." Within forty-eight hours he had resigned.[5]

During the period following the November elections when the size of the Nazi popular vote declined somewhat, I discussed the political situation with industrialists, editors, bankers, political leaders, university professors, labor leaders, economists and others. Almost without exception they insisted that Hitler had missed his hour. The claim of Hitler for the power of Mussolini was mercilessly ridiculed. "One cannot bargain for the power of Mussolini. One must be a Mussolini to have the power!" Hitler had made a fearful mistake when he had not accepted the terms offered by von Hindenburg and von Papen. A well-known professor of political science said to me, "I am certain that one can date the precipitous decline of the National Socialist party from August, 1932." In spite of the fact that I had come to Germany with the fixed belief that Hitler's coming to power was a virtual certainty,

5. I have written a detailed account in my *Germany Enters the Third Reich* of the extraordinary series of maneuvers which within a few months was to bring Hitler to power. That account was written some six months after Hitler became Chancellor. Reading it now, I am astonished to find how very little of it I would change if I were to write it today.

the fact that nowhere could there be found anyone outside the National Socialist movement who would even entertain the possibility momentarily shook this conviction.

Even as late as a month before Hitler became Chancellor, his cause was still accounted hopelessly lost by responsible opinion. Even as late as December, 1932, when I discussed the political and economic situation with German businessmen, they always considered it useless nonsense to discuss what the economic policies of the National Socialist party would be if it came to power. "Historical curiosity" and "the German Boulanger" were some of the terms applied to Hitler at this time. Two months later these same men were to insist publicly that he was a "real statesman," as they shivered in anticipation of his next move on the economic front. But until he was securely in power, they were all agreed that he had a biological aversion to the acceptance of responsibility, that his favorite role was that of the "drummer" who roused the mob, that his terms for entering the cabinet were so severe because he hoped thus to put off the day when he must abandon his "drumming" and make decisions. Events were to prove that this touchstone of Hitler's policy, of never accepting responsibility without the possibility of complete power, was the bedrock upon which his final triumph was built. After Hitler became Chancellor, he was to be acclaimed as a great statesman by many of those who had belittled him previously and as an evil genius by his enemies. I have had no experience more interesting than observing this judgment of a personality before and after the achievement of power.[6]

Hitler became Chancellor January 30, 1933. That night I watched a gigantic National Socialist demonstration in honor of the new cabinet. Hitler had been careful to see to it that the Nationalists were included in the celebration also. *Stahlhelm* detachments marched with the SA and SS detachments from the concentration point in the Tiergarten, through the Brandenburger Tor down Unter den Linden and through the Wilhelmstrasse, where the procession

6. This *ex post facto* discovery of genius is an almost universal experience. Thus, for example, the American ambassador in Russia on April 21, 1917, was to record in a cable to the State Department his first knowledge of the existence of Lenin, to whom the stature of genius is now almost universally accorded, "Extreme socialist or anarchist named Lenin making violent speeches and thereby strengthening Government; designedly giving him leeway and will deport opportunely." *Foreign Relations of the United States;* Papers Relating to the Foreign Relations of the United States 1918, Russia (Washington; U. S. Government Printing Office, 1931), I, 27.

was reviewed by President von Hindenbrug, Chancellor Hitler, and the other members of the cabinet. But the *Stahlhelm* detachments were lost in the sea of SA and SS detachments. Unter den Linden was packed with people as the torchlight procession went by. It seemed as though all of young Germany and middle-class Germany was there. The deep and fervent enthusiasm of this huge crowd as it sang the "Horst Wessel Lied," "Deutschland, Deutschland über alles," and the old Prussian marching songs made an indelible impression. This was the first and one of the greatest of those demonstrations of patriotism and enthusiasm staged by Hitler after his attainment of power, which were such an important feature of the conquest of the will of the Nationalist members of the cabinet and which rendered them incapable of opposing his desires. As the conservative Nationalist members of the Hitler cabinet surveyed this mass of humanity which had been roused to the highest pitch of emotional belief that here was the beginning of the Third Reich and the end of Germany's woes, they must have begun to realize a little that they were dealing with a movement which would sweep over and obliterate them if they were ever again to stand in its way.

I went down to the Unter den Linden to watch this gigantic torchlight parade which was celebrating Hitler's access to power. I had hoped to observe Hitler at close range as he reviewed the marching ranks of the SS, the SA, and the *Stahlhelm* from the balcony of the Chancellory on Wilhelmstrasse. I found, however, that guards prevented my following the parade past the balcony. By making a very long detour, I was able to come up under the balcony from the opposite end of the Wilhelmstrasse without being stopped. I watched Hitler from a vertical distance of about fifteen or twenty feet for some twenty minutes, as did half a dozen other persons who apparently had had the same idea as I. While we watched, a young girl in the group tossed a bouquet of flowers to Hitler, who caught it and bowed his thanks. I recalled at the moment that the concealing of a bomb in a bouquet was one of the oldest devices for assassination. Within a week, the tossing of bouquets was to be forbidden upon pain of being shot in the act, but the machinery of protection and repression of the new totalitarian régime had not yet been organized.

My impression of Hitler's personality was sharpened by watching him at this peak moment of his career. His fanatic's face was in sharpest contrast to the familiar picture of Mussolini posing in a standing strut on his balcony in Rome. Hitler's face reflected a mind which would never be content to find a secure place for himself and for Germany in a stable bourgeois world. My premonition of a coming holocaust for Western civilization was thus immeasurably strengthened.

It occurred to me then that I might have shot Hitler at the same moment with a very good chance of killing him since I was at that time a fairly good shot. I had the opportunity, but I lacked a pistol, the means. (I could perhaps have provided myself with one, but probably not without the help of some conspiratorial organization which would have at once increased the chances of prior detection of such an assassination attempt.) Above all, I lacked the will. It was not merely that I knew that I would probably be unable to escape and would be torn to pieces. I was not emotionally capable of sacrificing my life to save the world from a catastrophe which conceivably might have existed only in my own mind.

To kill a tyrant requires will, opportunity, and means. Rarely do these exist at one and the same moment. The combination of will, opportunity, and means to remove Hitler was never to occur in Germany until the assassination attempt of July, 1944, and this attempt was not successful. A modern totalitarian régime can almost guarantee that will, opportunity, and means will not exist simultaneously. We cannot, consequently, have the solace of knowing that if revolutions create tyrants, they can always be killed.

Chapter eleven. *The Nazi totalitarian state in action*

Some two weeks after Hitler became Chancellor, I revisited Soviet Russia for ten days. I was to find there not only a failure to realize the economic expectations of the spring of 1930 when I had last been there, but an increased terror and famine as well. The winter of 1932–33 was indeed the lowest period for the Soviet régime since the famine of 1921.

Since it was the dead of winter, and since Nazi-Soviet diplomatic relations had not yet reached a *modus vivendi,* the train from Berlin to Moscow had few passengers. Indeed, from Warsaw to Moscow there was only one other passenger in two *wagons-lits,* a Belgian named Bernard. The occasion of our train's coming to a long halt when its engine lost a couple of wheels served to throw us on each other's company.

I learned that he had lived in Moscow before the Revolution and had married a Russian wife. He had returned some years after the Revolution to serve as the head of an organization which operated in the most important ports of the world to certify the quantities and grades of bulk commodities such as grain and oil placed on board ship for export. He proved a very useful source of information. I was puzzled, however, that he, a foreigner, could have lived so long in Soviet Russia and maintained connections abroad without coming under suspicion. He must have been almost the last foreigner who had lived in Russia prior to the Revolution who had not been arrested or expelled.

We separated when we got to Moscow, and I did not find time to look him up later as he had suggested. Some ten months later, after I had returned to the United States, I read a dispatch from Moscow which said that he had been arrested as the head of a great international spy ring. He must, indeed, have been arrested almost immediately after his return to Moscow.

I did not hear the next chapter in his story until after the end of World War II. I happened to meet a friend with whom I had been in graduate school at the University of Minnesota. He told me that he had been Canadian Agricultural Attaché in Moscow at this time. I asked him if he knew Bernard and whether he knew what had happened to him. He said that he knew him well, and he gave me the next chapter in the story. After keeping him in prison for several years, the Soviet authorities in effect made a deal with Bernard. He signed a confession that he had plotted the sinking of a Soviet submarine which had been lost in the Black Sea! He was then released. He returned to Belgium and had just got a business going well when Hitler invaded that country. He fortunately managed to escape to the Argentine, and at last reports was successfully building up a new business there.

While I was in Moscow, I arranged interviews with some Soviet officials, and I made contacts with my friends among the newspaper correspondents who were still there. Although the Soviet government never admitted that famine conditions existed in the Ukraine and elsewhere at that time, everyone in Moscow knew of them. On the way to a performance of *Madame Butterfly* at the Bolshoi Theater, dozens of peasant beggars in the bitter cold of the Moscow night assailed me for alms. "*Gospodin*, for the love of God, a few kopecks!" These were obviously not the professional beggars, each at his accustomed stand, whom I had known before. In their full beards, their birch bark sandals, with their *lapti* wrapped around their legs, most of them speaking in the Ukrainian dialect, they could not be mistaken for anything other than refugees from hunger. It was an excellent performance of *Butterfly*. The audience wept at the sorrows of Cho-Cho-San, apparently uninhibited by the knowledge that hundreds of thousands of their fellow citizens were dying of diseases of malnutrition. There was indeed nothing they could do about it and no reason why they should not have expressed a safe grief for fictional sorrows.

I renewed my acquaintance with the Chamberlins, with Cholerton, Lyons, and Duranty. Lyons was in a terribly depressed mood. His Russian friends, some of them former Nepmen, were now being arrested and tortured. He condemned himself bitterly for staying on and sending dispatches from Moscow when he was not free to tell of terror and famine. He was later to redeem his self-respect with his remarkable *Assignment in Utopia.*

A recently arrived young British journalist correspondent of the *Manchester Guardian* named Muggeridge had been taken under Duranty's wing and had just returned from a trip with him to the North Caucasus. Muggeridge, whose father was a Labour M.P., had been very sympathetic to the Soviet régime. Now, as had been true in so many other cases, he was terribly disillusioned. He had witnessed the severe food shortages in the area. He had also learned of the deportation of several whole Cossack villages from that area of southern Russia to the northern wastes as a penalty for opposing collectivized agriculture. He was bitter against Duranty for his sophisticated attitude towards the sufferings of the peasantry. Muggeridge was to write of all this in a book, *Winter In Moscow.* He was to become a noted journalist and was to remain a leader of anti-Communist sentiment in newspaper circles in Britain.

I got into a conversation with a married couple in my compartment on the train when I left Moscow for Berlin. I fell into conversation with this couple when the other occupant of the compartment, an unattached Russian, was momentarily absent, and they unfolded to me a ghastly tale. He was of Ukrainian origin and his wife was Polish, but he had lived most of his life in the United States. He had been a highly skilled and well-paid mechanic in the aviation industry. They told me with pathetic pride of the two beautiful children who had been born to them and how they had provided them with milk and orange juice. They showed me the photos of the children with their own on their passport. "Where are the children now?" I asked. "They are dead," they said.

He told me how he had been sympathetic to Communism, and when the depression began in the United States, he had been recruited to go to Soviet Russia as a hired specialist. He had taken his family and his expensive tools with him and had eventually arrived in Moscow. To his chagrin, instead of being given work in the aviation industry, he was sent to Kazakhstan to work on a collective farm to repair agricultural machinery. The couple had lost all their peasant "know-how," so instead of drinking only tea for which the water had been boiled, they allowed the children to drink from some of the pretty little streams along the railway. Not long after they arrived in Kazakhstan, the children came down with typhoid fever. He got hold of a truck and drove with his family to the nearest town, but the hospital was crowded to overflowing. He drove on to another town. First the boy died and then the girl. Then he was faced with the ghastly problem of unwinding the red tape to get a burial permit and find a cemetery as he drove desperately from one place to another. Finally, it was done.

He and his wife were now sent to a collective farm. He reported to the Russian manager of the *kolkhoz*, and while they were talking, a number of emaciated Kazakhs turned up begging for food. The manager got rid of their importunities by setting his dogs on the natives. The Ukrainian-American protested, and the manager said, "Oh, those fellows are dying like flies. There are a lot of them piled up down there under the bridge." He could not believe it but went to look. It was indeed so.

Before he had got this far in his story, I had interrupted him. "You have a most important story, and I want to hear all of it. But it is not safe for you to tell it here. The other passenger may return at any moment. I do not know who he is, but he may be a member of the GPU. Where are you going? Perhaps I can come and talk to you after we are out of Russia." He explained that he and his wife were going to visit relatives in that part of the Ukraine which was now annexed to Poland. I promised that I would look him up later. I did, and he told me the story which I have given above. He further explained how after many appeals, through the intervention of President Kalinin, he had been given an exit visa and had been permitted to leave Russia. It was indeed fortunate that I had got him stopped talking, for when we went through the frontier customs inspection, our other passenger was standing behind the counter with other Soviet officials.

Almost at the hour of my recrossing the German frontier on February 27, after my return from Moscow, there occurred a spectacular and mysterious event. The Reichstag building was discovered to be in flames. The official account which was given out stated that one of the perpetrators of the arson had been apprehended in the act by the police. The perpetrator had been caught as he was trying to escape from the building after setting it on fire. When seized by the police, he was clad only in his trousers, having used his shirt as a torch to spread the flames. He had most considerately left his passport and membership book of the Communist party of Holland in his hip pocket as a means of identification for the police. It was established from these documents that he was one van der Lubbe.

The incident was dramatized very effectively by the National Socialists. Göring hastened to the scene and "took personal charge." Hitler, as he gazed at the mounting flames, cried, "It is a sign from Heaven that we must exterminate those dogs!" The police had raided the Karl Liebknecht Haus, the Communist headquarters, and "discovered" a fearful plot of fantastic ramifications. The burning of the Reichstag building was to have been the signal for a Communist uprising on a gigantic scale. The details of the planned uprising included poison, seizing of women and children as hostages, the assassination of prominent persons, and other fearsome acts. Just why the actual burning of the Reichstag building had not "touched off" this Communist *putsch* was somewhat unsatisfactorily explained by saying that the "lightning swift" action of the police had forestalled it. When it is remembered that the Karl Liebknecht Haus had been searched through again and again by previous hostile administrations, the ability of the police in this instance to discover the details of the plan, watch the burning of the Reichstag building, and then act in time so that the signal could not be obeyed was truly a magnificent demonstration of the efficiency of the Prussian police under the new régime.

Using the burning of the Reichstag building as an excuse, the new German régime rapidly duplicated the conditions of terror in Russia. Scores of thousands of Social Democrats, Communists, pacifists, Jews, Catholics, and monarchists were arrested. Sometimes these arrests were made by the police. Sometimes they were made by the SA and SS *Hilfspolizei.* In thousands of cases the arrests were made by SA and SS acting on their own authority. Often the victims had been beaten by the SS and the SA, and when their friends or relatives summoned police assistance, the victims were arrested. In fact, it was the almost invariable custom to arrest anyone who was attacked by the National Socialists. Many of the persons who were arrested were inhumanly beaten. The victims of these attacks were often Jews, but this was by no means always the case. Communists were usually more severely beaten than the Jews, although occasionally a Jew died from the effects of the beatings. Poles and Czechs, in hundreds of cases, received terrible thrashings. Jews sometimes had the swastika burned into their scalps and had their beards torn out.

The political maneuvers of Hitler immediately after he took power were extremely clever, yet his real intentions should have been evident. The extent to which he was able to follow the policy of paralyzing the will of his opponents in all parties and classes during the critical period when the National Socialists steadily took over control of every political and economic function in Germany is well-nigh incredible. His tactics consisted of issuing reassuring statements always accompanied by threats of what would happen if the will of the National Socialists were opposed. When the desired position had been conquered, the previously issued reassuring statement was blandly ignored and a new one was issued in reference to the next stage of the progress of the revolution. In these early days of the Hitler government, the assurances were not so thickly interlarded with threats as later, but the threats were always present even then.

These tactics were eventually to become almost 100 percent effective as they were developed into a form of sugar-coated terror. Men did not dare disbelieve the reassuring statements which were issued, and the statements made it easier for them to quiet their consciences when they acquiesced in some new act of force on the part of the National Socialists. The same tactics were to characterize the foreign policy of Germany under the National Socialist régime. In this field it was to have somewhat less success, for there was no irresistible force to compel foreign countries to believe the reassuring statements. Nevertheless, the way in which foreign diplomats who had interviews with Hitler came away with the statement "I have been very much reassured by my interview with the Reichskanzler" was amazing.

I can only conclude that the statements were really extraordinarily convincing because they appeared at least momentarily to be sincere. This conclusion leads to a second; namely, that the methods of Hitler were not completely a matter of cleverness but were also a species of self-deception which often characterizes the fanatic and which enables him at will to believe anything which at the moment appears convenient to have others believe. I have observed that this has been as characteristic of Soviet Russia as of National Socialist Germany. This synthesis of cleverness and self-deception which is so useful to the fanatic in the simulation of normal sincerity is a psychological phenomenon of first importance, and an understanding of it is essential to those who find it necessary to deal with fanatics.[1]

We left Berlin in late April for a few weeks in Munich, which had been the cradle of the Nazi movement. While there I carried out a number of interviews, including some with Nazi officials. I had an interview with the Chief of the Nazi Military Bureau. He suggested that he might arrange an interview with Hitler for me. I declined on the grounds that I was leaving Germany very soon, and, consequently, the time was too short. In fact, I had never wanted to interview Hitler even if it could have been arranged. I felt as deep a repugnance for him as I felt for Stalin, and to have had to be appropriately deferential to either would have revolted me.

I also had an interview with the Nazi Minister of Labor in the Bavarian government. He well illustrated the way in which the Nazis were trying to make the doctrine of Nordic leadership true retroactively. The Minister of Labor, dressed in the uniform of an officer of the SA, was a giant, at least six and a half feet tall. He was blond, blue-eyed, and fairhaired. He had what appeared to be a hole in his head, a large bluish-tinted scar on his forehead at the edge of his hairline, doubtless got in one of the innumerable street battles with the Communists. He obviously helped to pull up the Nordic average among the Nazi leadership, offsetting such non-Nordic types as Goebbels and Hitler.

My last interview before leaving for Italy was with a professor from the University of Munich. He criticized the Nazi régime freely. I became much alarmed for his safety. "I greatly appreciate your

1. To such an extent were these tactics successful that the *Berliner Tageblatt* severely censured the Communists for trying to call a general strike soon after Hitler's take-over because "to do so at this time would weaken the trade unions' effectiveness if conditions were to become so serious that a general strike could not be avoided."

frankness," I said, "but I must warn you that to speak frankly to a foreigner like myself could be most dangerous for you. I have lived for some time in Soviet Russia under a totalitarian régime like this one. The real danger is that a foreigner might not understand how seriously he would endanger you if he were to express criticism of the régime and then later happen to mention that he had been talking to you." "But to be silent is to be a coward!" the professor cried. "I know," I said, "but I feel that I must at least help you to realize what living in a totalitarian state means."

It is difficult indeed for anyone living in a country in which the principle that one cannot be deprived of life or liberty without due process of law usually holds good to understand the position of men who live under terror. Astonishment has often been expressed that hardly a voice was raised in all Germany against the acts of violence which occurred. But how could a voice be raised so that it would be heard? No newspaper would or could have printed such a protest. No man could have made such a statement in a public meeting without being interrupted before he could complete a dozen sentences and subjected at once to the extremes of physical violence. If he protested, even in private conversation, he was in danger of being denounced, and he would be fortunate if all that happened to him was to receive the legal penalty for spreading "atrocity propaganda." Just as likely would be a line in the press that Herr So-and-So had been arrested for spreading atrocity propaganda and "had been shot while trying to escape" or "had committed suicide in his cell." [2] Martyrdom may have a certain appeal if accompanied by court trials with attendant publicity from the sympathetic and liberal press, but it is quite another thing when it may take the form of summary and anonymous "justice" from a *Sturm Abteilung* which drags the "martyr" out of bed at three o'clock in the morning.

Terror of this sort is certainly effective. Once in control of the state apparatus, a group with very much smaller popular support than the National Socialists had who are willing to use unlimited force can control a country up to the point of defeat in a foreign war or of absolute economic collapse. Terror of this sort may be the negation of civilization. It may be that in the long run it

2. Such notices in the press were frequent. Thus the issues of the *Münchner Zeitung* of April 15 and 16, 1933, contain notices of three such "suicides."

destroys the individuals who wield it. But for a very long time, it is an all-powerful weapon against which the man of honor who is subjected to it is singularly defenseless.

When I first observed terror in action in Russia, I had been inclined to come to the comforting conclusion that it met with little resistance because of the long experience of the Russian people with it in one form or another. It would be as easy to come to the conclusion that terror had its way without opposition in Germany because of the long tradition of Prussian discipline. No doubt the Prussian tradition of discipline was an important factor in explaining why the National Socialists found at once so ready a respect for the authority of the state, regardless of the hand which wielded it. But a most disturbing doubt grew in my mind whether the situation would be very different in any land if the state power were seized by a sufficiently ruthless group.

In spite of the unreserved hostility to the Hitler régime of my *Germany Enters The Third Reich*, the Nazis did not hesitate to make propaganda use of it. They lifted several excerpts out of context and published them along with some favorable excerpts from British writers in a little brochure entitled *Germany in the Third Reich as Seen by Anglo-Saxon Writers*. The real attitude of the Nazis towards my book was shown in the summer of 1940, when, after overrunning the Low Countries and France, they published a special list of books which were to be seized and burned wherever found. My book was listed along with the publications of Marx and Lenin.

I already had a contract with my publisher, and since, because of the economic depression, it was possible to schedule an early printing, *Germany Enters The Third Reich* was in the bookstores by the middle of September, at least a year earlier than would normally have been true. Consequently, I was able at once to start destroying some of the dangerous clichés about the nature of the Nazi régime. My book made it clear that Hitler was something far more dangerous than a puppet of German reactionary capitalists, that he was likely to succeed in rearming Germany without starving the population, that his plans for German territorial expansion must be taken with utmost seriousness, and finally that the Nazi régime was an immediate danger to international peace and a grave portent of world catastrophe.

I had already determined to devote myself to awakening the West to the necessity for military preparation against Hitler. It was just as important and of greater immediacy to work for economic and political policies in the United States which would overcome our mass unemployment. I had written that it was the economic depression which had brought Hitler to power in Germany. I felt deeply that the survival of parliamentary democracy depended upon the ability of the government to carry out remedial economic measures while the people remained free. It was this profound feeling which now carried me into service in the New Deal.

Chapter twelve. *The New Deal*

I found upon my return to the United States in June, 1933, that the country was in the grip of a depression as deep as that which I had just witnessed bring Hitler to power in Germany. I was obsessed with the fear that a similar revolutionary situation would now arise here. Indeed, the signs of such a crisis had already begun to appear. The firing on the "bonus marchers" in Washington, the threatened lynching of a judge by farmers in Iowa at the sale of a farm on which the mortgage had been foreclosed, and other acts of violence were ominous.

The "Hoover villages," occupied by the transient unemployed, which began to appear on the edges of towns and cities; the "Hoover buggies" of the farmers, who put the wheels of cars which they could not afford to repair on the axles of old buggies which they dug out of their sheds; the bitter stories about "the Great Engineer who surveyed, ditched, and drained the country" reflected the prevailing mood. President Hoover, who had said that "prosperity is just hovering around the corner" had had his words twisted by the comic, Ed Wynn, into "Prosperity is just *hoovering* around the corner." Yet President Hoover in his policy of attempting to balance the budget, in avoiding governmental intervention in the economy as long as humanly possible, was faithfully following the precepts of the orthodox economics of that day. I did not agree with this policy for a moment. I was convinced that to follow it to the end meant certain disaster.

I was no longer an orthodox economist. I had become a

"Keynesian" as early as had Keynes himself. I had previously written one of the essays in the prize contest of critical reviews of Foster and Catchings' *Profits.* This book embodied ideas crudely similar to those of Keynes. In writing my criticism of Foster and Catchings, I became more convinced than ever that their concept of a deficiency in consumer purchasing power, while incorrectly related to profits, was essentially valid.[1] I consequently was convinced that a general deficiency of demand, such as existed during the Great Depression, could be cured by massive creations of purchasing power through deficit financing.[2]

In repudiating the economic policy of Herbert Hoover, I would have voted for Franklin Roosevelt in the election of 1932 if I had been in the United States. The logic of my attitude is not immediately apparent to those who remember the campaign. Although it has been almost entirely forgotten, Roosevelt denounced Hoover for incurring a huge budgetary deficit and promised to balance the budget himself. There were indeed proposals for a new agricultural policy, accompanied by denunciations of past governmental intervention in agriculture by the Hoover administration by means of the Farm Board. There was, however, hardly a hint of Keynesian doctrines in the Democratic platform or in Roosevelt's campaign speeches.

Indeed, there was a certain similarity in the political strategy of both Hitler and Roosevelt in denouncing the policies of previous administrations while avoiding committing themselves to specific economic programs until victory had been won. When the party in power has failed, the maximum volume of votes can be mobilized by bringing together all the dissatisfied, even though there may be hardly any agreement at all among them on the measures which should be taken to solve national problems. Far more freedom of

1. When I had seen Keynes in London in the summer of 1930, we had discussed the possibility of my bringing out a book of my largely parallel ideas simultaneously with his *General Theory.* Since I became caught up in the administration of the New Deal, this was not to be feasible.

2. In this belief I was flying in the face of the opinion of the most distinguished American economists of the day. The Hearst newspapers had queried some fifty leading American economists about the advisability of a ten-billion-dollar bond issue to finance a great program of public works as a remedy for the depression. They received the almost unanimous reply that it would destroy the credit of the United States government by driving us off the gold standard. Furthermore, it would not create additional employment since such funds would only be taken away from their normal employment in industry. The economists who gave this reply included a number who later became convinced Keynesians.

action and of maneuver is preserved for an incoming administration if it has not had to commit itself to specific legislation.

I was convinced, moreover, that if the revolutionary situation was to be prevented from developing, the first thing necessary was to have a change in the administration—a change for its own sake, if you will. People would then feel that something different might happen. Inaction constituted the really desperate danger.

I sensed, and I think the American people sensed also, that Roosevelt would try anything rather than sit quietly while stagnation spread further over the country, regardless of the economic theory involved. After the necessary emergency action had been taken, Roosevelt was always confident that it could be rationalized. Hoover had feared that massive budgetary deficits would produce violent inflation. It was his tragedy that he did not understand that governmental borrowing could create bank deposits just as did borrowing by businesses. Above all, he did not understand that the money thus created could result in an increased production of goods, thus limiting the price-raising effects of money creation.

I used to say that Roosevelt if confronted by the choice between the *rigor mortis* of economic depression and the *delirium tremens* of inflation would choose *delirium tremens*. I was personally convinced that violent inflation was by no means the inevitable concomitant of the kind of budgetary deficit required for economic revival. As I viewed from abroad the economic depression deepen and culminate in the closing of the banks immediately following Roosevelt's inauguration, I had felt an ever greater sense of urgency for governmental action which would forestall the kind of catastrophe which I was witnessing at that moment in Germany. The situation required a political figure who would be willing to take the risk of inflation which almost all responsible people thought existed. Roosevelt turned out to be this man.

As an economist, I felt that the New Deal policy of reducing production in order to maintain prices as was sometimes attempted under the National Recovery Administration in industry, or as carried out vigorously by the Agricultural Adjustment Administration was repugnant, but that it was temporarily necessary.[3] This

3. See my "The 'New Deal' in the United States. I. The Agricultural Adjustment Act: Principles, Practices and Problems," *The Economic Journal,* XLIV (Dec., 1934), 567–590.

policy of reducing agricultural production to maintain prices could be justified only on the assumption that it was necessary to prevent a downward spiral of prices and wages, that it would somehow restore an equilibrium between prices of farm products and manufactured goods. Such justification depended on the further assumption that any reduction in total production brought about by governmental action would be only temporary. I had the uneasy feeling, however, that it might prove very difficult to wean farmers away from a policy of reducing production to raise prices so that such a governmental policy might become permanent. I further realized that there was a danger that such a program would come to be of benefit primarily to the more well-to-do farmers.

In retrospect, it would have been far better if the Roosevelt administration could have depended from the beginning on doing whatever was necessary to restore purchasing power by deficit financing and other means and so have avoided permanent involvement in production controls. The decision of the Supreme Court declaring the NRA unconstitutional was to extract the government from the morass of price and production control in industry, but for special reasons the similar decision of the Supreme Court with respect to the AAA did not have this effect.

I hoped that the new administration would have the opportunity both to improve the balance of power of labor versus industry and to lessen the inequality in the distribution of income. These ends were not to be attained until later through the Wagner Act and the Social Security Act in what has sometimes been called the "Second New Deal." The Wagner Act was indeed for a time to more than equalize the bargaining power of managements of labor unions and that of the management of industrial corporations, but this was all in the future.

It was not until late in 1933, however, that an opportunity was offered for me to participate in the formulation and administration of governmental economic policy. I was invited by Rex Tugwell to become an economic consultant in the Agricultural Adjustment Administration. My appointment was delayed for some weeks by the first of those internal convulsions in the "Triple A" by which the first administrator, George Peek, who was a conservative, was forced out. He was succeeded by Chester Davis, whose policies were more in accord with those of the Secretary of Agriculture,

Henry Wallace, and of the Assistant Secretary, Rex Tugwell.

More diverse personalities than these three could hardly be imagined. Rex Tugwell was a professor of economics at Columbia University, the leading member of the Brain Trust, after Raymond Moley had been forced out of the administration. Tugwell was well known as an author of books and articles favoring economic planning and an increased role of government in business and industry. He had easy access to the White House, since he had been one of the principal speech writers for Roosevelt during his presidential campaign. He was not in the least a fanatic, nor indeed, even an emotionally dedicated reformer. He was neither arrogant nor pretentious. Although an intellectual, he was a man of the world and refused to assume a pose of solemn dedication. Instead, he was inclined to be flippant. This quality naturally endeared him to Roosevelt, but not to the farm leaders and other politicians with whom he had to deal. Young looking, well dressed, articulate, he came more than anyone else to represent the Brain Trust to the American public.

Tugwell was widely believed to be a socialist, and conservatives of both parties even charged him with being a Communist. He did indeed believe that American capitalism was going through an evolutionary change which eventually might become almost indistinguishable from socialism. He certainly was not a doctrinaire socialist and not at all a Marxist. He was too sophisticated for that. Likewise, the Soviet economic and political system was quite unacceptable to him, although he did not feel the deep repugnance for Communists and the Soviet regime which I did. He had visited Soviet Russia briefly, but had not had the opportunity to observe the growth of Stalinist terror so intimately and over as long a period as had I.

Tugwell, nevertheless, got the credit for any new legislation which involved increased governmental controls regardless of whether he had really favored such legislation or not. The Bankhead Act is a case in point. Proposed and pushed through Congress by the cotton growers of the South, it was superimposed upon existing "Triple A" controls and complicated the administration of the cotton program immensely. Both Tugwell and Wallace opposed it, but were helpless to prevent its enactment. But Tugwell and the Bankhead Act were indissolubly linked in the minds of the opponents of the New Deal. Tugwell came to be the principal whipping boy for the New Deal and diverted to himself a good deal of the criticism which otherwise would have fallen on the President.

As usually happens in Washington, social dowagers were eager to exhibit prominent figures of any new administration at their dinners. Since Tugwell had become a celebrity, he was earnestly pursued by these socialites even though they detested everything he stood for. On one occasion his hostess accused Tugwell of being a socialist. Tugwell inquired with amusement what her definition of a socialist was. The dowager thought a moment and then replied, "A socialist is anyone who tries to get my dividends reduced!" Tugwell thought very highly of her definition. Although his economic and social philosophy was to the left of mine, we got on well and were on very friendly terms.

Henry Wallace was the grandson of the founder of an Iowa newspaper, *Wallace's Farmer.* His father had been Secretary of Agriculture in the cabinet of President Coolidge. He had left the cabinet after a dispute with Coolidge over the McNary-Haugen Bill. Now his son, Henry, felt that he had a mission to restore the American farmer to a position of economic parity with city dwellers.

Wallace possessed a strain of mysticism. He was very religious, although in a non-conventional way. This mysticism was to be responsible for his strange relations with a Russian-German psychiatrist-philosopher, Roerich, a charlatan. This relationship with Roerich probably was responsible for his replacement as Vice President by Harry Truman, and hence perhaps cost Wallace the presidency.

I was always on friendly terms with Wallace. I never knew anyone who seemed at ease with him, and I never observed him to be at ease with anyone. He would sometimes appear to fall asleep in conferences. His tousled hair topped off a kind of Henry Thoreau rural-philosopher appearance. He was not timid, however, nor was he cowed by difficult problems or embarrassing situations.

Wallace had a very high I.Q. He was competent in mathematics, and was a highly qualified geneticist. He was well informed on all aspects of American agriculture and its problems. He had a fertile imagination and was given to grandiose, if often vague, ideas of social reform. He would try out new diets, perhaps milk and peanuts, not for their personal benefit to him but to investigate the possibilities of new uses for agricultural products in low-cost diets.

He never allowed himself to be limited by narrow considerations concerning the expenditure of funds appropriated for the Department of Agriculture and the Agricultural Adjustment Administration. He had A. E. Russell brought over for consultation on the possibilities of the co-operative movement. "A.E.," as he was always called, with his huge beard, and his ideas about the population-death function of cities, both looked and acted the role of the Irish poet-philosopher which he was. I remember his telling me that only one fourth-generation Londoner had ever been found, and that he was a miserable, shriveled-up specimen of humanity.

Wallace also financed the sending of an expedition to Inner Mongolia, headed by Roerich, ostensibly to search for drought-resistant grasses which might be adapted for use in the drought-stricken areas of the United States. Roerich holed up with his retinue in an ancient Buddhist monastery. He sent infrequent letters back referring rather casually to his travels in search of new varieties of grasses. I came to know of this expedition because the only map of the area which was in anything like sufficient detail was in Russian. The impression everybody had was that he was traveling over wide areas in his search. When I spotted the places he mentioned on the map, it became apparent that he was actually confining himself to a very limited area in Mongolia. Not only did money have to be sent to him—he soon requested that machine guns be sent also! Since this area was one of conflicting territorial interests of the Japanese and Russians, it was felt that this request could hardly be honored. It was later rumored that the whole Roerich expedition had had some esoteric motivation, involving the appearance of a "New Redeemer" who was to arise in Asia. At the time, however, I had no inkling of this.

Chester Davis was a sharp contrast to both Wallace and Tugwell. He also was an Iowan and had been editor of a farm journal and had been an executive of various farm organizations. He had had an active role in pushing for governmental aid to farmers. A college graduate with an excellent mind, he was not an "intellectual," but was the best administrator with whom I have ever been associated. He worked well with Congress and was both respected and liked by farm leaders and other politicians. He was to come into conflict with a group of young radicals—Lee Pressman, Jerome Frank, and Gardiner Jackson, among others—not so much over economic philosophy, but for his insistence on responsible and orderly procedure. Chester Davis was much less visionary than either Wallace or Tugwell, with a far better sense of what was politically and administratively feasible. Since both Wallace and Tugwell realized this, in a controversy between the leftists and the conservatives in the department, however reluctantly, they eventually backed whatever policy Davis decided upon.

At the moment of my joining the "Triple A" the problem of the displacement of agricultural laborers, sharecroppers, and tenant farmers by the acreage-reduction program under the Agricultural Adjustment Act had begun to attract much public attention and criticism. This problem was particularly acute in the South in connection with cotton and tobacco acreage reductions. It was indeed, not merely a question of the displacement of manpower, but a question of the division of the benefits of the program among the various classes of laborers, tenants, and landowners.

Since I was the only economist among the economic advisers who lived in the South, and had had experience as a "dirt farmer," I was asked to make an economic survey and analysis of the situation. I spent about a month at the task. At the time I was still working only half of each week in Washington, returning each week to Duke University to teach my classes. Now, during the half of each week I had been spending in Washington, I traveled through the South instead. I talked with county agricultural agents, local directors of the Emergency Relief Administration, plantation owners, sharecroppers, and displaced agricultural workers.

I found that there were indeed some thousands of these displaced workers. Surprisingly enough, however, most of them had been displaced *before* the acreage-reduction program had been undertaken. They had been displaced simply because at the previously existing low prices for cotton, plantation owners could not afford to take them on in sufficient numbers to keep pace with population increase. The disappearance of job opportunities in industry in the face of the depression had made their situation more desperate. Thousands of these displaced agricultural workers and their families were living in tumbled-down hovels. They now were, however, receiving emergency relief and so were better off than they had been before the New Deal.

I noted this in my report, but I also pointed out that the acreage-reduction program had been intended to benefit farmers in general and not merely landowners, that it was intended that benefit payments and parity payments by the government to induce acreage reduction should be divided among tenants and sharecroppers as well as landowners.

My report, "Human Problems in Acreage Reduction in the South," was launched at a press conference. The demand for it was enormous. It was put out only in mimeographed form, but I think more copies by far were distributed than of anything I have written since that time. It also proved a striking example of the authority of the first written word on a currently pressing problem. Although not intended in the least as a manual of regulations, visiting delegations of cotton farmers during the succeeding months would refer to the "Report" and say that they were operating under its provisions.[3]

I continued to be haunted by the specter of these displaced persons, living on bare subsistence, at a time when we were taking land out of production to raise prices of farm products. If only the land idled by production controls could be used by these people to raise food for themselves! I did succeed in getting agreement that these acres could be used for raising food and feed for non-commercial use. I likewise examined the possibility of developing "subsistence farms" for these people. Such farms had already been set up for unemployed urban workers. I worked with Clark Foreman, an advisor in the Department of the Interior, in this venture. We visited an old run-down plantation known as "Bricks" in North Carolina to see whether a sort of model subsistence farm could be set up. We found that only an inconsequential number of displaced sharecroppers could be settled, and the project never got going. Indeed, there was no way in which the acres idled by the reduction in production could be assembled into subsistence farms. The whole effort was to prove unfeasible.

3. For an account of the controversy over the sharecropper and of my own relation to the controversy and of the later "purge" of radicals, see Arthur M. Schlesinger, Jr., *The Coming of the New Deal* (Cambridge, Mass.: The Riverside Press, 1958), pp. 77–83.

I continued to press for measures to improve the lot of sharecroppers and other tenants. With the earnest support of Secretary Wallace, Chester Davis, Rex Tugwell, M. L. Wilson and others, the Bankhead-Jones Farm Tenant Act was formally passed in 1937. The bill provided long-term loans to tenant farmers to buy land at low interest rates. On September 1, 1937, Dr. Will Alexander, with whom I was to be closely associated in later years, was appointed Administrator of the Farm Security Administration under authority of this Act. This Administration, under a changed title, is still in existence and has made it possible for hundreds of thousands of tenant farmers to become land owners.

Shortly after my report on the farm-tenant problem in the South, a letter to Secretary Wallace on this subject from Norman Thomas, the leader of the Socialist party, was referred to me to prepare a reply for Secretary Wallace's signature. The letter had been received several weeks previously, and various other people in the AAA had tried their hands at drafting a reply. None of these drafts had been satisfactory, and now the whole file came to me. By a curious coincidence, there simultaneously arrived a letter on the same subject from Norman Thomas addressed to me since he had read of my report in the press. Consequently, on the same day, I wrote two letters on the same subject, once as myself and once as Secretary Wallace. I took care that the letters should not be the same, since the official position of the Secretary of Agriculture had to be stated much more cautiously than my own.

This was but one of the jobs of "ghost-writing" which I did, preparing drafts of letters for the signatures of Wallace and Tugwell, and sometimes preparing portions of speeches. Later, when I became Consumers' Counsel, many letters and sometimes speeches were ghost-written for me. At first the task of ghost-writing was exceedingly distasteful. Yet I quickly realized that the practice was an absolute necessity. No cabinet officer can possibly take the time to prepare any large fraction of the letters, the directives and regulations, and the speeches for which he is responsible. However, this mass of ghost-written material goes through a number of hands for checking and authentication, and is supposed to be initialed by all responsible officials, together with any comments or objections. Nevertheless, historians who may review the papers of presidents and cabinet ministers need to remember that changes in style, subject matter, and even policy positions taken, may occur overnight simply because a different set of ghost writers has been employed.

While I was traveling extensively in connection with my study of the farm tenant situation, I had an opportunity to observe the extreme extent to which support of or opposition to the New Deal had developed along class lines. This was shortly before the Congressional election of 1934, which produced a New Deal landslide. However, if one had forecast the election on the basis of the political sentiments of those who rode in the Pullman cars, a Democratic defeat would have seemed inevitable. Apparently the only pro-Roosevelt passengers were those like myself who were traveling on government transportation.

On one occasion I fell into conversation with a businessman who was the holder of a Coca-Cola bottling franchise in one of the Southern states. He had prospered greatly and had bought a large plantation on which he lived. He denounced President Roosevelt and all his works. He said that he hoped that Roosevelt would be assassinated before he had ruined the country irrevocably. He ended by saying that he thought the country was going Communist and that the country deserved to have this happen as a punishment for electing Roosevelt. If the country did go Communist, he said he planned to retire to his plantation and let the country stew in its own juice! I thought of writing an article for *Harper's* which I would have called "The Pullman Vote," but I did not have time to do it. Shortly after the 1934 election, someone else had essentially the same idea and published an article which he called "The Tuxedo Vote."

Soon after I had completed my report on "Human Problems in Acreage Reduction in the South," Tugwell suggested that I take a look at the extremely severe drought which had begun to devastate the cattle- and wheat-raising areas. Black clouds composed of top-soil blown off the land in the Dakotas, Montana, and Minnesota had begun to darken the sky even in Washington. Such a black cloud one afternoon had indeed produced the decision for me to make an investigatory trip. I spent some ten days traveling in the area and was appalled at what I saw. The ruthless plowing up of the buffalo grass and grama grass to put land into wheat had led to wind erosion which aroused memories of what I had seen on the steppes of Central Asia only a few years earlier. It had already been proposed that the government should undertake a cattle-buying campaign in order to prevent price demoralization as ranchers and farmers without adequate feed and water began to ship their cattle to the Chicago and Omaha markets. I now strongly urged that this program be speeded up and intensified.

After a short interlude in which I gave three weeks of lectures at Utah State Agricultural College, I once more returned to Washington. In traveling from Salt Lake City to Washington, I passed by thousands of acres of corn which were "firing," and which it was evident would produce no grain at all. The drought had moved into the western Corn Belt. The corn crop was cut almost in half that year, and all grain production was drastically reduced.

I reported on what I had seen to Tugwell, Wallace, and Davis and urged not only that all thoughts of production restriction must be temporarily abandoned, but that a comprehensive program involving heavy expenditures of federal funds must be put into effect without delay. My personal report coincided with similar information which was now pouring in from the drought area. Far from resisting my recommendations, Tugwell, Wallace, and Davis moved with unprecedented speed in setting up such a program. Harry Hopkins, Federal Relief Administrator, and W. I. Myers, Administrator of the Farm Credit Administration, together with Wallace and Davis, were chosen to make up the President's Drought Relief Committee, with Wallace as Chairman. I became the executive secretary of the committee. It was decided that a working committee should be set up to administer the program of the President's Drought Relief Committee. It was also decided that there should be no public announcement of the formation of the President's Drought Relief Committee in order to avoid public alarm. Instead, the working committee was given the name of the Livestock Feed Committee. I was appointed chairman of the committee, and all public references to its work thereafter referred to measures necessary for feeding livestock and not people. This procedure was justified because, fortunately, a serious shortage of food did not arise.

I took the position that the more rapidly we bought cattle and slaughtered them, the less we would have to slaughter in the long run since the sooner the cattle were slaughtered, the more feed would be left for the remaining cattle. I called in representatives of the meat packers for a number of conferences. They were urged to make their maximum facilities available with all speed. Although they were at first very doubtful of their ability to process these additional millions of cattle, all available resources were utilized, and no cattle carcasses went to waste because of lack of packing facilities.

Some hundreds of thousands of cattle were also shipped from the drought-stricken areas to pasturage east of the Mississippi. In all, some eight million cattle were slaughtered. Some four million sheep and goats were also purchased and slaughtered. I insisted that all salvageable meat should be canned for distribution to people on relief. This was done. However, somewhat more than a million head of cattle which were either diseased or too emaciated for use were simply shot and buried. I urged that this also be carried on with all possible speed in the interests of conserving feed and forage. Every possible sort of feed was utilized, including straw, corn stocks, and "Russian thistles." Cheap "black strap" molasses, a by-product of sugar refining, was used to make this low grade forage palatable and more nutritious.

A total of $525,000,000 was recommended for allocation to the various governmental agencies co-operating in drought-relief measures. Congress appropriated this sum. A fund of $100,000,000 was allocated to the Farm Credit Administration to be loaned as emergency feed loans to farmers in drought areas. These funds were loaned without security and enabled farmers to keep through the winter cattle which they would have otherwise have had to let die or would have had to dispose of at ruinously low prices. I have since thought of this loan arrangement as one case in which I could feel that I had personally been responsible for saving the government some millions of dollars. In view of the catastrophic situation, it had been proposed that substantially all funds should be direct governmental expenditure or grants. I insisted that the $100,000,000 loan program should be set up, since I knew that once the drought was over most of the farmers would be able to repay the money they needed for feed. This proved to be true.

The governmental program for dealing with the drought was successful enough that it largely offset the criticism of the agricultural adjustment program which naturally accompanied the drought. It had even been argued that the drought was the punishment which the Lord inflicted upon us for trying to reduce food production. All programs involving the reduction of grain production were momentarily stopped. It was profoundly more satisfying to be able to put all my time and effort on conserving food and feed instead of helping to limit its production.

All during my service in the Agricultural Adjustment Administration, I was to observe that every extension of governmental authority in the economy was used both as the occasion for still further extension of that authority and for the advantage of special interests. In order for the government to purchase cattle in the drought areas, it was necessary for each county in which such purchases were to be made to be declared an emergency area. Tugwell had noticed that several counties in Florida had been declared in a state of emergency and cattle were being purchased in these counties. Assuredly there was no drought in Florida. We discovered that these counties had been declared emergency areas on account of floods! Further inquiry showed that no serious flooding had occurred in these Florida counties. Political pressure had simply been used to get the government to purchase some very low grade cattle at prices higher than otherwise could have been obtained. Further, we discovered that cattle from the drought areas of the Far West were being shipped into these counties for pasturage. Finally, we discovered that some small packing plants in these counties had received contracts for slaughtering and processing the slaughtered cattle. I was outraged at this, and I demanded that the purchase and slaughter of cattle in these counties be halted. Even though I took the matter directly to Secretary Wallace, who immediately agreed, it was some weeks before the purchase and slaughter of these cattle could be stopped. I suspect that by that time all the cattle which the people in that area wished to sell had been disposed of.

At this time also I received scores of telegrams from one county in New Mexico, urging that turkeys be included in the emergency purchase program and setting forth in varying detail the individual impact of the turkey emergency. These telegrams were signed by individuals, farm organizations, chambers of commerce, and, indeed, by almost every conceivable sort of organization. About a year later I was to travel through this area surveying the results of the drought of 1936, which then affected the South-west instead of the Northwest as in 1934. I happened to fall into conversation with the secretary of the Farm Bureau of the county. The young lady asked me whether I remembered getting all those telegrams about purchasing the turkeys. I remembered that they had indeed come from this particular county. "I wrote those telegrams," she said with quiet pride; "then I called everybody up and asked if I could use their names."

Just as the drought crisis was brought under control, an internal crisis developed in the Agricultural Adjustment Administration itself. Some of the more radical young people in the Agricultural Adjustment Administration took advantage of a few days' absence of the Administrator, Chester Davis, to issue a ruling that landowners who signed contracts to reduce cotton acreage must not displace any of their sharecroppers or other tenant farmers without their agreement. There had previously been a provision by which landowners who signed contracts undertook to avoid as much as possible reducing the number of their tenants. However, it had been recognized that a landlord could not be required to keep a particular tenant any more than a tenant could be required to remain with the same landlord.

Chester Davis demanded that Jerome Frank, the General Counsel, generally considered the leader of the radicals, be dismissed. Wallace unwillingly agreed. Lee Pressman, Gardiner Jackson, and Fred Howe, Consumers' Counsel, were also dismissed. Curiously enough, Alger Hiss, who had drafted the reinterpretation of the tenant clause in the AAA contract was not fired, nor did he resign in sympathy with those ousted. Hiss was blamed by Jerome Frank for his failure to resign. Undoubtedly, Frank did not know that Hiss was a member of the Communist party and had presumably been ordered by the party not to resign since he was needed for the services to Soviet Intelligence, which he was later to render.

Fred Howe, Consumers' Counsel, who was an old style social reformer, softhearted, and rather soft-headed, had been needlessly involved in the controversy, since the issue would not normally involve the Consumers' Counsel. Howe had apparently been manipulated by some of his staff who were party members and others who were at least "fellow travelers."

I did not suspect any of this group of radicals of being Communists, with the exception of Lee Pressman. It was rumored at the time that Pressman was a Party member, and his personality and attitude made this easy to believe. Years later, he confessed he had been a member at this time. Nathaniel Weyl, who had been on the staff of the Consumers' Counsel and who was to turn against the Party, later stated that both he and Alger Hiss belonged to the Party cell which existed in the Department of Agriculture. The conviction of Hiss in the later perjury trial and the accompanying revelations of Whittaker Chambers confirm this.

I simply could not believe that a quiet, intelligent, highly educated man like Hiss could be a Communist. Did he not know the facts of Stalin's Soviet terror, of the complete suppression of individual liberty, of his forced collectivization of agriculture, of the complete absence of free elections? Since I was so intimately acquainted with the Soviet tyranny, I assumed that the facts were well known. Only later did I come to realize the efficiency of Marxist doctrine in totally obscuring to many intellectuals the fate of the individual in Soviet society. Further, since according to Marx, the overthrow of capitalism and the triumph of collectivism was to come about by deterministic forces, outside the control of individuals, Marxist-dominated intellectuals were spared any responsibility for the lives and feelings of individuals. I was to find that almost without exception, intellectuals who had joined and remained in the party had one trait in common, a lack of personal warmth and an equal lack of sympathy for individual unhappiness or suffering. Intellectual arrogance was another quality which I have found to be almost universal among Communist intellectuals. Curiously, this personal arrogance has usually not been a bar to the acceptance of complete party discipline by intellectuals who join the party. In retrospect, I could see how Hiss could simply disregard evidence of Soviet brutality, at once denying its existence and feeling that it was unimportant even if it did exist.

Chester Davis, Henry Wallace, and Rex Tugwell asked me at this time to take over the post of Consumers' Counsel, now that Howe had been moved out and into a sinecure in the AAA. Presumably I was chosen because I was known as sympathetic to the position of the sharecroppers in the South (although this really had nothing to do with the job of the Consumers' Counsel), and because I had been a farmer and could be counted upon to deal sympathetically with the interests of the farmer while somehow protecting the interests of consumers.[4] My acceptance of the position also entailed membership in the nine man "cabinet" which developed and administered general AAA policy.

The position of Consumers' Counsel was the result of writing a so-called "Consumers' Protection Clause" into the Agricultural Act: "To protect the consumers' interest by readjusting farm production at such level as will not increase the percentage of the consumers' retail expenditures for agricultural commodities, or products derived therefrom, which is returned to the farmer, above the percentage which was returned to the farmer in the pre-war period, August 1909–July 1914."

Secretary Wallace had been responsible for the language of the clause. The Consumers' Counsel was expected to see to it that the consumer got a "fair deal" vis-a-vis the farmer. But the Agricultural Adjustment Act was intended to raise prices to the farmer by means of reducing production. Thus the intent of the Act apparently was *ipso facto* contrary to the interests of the consumer. However, Fred Howe, my predecessor as Consumers' Counsel, and his staff had tried to provide a modicum of protection to the consumer by attempting to limit the returns to the middleman-processor of agricultural products. This was attempted by having a representative of the Consumers' Counsel sit in on the hearings which were held whenever a price increase was proposed under one of the marketing agreements or codes administered by the AAA. This representative usually attempted to see to it that if, for example, the price of milk was to be increased by one cent, as from eleven to twelve cents per quart, as small a share as possible went to the distributors and as much as possible went to the dairy farmers.

I continued this policy, together with the requirement that a case must be made to justify any increase at all. I often participated in these hearings personally, and it was interesting to observe the reactions of the representatives of the farm organizations and the distributors when they first became aware that a representative of the consumer was participating in the hearings. Here both producers and distributors were unselfishly agreeing to co-operate in

4. See also Murray R. Benedict, *Farm Policies of the United States 1790–1950* (New York: The Twentieth Century Fund, 1953).

raising the price of a quart of milk and now this busybody of a Consumers' Counsel was trying to sabotage this splendid co-operative effort!

However, the Consumers' Protection Clause could always be appealed to, and grudgingly my presence at the hearings was accepted. Fortunately, it was some months before I subjected the Consumers' Protection Clause to close analysis. I then discovered that the "protection" in the famous clause was actually a protection to the *distributors*, not the consumers, although this had naturally not been the intention of the draftees. In drafting the clause, Wallace and his associates had apparently carried over a sort of primitive concept of the division of society into farmer-producers and processor-distributor-urban consumers. If one limited the percentage of the consumer's dollar which went to the farmer-producer to that of the parity period (1909–1914), then the rest of the dollar would be guaranteed for the urban consumer in his role of processor-distributor.

What the Consumers' Counsel had been doing was to try to limit the share of the consumers' dollar going to the processor-distributor. In addition, I had been dragging my feet on raising the price of agricultural products by trying to require justification for each increase in price. In so doing, I was indeed making an attempt at protecting the consumer. However feeble the powers wielded by the Consumers' Counsel in trying to limit the share of the middleman or in slowing down the increases in the price of milk and other products, I was shaken when I came to realize that the policy and procedures I had been following had no legal support in the Consumers' Protection Clause. Fortunately, no one else discovered this illogical flaw in the Agricultural Adjustment Act. I said nothing about it, since the policy I had been following was one which was consistent with the original intention of the framers of the Act, and it was approved as the correct policy by Secretary Wallace and by Chester Davis. It was decidedly *not* approved by some other officials of the AAA, however, who resented any real effort at the protection of the consumer. In a sense, they could not be blamed, for the position of Consumers' Counsel in the Agricultural Adjustment Administration was anomalous if not completely self-contradictory.

The position of the Consumers' Counsel in attempting to limit the share of the processors and distributors of farm products in the consumer's dollar, however, was doubtful not only on legal grounds. Not only the farmers but substantially all consumers tended to think of the "middleman" as a sort of parasite who stood between producer and consumer and took his toll. This was inherent in the concept of "the share of the consumer's dollar" which is still regularly computed by the Department of Agriculture. As I write (1963) "the farmer's share" is 37 cents. The 63 cents which does not go to the farmer used often to be referred to as the "middleman's profit," which is ridiculous. This 63 cents includes the cost of transportation (mostly labor), processing, and distribution. Since food is typically transported farther and farther from where it is grown, more highly processed, elaborately packaged, and accompanied by trading stamps, it is inevitable that the farmer's share of the dollar should decline over time.

When prices of farm products fall during a depression, however, the processor-distributors' returns fall much less, since these costs are far more rigid. Thus the share of the consumer's dollar going to the farmer had fallen from 47.4 cents in 1929 to 33 cents in 1932. It was indeed essential that when the AAA was using governmental powers to raise farm prices, these powers should not be utilized to maintain the abnormally high share, 67 cents, which processor-distributor had been receiving at the bottom of the Great Depression. Some success was achieved, since the farmers' share of the consumers' dollar had risen to 37.5 cents from the low of 33 cents. In addition, farmers were receiving benefit payments from government. It was frustrating, however, to have to rely on this clause in the Agricultural Administration Act which gave the Consumers' Counsel the duty of limiting the rise in the farmer's share of the consumer's dollar and which meant guaranteeing that the processor-distributor's share of the consumer's dollar should not go below that of the base period, 1909–1914.

In an effort to protect the consumer's interests in a less illogical way, I proposed the following amendment to the Agricultural Adjustment Act:

> To protect the interest of the consumer by (*a*) preventing the rise to or continuance of prices to farmers at a higher level than that which it is declared to be the policy of Congress to reestablish in subsection (1) of this section, (*b*) making available for annual consumption such quantity of any agricultural commodity or prod-

> uct which was annually consumed during the period 1925–1929, plus or minus such additional quantity as will reflect any trend in the consumption of such commodity or product thereof, relative to the consumption of all agricultural commodities and products thereof, during the period 1926–1929, and (*c*) insuring the availability for domestic consumption of such average quantity (corrected for trends as hereinabove provided) of any basic agricultural commodity by establishing surplus reserves out of current production in excess of current domestic consumption.

Subsequently, the essence of this proposal was incorporated in amendments to the Act.

My admiration for the old-fashioned "free market" as the protector of the consumer in comparison with what I could do to protect the consumer under governmental regulation of prices became positively nostalgic. I had to remind myself that the free market *had* broken down during the Great Depression. I recalled the milk-price war which had raged in Los Angeles just prior to the New Deal. The retail price of milk had fallen momentarily to one cent per quart. The limit of absurdity had been reached when the customer of a milk seller who offered to buy a quart of milk was given a penny on condition that he would buy from his competitor, thus hurrying him the more rapidly into bankruptcy. I became more convinced, however, that the answer to these failures of the free market to function was to cure the economic depression by monetary and fiscal means rather than to try to substitute regulated prices for the free market.

It might be thought that since everyone is a consumer, the political and economic power of the consumers' representatives in the hearings on price fixing in the marketing agreements and codes would have been overwhelming. Quite the contrary. The political power of consumers is so diffuse as to be all but useless when applied to a particular governmentally controlled pricing process. Thus, even in the case of the price of bread, for example, the interest of any particular consumer will not warrant his coming to Washington to appear before a Congressional Committee, or to vote for his representative in Congress on the basis of some vague idea of the representative's position with respect to matters which could affect the price of bread. Even more to the point, the consumer of bread is not going to hire a lawyer to represent him at a hearing, nor is he likely to join with other consumers in so doing.

Since the marketing agreements and codes with which we had to do included such highly varied products as ripe olives, red sour cherries, Georgia watermelons, and Colorado cling peaches, one can see that the likelihood of having representatives of the consumers of these items support the efforts of the Consumers' Counsel to protect the consumers was nil. Once more one felt nostalgia for the market place where, when it functioned freely, consumers were protected by the self-interest of producers and distributors competing for the "dollar votes" of the consumer.

Still another incident illustrated the tendency to extend governmental control of prices once the process had begun. It must be remembered that the AAA was intended to *raise, through governmental action, agricultural prices* relative to the prices of goods which the farmer bought. The measure of success of governmental policy was to be measured by the "parity index," or the ratio of the prices of goods that farmers sold to the prices of goods which the farmer purchased, with the base period 1909–1914 taken as 100. My friend Dr. Don Humphrey, at that time on the staff of the Consumers' Counsel, discovered that a proposal was being advanced for an "Anti-Hog-Cholera Serum and Virus Code" allegedly for the purpose of insuring an adequate supply of serum and virus for the prevention of hog cholera. This was to be done by permitting the producers to agree upon prices to be charged farmers who purchased the serum and virus.

Here was a case of enabling producers to enter into agreements otherwise clearly illegal under the Sherman Anti-Trust Act to set the most profitable prices. It was extraordinary that many officials of the AAA had got so conditioned to co-operating with farmers and farm organizations in trying to raise farm prices that these minor officials saw no reason why they should not co-operate with other producers in raising prices even though the only purchasers would be farmers. The Consumers' Counsel vigorously opposed this proposal, with the result that the administration of the code was transferred entirely out of the AAA to the Bureau of Animal Industry!

In my service in government, which was to stretch over some thirty years, one of the less admirable aspects of the staffing of governmental bureaucracy was the adulation, which often attained the level of sycophancy, accorded cabinet members. None of us is invulnerable to flattery. "Stuffed shirts" are, of course, particularly vulnerable. Wallace was, however, anything but a "stuffed shirt." He was shy, introspective, withdrawn, even though deeply concerned with the welfare of the "common man." In appearance and in thought processes, he was the ideal "farmer-philosopher." In a real sense, he was a very modest man. Yet sycophants around Wallace seized upon his modesty as the vehicle of their flattery. They proclaimed him as an intuitive genius, one of the great philosophers of all time, and withal *the most modest man alive.* Flattery is like a habit-forming drug: constantly heavier doses are required to maintain its potency. It became noticeable that the early flatterers of Wallace were displaced by those who did not scruple to lay it on more thickly. Finally, the Communists took over the process. As Walter Reuther has said, "The Communists will furnish a complete valet service. As long as anyone is useful to them and will follow their lead, there is no limit to the flattery they will provide." I am convinced that this vulnerability of Wallace to being acclaimed as the most modest of men was a major factor when in later life he unwittingly came under Communist domination and headed the Progressive party in the election of 1948. It is to his credit that eventually he came to understand something of the true nature of the Communist party and repudiated it.

My experience with the AAA, to be supplemented by many years of experience in other branches of the government, was a revelation to me of the complexity and subtlety of the governmental process by which men are ruled. I had realized, of course, that the simple doctrine of legislative representation of the will of the majority of the citizenry did not reflect reality. I realized that, assuming a score of significant issues, there might be as many different majorities, overlapping in greater or lesser degree, and that a given measure before Congress might be supported or opposed by those making up a legislative majority for different or even opposite reasons. These and many other complexities prevented the legislative process from ever reflecting some sort of simple and stable majority of the voters.

What I had not realized was the extent to which the legislative, executive, and judicial processes were all affected by a nonelected bureaucracy, and indeed, by a bureaucracy whose members were almost entirely anonymous as far as the public is concerned.

Just as in the case of ghost-writing for cabinet members and other high officials, legislation and administration by a non-elected and faceless bureaucracy is largely inevitable. Neither Presidents nor cabinet officers can possibly devote much of their time to reading the text of even the most important legislation, not to mention devoting much time to the actual analysis and writing of such legislation. Even the justices of the Supreme Court depend largely on their young lawyer assistants for writing the text of their opinions. Senators and Representatives must depend upon the staffs of the committees on which they serve to prepare for Congressional Hearings and then to write the detailed legislation. Finally, a great part of the regulations by which the economy is governed comes into being and is administered by commissions which are not subject to the legislative process at all. The members of these commissions in turn must depend upon their staffs for their actual functioning.

I soon realized the difficulty which every new administration encounters in trying to inaugurate and administer new policies with the previously existing governmental bureaucracy. This difficulty is, of course, accentuated when the changes in policies are as fundamental as those involved in changing from the past Republican administrations to the Roosevelt administration. However, this accentuation of the difficulty was more than offset by the circumstance that the policy of increased governmental intervention and control by Roosevelt meant that thousands of new government employees had to be hired. It was inevitable that the new employees should be far more in tune with the new policies than were those civil servants inherited from previous administrations.

Through the years I was to observe the process of adding on new layers of governmental personnel with every new administration. I came to call this the "Coral Reef Effect" since the new organisms always grew upon the bodies of the ones previously deposited. However, whenever a new administration, such as that of Eisenhower, wants to reduce governmental controls somewhat, it faces at once the problem of how it can possibly do so without adding personnel sympathetic to the new policy. But new personnel always has to be added to the existing personnel, which means the expansion of the federal bureaucracy, contrary to the policy of reducing the role of government.

The shock which I felt as I came to realize the complexity of the governmental function and how far it departed from some simple model of representative democracy is almost universal among academic people who come into government as advisors.[5] This is not to say that our governmental process is totally undemocratic or hopelessly ineffective. Assuredly, when compared with the processes employed by any other government, ours are quite satisfactory. Above all, compared with the governmental processes of totalitarian governments, ours is not only far more representative of the people's will, however diffuse and amorphous that will may sometimes be, but it is even more efficient.

However, the importance of the role of the anonymous bright young man in the legislative, administrative, and judicial bureaucracy does mean that any tightly disciplined minority if it extends over all three branches and over several departments can play a role totally disproportional to its size. This is why the influence of the Communist party could be of so much importance.

While I was still acting as economic advisor and had not yet taken on the responsibility of dealing with the drought crisis nor of Consumer's Counsel, John Maynard Keynes arrived in Washington in the later spring of 1934. We renewed the friendship which had begun when we had met in London in the spring of 1930. The first thing he asked me was "What is this 'Brain Trust' I read about?" I described the group as well as I could, explaining that Tugwell was now the informal head of the "Trust" after the departure of Raymond Moley. I also told him of my own role in the AAA and the Department of Agriculture. "It's no good being an economic advisor," he said. "I had that job for a while in the British Treasury in World War I. No cabinet minister can possibly listen to you for more than an hour, and it is impossible to explain the economics involved in proposed legislation in such a brief time. If you want to have any real effect upon economic policy, you must take a responsible operating job." It was this advice which largely motivated me in becoming first the Secretary of the President's Drought Relief Committee and later Consumers' Counsel.

Keynes strongly believed that the normal condition of an

5. As Arthur Schelsinger put it after his own experience as a participant in the Kennedy administration, "Nothing in my own recent experience has been more chastening than the attempt to penetrate into the process of decision." Arthur Schlesinger, Jr., "The Historian and History," *Foreign Affairs*, XLI (April 1963), 493.

affluent capitalistic country was that of underconsumption. This was well illustrated one night when we had both been invited out to dinner and then the dinner was called off. He telephoned me and invited me to have dinner with him in his suite in the Mayflower. While I was washing up in the bathroom, he genially ridiculed my niceness in selecting a towel from the rack so as not to muss the others. He made a sweep with his arm and knocked two or three on the floor. "I am convinced," he said, jokingly, "that I have served the economy of the U. S. A. better by stimulating employment through mussing up these towels than you have by your carefulness in avoiding waste." His insistence during World War II on limiting disposable consumer income apparently did not change this fundamental point of view. In London during the war (I cannot be sure whether it was in 1942 or 1943) Keynes told me that he had become convinced that after the war the "answer will lie in increased consumption." He went on to say that he believed that after the war it was going to be necessary and desirable to take action to increase the consumption of the lower-income groups rather than to depend upon maintaining full employment by means of measures to encourage the expansion of investment.

Keynes was by nature impatient with anyone who argued that the same policy was appropriate for all occasions and circumstances. He was in essence a believer in the simple efficacy of the barmaid's turning the spigot on and off to regulate the flow of beer, to accommodate fluctuations in the thirst of the customers in the pub.

Keynes spent a week or so in Washington before going on to Columbia University, where we both received honorary doctorates. I gave the Phi Beta Kappa address there, and Keynes gave a lecture which was also part of the commencement activities. In this lecture he paid tribute to the economic policies of the Roosevelt administration. However, he referred to the current monetary policy as resembling "the gold standard on the booze" rather than a managed currency of the sort he would have favored.

He had had his hour with President Roosevelt before leaving Washington and had felt that he had not succeeded in explaining adequately his monetary theories in connection with deficit financing. However, this hour was to bear fruit, because eventually the Roosevelt administration did adopt the Keynesian justification for deficit financing. After deficit financing on a large scale had become a necessity for the administration, those of us in the administrative apparatus who were Keynesians, Rex Tugwell, Gardiner Means, and I, were able to provide an *ex post* rationale for the policy.

I had originally agreed to serve as economic consultant to the AAA on a part-time, temporary basis. I had accepted governmental employment only because of the grave economic emergency. It had soon become apparent that I would have to devote full time to my governmental responsibilities; so I obtained a leave of absence from Duke University and moved my family to Washington. As the academic year 1936–37 approached, I had now to decide whether I should remain with the government or return to the university. Although difficult problems of policy and administration remained, the emergency aspect of the agricultural situation had by now largely resolved itself.

I had no taste at all for becoming a permanent member of the federal bureaucracy concerned only with administration. To have continued in a policymaking position would have required my identifying myself with the Roosevelt administration's political future. I would have had to have become, in effect, a politician, often taking positions in which I would have to compromise, not only my professional principles as an economist, but my concepts of right and wrong. Further, I would have had to recognize that I could not let loyalty to personal friendships override the national interest, political party interest, or even the interest of one's immediate superior. All these things politicians must do at times. The governmental process could otherwise not be carried on.

Up to this time, I could always decide whether or not the principles involved in a controversy were important enough to warrant my resignation if the issue went against my principles. I could always withdraw to my permanent university connection. Since this was well known, my position as an advisor on economic policy had been much stronger than it otherwise would have been. Furthermore, I could take and state my position without having constantly to "carry a chip on my shoulder" or indulge either in violent controversy or in intrigue in order to get my position accorded consideration. Once I abandoned my university connection, this would no longer be true. Granted that I could and would resign if the principles involved were important enough, my position would have become much weaker if I had stayed on. My position had been strengthened too by the fact that I was a writer. But if I had stayed on in the government, this would have become a wasting asset also since I would not have been able to continue as an independent writer.

A possible alternative would have been to enter politics outright and try to get myself elected to Congress. But for this, I had neither opportunity nor taste. So I returned to Duke University and academic life. I did not realize that I was to have a breathing space of only about four years before an even greater emergency would call me back into government service, and that, indeed, I was never permanently to escape.

Chapter thirteen. *The coming of World War II in Europe*

After resigning as Consumers' Counsel and Economic Advisor with the Roosevelt administration, I resumed my career as a teaching and research economist. My interests continued to be regional as well as national and international. My regional interests were now carried out largely through the Southern Economic Association, of which I became President in 1937.

In the meantime, the Civil War had broken out in Spain in 1936. My sympathies were from the outset wholly with the Republican government. My attitude was primarily due to the fact that the rebel forces were aided from the very beginning by the Nazi government of Germany and by the Fascist government of Italy. The heavy dependence upon Moorish troops by Franco also made it plain that the rebel régime did not have the support of the majority of the Spanish people.

The support which the Soviet government soon began to furnish the government of Spain did indeed provide the channel by which the Communists came to exercise a dominant role on the Republican side. I felt, however, that the Republican government had turned to the Soviet government for aid only after Nazi and Soviet intervention in the conflict and after it had proved impossible for the government to purchase arms from France, Great Britain, or the United States. The solemn farce of "non-intervention" which European governments agreed to disgusted me.

I followed the war battle by battle, rejoicing when Franco's advance on Madrid was stopped. The humiliating defeat of the Italian Fascist divisions in their attempt to break through to Madrid was also a source of personal satisfaction. I felt a great admiration for the fighting qualities of the International Brigades, even though I realized that a large proportion of the membership were Communists. I followed the fortunes of the International Brigades with all the more interest as I learned that my Russian companion on the Turk-Sib trip of 1930 was now commanding the Brigades as "General Kleber." [1]

I did have some inkling of the divisive role which the Communists were playing in the Republican forces. It was only later, however, that I came to realize the extent to which Stalinist terror and purges had been introduced into Spain so that finally the defeat of the Republican forces could be attributed in large degrees to the Communists. The bombing of the civilian population of Guernica by Nazi flyers, and similar exploits, served to sustain my sympathy for the Republican regime in Spain.

I viewed the defeat of the Republican government and the triumph of Franco in the spring of 1939 as a victory for Hitler and Mussolini. It worried me deeply that the democratic governments of Europe apparently lacked the will to resist. I assumed that Spain had now been added to the *de facto* Nazi-Fascist alliance.[2]

From the beginning of the Civil War in Spain, my concern over the aggressive and expansionist policies of the totalitarian states began to override my interest and participation in our own domestic economic and political problems and policies. The success of the New Deal in bringing about economic recovery from the Great Depression had prevented the collapse of capitalism and democratic institutions in the United States. Without this rescue of capitalism and democracy in the United States, there would have been little chance for its survival in any other country. While the immediate danger of the further progress of totalitarianism through revolution due to internal economic causes in the West had now passed, the threat of conquest by totalitarian states began to be a most serious one.

The difficulties which had resulted from the forced collecti-

1. See pp. 120–122.
2. In retrospect, this was an oversimplification. As it turned out, Franco did not enter World War II on Hitler's side, and his failure to do so may have been crucial.

vization of agriculture in Soviet Russia, culminating in the famine of 1932–33, followed by the Stalinist terror and purges, had even raised in my mind doubts of the survival of the Soviet régime. As I wrote in 1937:

> If the Soviet regime is overthrown as a result of the present frenzy, either by an internal coup or by a new regime set up under foreign tutelage, among the exploited of the earth a legend will grow of a free, socialist society, once created by the heroism of the toiling masses, later done to death by capitalist assassins. The bitter irony of this legend will lie in the fact that such a society had never emerged from the dictatorship of the proletariat which was to have been its chrysalis. Instead, the dictatorship of the Communist party emerged and developed into the tyranny which now exists. A fascist coup in Russia could not produce a regime more absolute, more ruthless, or more violent than the one descended in unbroken line from that given birth by the October Revolution.[3]

The victory of Franco in Spain, the reoccupation of the Rhineland by Hitler, and his subsequent occupation and annexation of Austria completed my conviction that the Nazi and Fascist totalitarian systems had now become a more immediate threat to the democracies than was the Soviet totalitarian system.

Throughout the Western World there had been a failure to recognize the basic similarities between the Nazi and Fascist economic and political systems and the Soviet totalitarian system. Curiously enough, extreme conservatives and Communists were largely agreed about the nature of the Nazi system.[4] Many American and British industrialists found it comforting to believe the Communist charge that Hitler was simply a "stooge" of the German industrialists and Junkers. While very few indeed among American or British industrialists would have favored anything like the Nazi movement for their own countries, many did feel that the Nazi movement was the very antithesis of Communism. They believed that "Big Business" and extreme conservatism held the whiphand over Hitler. Some, doubtless, even felt some nostalgia for the kind of old fashioned "no nonsense" capitalism which they believed Hitler had restored in Germany. The thought of big business con-

3. *Dictators and Democracies* (New York: Macmillan, 1937) pp. 39–40.
4. The Nazi system was, of course, of far more importance than the Fascist system, and henceforth my analysis will refer specifically to the Nazi system.

trolling government instead of government controlling big business, of smashed labor unions with corporate management once more master in its own house, was nostalgically sweet. Most American and British industrialists realized, however, that such a relationship between government and business and between management and labor was not only a thing of the past—it was contrary to modern enlightenment.

What industrialists outside Germany did not realize was that their picture of the Nazi system was fundamentally false. Big business did not control the Nazis; the Nazis controlled, even terrorized, big business. Far from restoring the laissez-faire for which businessmen always proclaimed their admiration, the Nazi system had both intensified existing governmental controls and had added others. Far from the regime of law and order which capitalists have always admired and needed, there existed instead a *Revolution of Nihilism* [5] in which neither life nor property was safe, in which legal and constitutional protection by the courts had disappeared. Above all, and contrary to the stereotype, German industrialists flinched from contemplating the threatened European war, which they feared because they realized that Germany could not win.

I now devoted myself to trying to explain the true nature of the Nazi system and its threat to the Western World through public lectures and magazine articles. I wrote a series of articles for the *Virginia Quarterly Review* on the nature of the Nazi and Soviet totalitarian systems. At the urging of the editor, Mr. Lambert Davis, I published these articles, together with a couple of additional articles with the Macmillan Company under the title *Dictators and Democracies*. The last sentence of that book reflects the gravity with which I viewed the international situation: "Nevertheless, whatever the risks to non-totalitarian states of opposition to Hitler and Mussolini, such a policy affords well-nigh the only prospect for the survival of parliamentary government on the continent of Europe."

I returned to Europe in the early summer of 1939. I realized that I might be caught in either Germany or Russia by the war which I expected to break out at any moment. Nevertheless, I was so eager to have a look at Europe on the eve of war that it seemed worth

5. See Hermann Rauschning, *The Revolution of Nihilism* (New York: Alliance Book Corporation, 1939).

taking the risk. The immediate occasion of my going to Europe and the major means of financing the trip was a conference to be held in Bergen, Norway, in September with delegates from most European countries. I was one of six American delegates to the conference. I was accompanied by Henry Oliver, an instructor at Yale University, one of my former graduate students. We arrived in London in early June. I had a letter of introduction to Harold Macmillan from my publishers, the Macmillan Company in the United States. I had greatly admired Macmillan because of the stand he had taken together with Anthony Eden and Duff-Cooper against Chamberlain's policy of appeasing Hitler. My meeting with Macmillan was a disappointment. We had no disagreements, but I found him a cold fish. I was to meet him again in London ten years later, and I got the same impression. Somehow we simply did not hit it off.

I had written Keynes of my intention to have another look at the economic and military situation in Germany, and we arranged a meeting as I passed through England.[6] We analyzed the success of Hitler's rearmament program in restoring full employment in Germany and of the success of President Roosevelt's policy of deficit financing in pulling the United States out of the depression. We agreed that what had occurred in both countries was in accordance with Keynesian economic doctrines and with my own which had developed along largely parallel lines. Keynesian ideas had by that time strongly influenced current economic policy in both countries.

Crossing over to Paris, I got in contact with Georges Blumberg, who had translated my *Economic Life of Soviet Russia* and *Germany Enters the Third Reich* into French. I wanted to meet some of the writers who were influencing public opinion in France, particularly those who were Communists. Blumberg arranged for me to meet a Communist journalist. The interview took place in the Sèvres-Vanneau, a Left Bank hotel. The journalist was anything but cordial at first. He did not conceal his astonishment that the Soviet government had given me a visa to revisit Russia, in view of the critical character of my books and articles. However, he quickly became friendly and offered to arrange an interview with the famous French author Jules Romains, who was at that time

6. Letter from Keynes, May 11, 1939.

carrying on a liaison with the Communists. He remarked, however, as he looked about the small hotel room, "Of course, I could not ask him to come here." The remark epitomized the utter contradiction between the stereotype of the Communist party embodying the dictatorship of the proletariat and the Communist party as the "New Class" which was taking to itself the perquisites of a ruling class. I replied that I was unfortunately leaving for Berlin to go on to Moscow before the meeting with Romains could be arranged.

After a brief stop in Berlin, I went on to Moscow, where I stayed only some ten days. Living conditions had improved from February, 1933, which was the year of the famine in the Ukraine, but were not better than they had been in 1929–30 when I had lived in Moscow. Furthermore, the pall of the Stalin purges still hung over Russia, and I did not dare try to make contact with Russians whom I had formerly known.

The threat of war with Hitler was in the air. The contrast between the highly disciplined, smartly uniformed German soldiers whom I had just seen in Berlin and the Soviet soldiers whom I saw in Moscow was marked. When Soviet troops were later to make such a poor showing in the early days of the invasion of Finland, I recalled their unimpressive appearance. This confirmed me in an underestimate of the fighting quality of Soviet troops.

On my way back to Berlin, I stopped off in Warsaw long enough to purchase railroad tickets for Germany. These tickets could be purchased at reduced prices outside Germany. I insisted at the Polish travel bureau on purchasing a ticket from Berlin to Bergen, Norway, which would take me through Danish Jutland. The Polish travel agency exclaimed, "No one travels that way. Much better to go by ferry from Warnemünde to Gedser." "I want to be sure that I can get out of Germany by land rather than by sea," I replied. "But why?" asked the agent. "On account of the war," I said. "What war?" he asked. "The war which is just about to break out," I replied. I have rarely seen a man so shaken. Although Poland was already mobilizing, he could not really believe in the monstrosity of war, although I found on further conversation that he had been an officer in the Polish army and had participated in World War I and in the Soviet-Polish conflict.

Upon my return to Berlin, I found Germany in the last stages of rearmament, just prior to the outbreak of World War II. The

"West Wall" which was intended to hold the Rhineland against any attack by the French and British while the Nazis settled matters with the Poles was being built with feverish energy. Yet the whole Western World was still under the delusion that Chamberlain had secured "peace in our time" by his appeasement of Hitler. Countermeasures of rearmament by the Western powers were consequently totally inadequate.

Ironically, the most extreme anti-Nazi writers in the world press had played a role in inhibiting preventive rearmament by France, England, and the United States against the Nazi military threat. The efforts of the Nazis to bring about economic recovery in Germany were ridiculed. Indeed, the picture was painted of a Germany in which the Nazi armaments program had been carried out only at the cost of the working class and of near-starvation by the whole civilian population. It would be perfectly safe for Britain and France to stand up to Hitler even without additional armament. A régime faced by the mass hostility of its people and threatened with starvation could not be a strong military power. Typical of such magazine articles was one which appeared in June, 1939:

> "*Auf den Hund Gebracht* (To the Level of a Dog). It is no secret that meat can be bought only at fabulous prices in Germany. There are few dogs left; one by one they have disappeared into the stewpot.—The slogan has spread like wildfire across Germany. As if by magic, stickers printed with the slogan appear on billboards, on shop windows, on automobiles." [7]

The reality in Germany was far different. It is small wonder that Hitler, once in power, had been successful in winning a large fraction of German industrial workers to his support. He had succeeded in eliminating unemployment in Germany some time before World War II. By 1939 it was estimated that there were some two million jobs available which could not be filled because of lack of manpower. He had accomplished this without causing serious inflation.[8]

Industrial production in Germany in 1938, during the year just

7. Quentin Reynolds, "To the Level of a Dog," *Readers Digest*, Oct., 1939, p. 44, condensed from *Collier's*, June 24, 1939.

8. For an account of how German rearmament and the general expansion of the German economy was financed, see Samuel Lurie, *Private Investment in a controlled Economy: Germany, 1933–1939* (New York: Columbia University Press, 1947).

before the outbreak of the war, was more than double what it had been in 1932, the year before Hitler came to power, and about one-fourth larger than in 1928 at about the peak of predepression prosperity. Agricultural production was about 10 per cent higher in 1938 than in 1929. On the average, real wage rates were by 1938 substantially the same as in 1929 before the depression. Total employment of wage and salary earners had increased from 12,680,000 in 1932 to 20,360,000 in 1938, or by some 7.6 million. Their total income, measured in reichsmarks of constant purchasing power, increased from 21,905,000,000 RM in 1932 to 40,997,000,000 RM in 1938, almost doubling.

The increase in the production of capital goods was much greater than the increase in the production of consumer goods. Armament production was the dynamic element which sparked the increase in production, yet the statistical evidence is clear that the population of Germany substantially improved their status as consumers prior to World War II, compared with the pre-Hitler year of 1932. This improvement included food as well as other consumer goods.

The proportion of national income going to wage and salary earners, however, had fallen from 68.8 per cent in 1929 to 63.1 per cent in 1938 [9] —a decline which was accompanied by a large increase in the size of the labor force. The decline in the share of a greatly increased national income going to wage and salary receivers reflected to a large extent the reinvestment of increased corporate profits in capital goods and armament industries. Under Hitler a country with severe unemployment had become a country of full employment, with the effects on national income which could be expected.

I had indeed believed that the picture of the near-starvation of the German people was an exaggerated one. However, the statistics which I have just quoted were not fully available at the time, and it was a shock to me to find few signs of consumer de-

9. The larger decline from the abnormally high figure of 77.6 per cent in 1932 to the level of 63.1 in 1938 was a phenomenon which commonly characterizes changes in the business cycle in all industrialized countries. The statistical decline in the percentage of national income going to wage and salary earners in the United States between the same dates was similar, although the data are not strictly comparable. See Otto Nathan's, *The Nazi Economic System* (Durham, N.C.: Duke University Press, 1944), chap. x, "The Effect of the Military Economy on Civilian Consumption."

privation. Only a very few food products were rationed. No ration cards were required for eating in restaurants or hotels. There was, indeed, an air of prosperity, conditioned, however, among the upper classes by a general sense of personal insecurity and fear of impending war.

I renewed my contacts with German friends and at once came in touch with their personal tragedies. When I visited the home of one old friend, I found that his daughter, who was taking training as a ballet dancer, had been expelled from her school. The fact that he was from an old family which had served the German government for generations, that he had been an infantry captain and was crippled from severe wounds received in World War I made no difference. His wife was Jewish and that was enough.

I took rooms in a pension in Lichterfelde West quite near where I had lived during 1932–33. The residents of the pension were all upper middle class, including a German general who had just returned from serving in China as military advisor to President Chiang Kai-shek. After a couple of weeks, it became apparent that there were only two Nazi sympathizers among the some thirty persons. One of these was a businessman who was a member of the Nazi party. When he came in to dinner at night, he would quickly give the Nazi salute in a kind of shame-faced way, mumbling "Heil Hitler!" No one ever answered beyond giving a kind of noncommittal grunt. The other was a white bearded retired Herr Director, and he was indeed a red-hot Nazi. He invited me to his room to listen to the Nazi propaganda campaign being carried on in Danzig, and he reveled in it.

By contrast to the great majority of the pensionaires, the servant girls in the pension were fervently Nazi. This was reflected in a somewhat hostile attitude towards Americans which I had never experienced before in Germany. I noticed the same attitude when I dropped in at a *stube* in a working class district for a glass of beer.

I was invited to dinner by our old housekeeper in the same apartment in which we had formerly lived. I noticed that the signs *Eingang nur für Herrschaften* which had adorned the entrance of our apartment house as well as the entrances of the other houses in aristocratic Dahlem during our previous residence in Berlin had been removed. Apparently this snobbish way of discouraging the delivery of groceries at the front door was no longer tolerated under National Socialism.

A sergeant from Hitler's SS bodyguard had also been invited to the dinner. He had heard that I had just returned from Moscow, and he asked me what I thought of the Soviet regime. I wished to avoid controversy, so I said that since we Americans lived in a capitalistic society, we did not care much for a Communistic regime. "Well," said he, "although our society is national, it is also socialistic, so I suppose you do not like Nazi Germany either." I succeeded in changing the subject, and the sergeant told with pride how he had been on guard at Berchtesgaden when the noted industrialist Krupp von Bohlen had called on Hitler. He commented with deepest satisfaction, "Krupp von Bohlen was so scared his knees knocked together."

I used to buy three or four newspapers every morning to read during breakfast, including the Nazi newspapers *Der Angriff* and *Voelkischer Beobachter* at a small newsstand nearby. The news vendor was not a man of much intelligence, but he was curious at my buying the Nazi newspapers. He inquired if I were Dutch, and I told him, "No, I am an American." As the summer wore on, the headlines became ever more violent. Late in August *Der Angriff* carried a black headline *Polonia wahrt dich ab*! ("Poland beware!") The little news vendor remarked to me when I bought the paper, "*Es fängt an zu rauchen.*" ("It is beginning to smoke!") The situation could not have been more aptly described. He added with bitterness, "I suppose now Roosevelt will blame us!"

At this time I wrote to President Few at Duke University and said, "If Danzig is not surrendered to Germany by September 1, there will be war." I hoped that Danzig would not be surrendered, but I was not at all sure that Britain and France would support Poland in the face of a German ultimatum. Indeed, as it turned out, if Hitler had been willing to content himself with Danzig, it seems likely that the British and French governments would have pressed the Polish government to capitulate, as they had done at Munich in the case of Czechslovakia.

From day to day signs of the impending war became more evident. Reservists with field boots strapped to their suitcases were catching trains to report to their regiments. German friends, visiting relatives near the Polish frontier, reported on their return that the villages were "stuffed with troops." I commented to Henry Oliver, "I smell war. I think you had better get out of Germany at once." When he asked why I should not leave also, I replied that I had to attend a conference in Norway in early September and so would wait until then to leave.

At this time there occurred in Berlin the first practice "blackout." I suspect that this was part of the war of nerves to convince the British and French that the Nazis were ready to go to war to enforce their demands on Poland. We participated in the exercise by going into the cellar of the pension with the other residents where all lights were extinguished and the windows had been covered with black cloth.

Afterwards, we went to a neighborhood movie house to see the film *Kampf gegen den Weltfeind; Deutsche Flieger in Spanien* ("The Struggle Against the World Enemy; German Flyers in Spain"). Up to this time, Hitler had represented the Nazi regime as the defenders of the whole world against the Communist menace. Nazi intervention in the Civil War in Spain had been justified on this basis. The film showed the bombing of Spanish towns by the Luftwaffe, followed by the triumphal return of the German flyers to a splendid welcome in Germany. Undoubtedly, the audience was supposed to show their patriotic fervor by appropriate applause. It was too much to expect an audience which had just come out of a practice blackout to show the expected fervor of patriotic applause. One could have heard a pin drop both during the film's showing and as the audience filed out.

Actually the advance showing of the film had been an error. It was never shown again, since it was totally out of synchronism with the radical change in Nazi foreign policy which was soon to be announced. The whole expensive film was junked.

At the end of August I took the express train appropriately known as *Der fliegende Hamburger* for Hamburg on my way to Copenhagen and then on to the international conference in Bergen. I had some extra "travel marks" which could not be redeemed for foreign currency, so I gave them to the old porter who carried my bag. He was apparently surprised and, of course, pleased. His reaction, however, was unexpected. He said earnestly, "You must be very careful tomorrow morning, sir; a tremendous thing is going to happen!" "What is going to happen?" I asked; "I can't be careful about something when I don't know what it is!" "Oh, I must not say another word," he replied, and I could get nothing further out of him. I decided that he had simply had a glass of schnapps too many.

However, when I bought a paper in Hamburg next morning and saw the headline—"Nazi-Soviet Pact Signed," I concluded that the old porter had overheard something when he had carried somebody else's bag. He probably had not understood what it was all about, but he knew it would be dangerous to talk about it. His goodwill had partially overcome his caution.

The removal of the danger of war on two fronts by the major powers meant that the Nazis were now free to move. In the meantime, I continued on my way to Bergen to the conference. I traveled by way of Copenhagen and Oslo. I shared a compartment on the train from Oslo to Bergen with a Britisher who was taking a holiday in Norway. Although he seemed to have a built-in anti-American attitude which would have precluded much conversation in ordinary circumstances, the probable imminence of war overcame his inhibitions. He asked my profession, and I admitted that I was an economist. When I asked what his profession was, he hesitated, then answered, "I am afraid I do not have one." It turned out that he was an incredible stereotype of the British upper class. He had an estate in England, but he spent the late fall and winter on the Riviera. He skied in Switzerland; he fished in Norway.

He had been an officer in the Black Watch in World War I, and he was utterly appalled at the thought of Britain's participating in another war. "How could we get out of it, do you think?" he asked. "Well, if you would be willing to turn the British Empire over to Hitler, I think he might let you off," I replied cruelly. "Perhaps we should let him have it," he answered thoughtfully. Such a caricature of the "Cliveden Set" I had never expected to meet. It turned out that what principally appalled him was that plans had been made to evacuate the children from the slums of London in case war broke out, and that Ye Olde Manor House was going to have to be turned over to house the brats!

The American delegation to the International Studies Conference consisted of Henry Wriston, President of Brown University; Jacob Viner, Professor of Economics, University of Chicago; Francis Miller, Director, Committee on Foreign Relations of the Council on Foreign Relations; Percy Bidwell, Director of Research, Council on Foreign Relations; Malcolm Davis, Associate Director of the European Center of the Carnegie Endowment; Vera Micheles Dean, Foreign Policy Association; and myself. I had had and was to continue to have close personal associations with almost all of the American delegates. Substantially all important European countries in addition to the United States were represented at the conference.

Our conference was held immediately after the German army marched into Poland, and just as the United Kingdom was making the decision to enter the war. While we were waiting for the conference to convene next day, an old friend, Colonel Francis Miller, and I went to a movie in Bergen. The movie was *Den Siste Danse* (It had been "The Dancing Castles" when originally shown in the United States.) In one sequence showing Vernon Castle just before he enlisted for the flight training in which he was to be killed, a copy of the first page of the *New York Times* was flashed on the screen. The headline read "Britain Declares War on Germany!" It took us an instant to realize that the headline referred to World War I. Doubtless the same headline was appearing that very day in New York, but the reference was to World War II.

The conference opened in an air of extreme crisis. Neither the German nor the Polish delegations arrived. The French delegation left after the first day, and the conference had to be adjourned. The American delegation now awaited the arrival of the *Oslofiord*, the ship on which we had booked passage home. In the meantime, the Hotel Norge was jammed with tourists who were trying to return to their diverse homes. There was only one radio in the hotel. When someone got a French station tuned in, he had only to turn his back and the radio would be broadcasting in Italian or Swedish or once in a while in English. It was in an English broadcast that we learned of the sinking of the *Athenia* by a German submarine.

When the *Oslofiord* arrived, she was jammed with American tourists returning home. For some unknown reason, I had been assigned a cabin to myself, but I quickly volunteered to share my cabin with one of the crowded refugees. By an ironic coincidence, the sea was like a mill pond with scarcely a ripple, and I have never had a more comfortable passage. We sailed with all lights ablaze, with searchlights focused on our Norwegian flag. It was still believed that neutral ships would not be torpedoed. Within six weeks the *Oslofiord,* a beautiful new white ship, had been torpedoed and sunk. We returned to an America which was determined to remain neutral and which had hopes of a compromise peace to end a short war.

Chapter fourteen. *We enter the war*

My friend Francis Miller had asked me on our voyage home from Noway immediately after the outbreak of the war in Europe, "Do you think the Poles have any chance against the Nazis?" My answer was simply "No." My estimate of the might of the Nazi armies was proved correct by the Nazi blitz which so speedily crushed the gallant Polish forces. The Polish armies might have been able to resist for some weeks longer if they had not been attacked in the rear by the Soviet forces which occupied eastern Poland.

Yet public opinion in the United States, in England, and in the rest of Western Europe still continued to underrate Nazi military power utterly. From what I had seen of the German army on the one hand and of the level of British and French preparation for war on the other, the Allied defeats in Norway and later in Belgium and France came as no surprise to me. In a series of public lectures in various cities throughout the country, I had tried to prepare the American public for the possibility of defeat of the Allies by the Nazis, and above all to build up sentiment for the rearming of the United States at top speed. Since I was almost the only commentator in the United States, or, indeed, in the Western World who foresaw the Nazi military victories, I fear that I had come to feel that I had a quasi-magic power of analysis. This was to result in an overconfidence which was later to lead me astray in assessing the relative military power of the Nazis in relation to the Soviets.

The failure of public opinion to recognize the Nazi success in attaining full employment levels of production in Germany or to understand how it had been accomplished hampered my efforts to explain the desperateness of the situation almost hopelessly.

I wrote a number of articles in which I tried to explain how Germany had been able to increase production of both capital equipment and military equipment without diminishing aggregate civilian consumption. I wrote an article in the *New York Times Sunday Magazine* entitled "Guns *and* Butter," a title derived from Göring's "Guns *or* Butter."[1] I pointed out that so long as a country had large unemployed resources, it was not necessary to diminish the production of civilian goods in order to carry out an armament program. Indeed, in the first stages of an armament program in the United States, both the demand and the supply of consumer goods would almost certainly increase. Even in Germany, where the choice had been made to sacrifice civilian goods production for armament, if necessary, aggregate consumption had substantially increased up to the outbreak of the war. My realization of the economic strength of Nazi Germany enabled me to understand how the Nazi military machine could have been built. It enabled me to understand, too, that we were confronted by a German population who, if they were indeed unenthusiastic about fighting another war, were at least not half starved and ready to revolt at the first opportunity.

I did not immediately draw the logical conclusion from my analysis of the relative strength of Germany vs. the Allies. I did not at once decide that it would be in our national interest to enter the war on the side of the Allies against the Nazis. It was only after my fears had been confirmed by the German occupation of Denmark and Norway and by the crushing defeat of the Allied armies, followed by the fall of France, that I saw that our active participation in the war could not be avoided.

First I joined William Allen White's "Committee to Defend America by Aiding the Allies," which favored giving the financial and economic aid for which Churchill was pleading. I soon took a further step. In the early summer of 1940 I joined a group of thirty prominent Americans who signed a manifesto advocating our immediate entrance into the war against Germany. The manifesto was published in the New York newspapers and commented upon

1. *New York Times Magazine,* Feb. 16, 1941, pp. 3, 18, 21.

widely in the press.[2] Thereupon, I received a number of letters and telephone calls denouncing me as a warmonger.[3]

I have asked myself many times whether I was justified in advocating our entrance into the war against the Nazis. By our defeat of the Nazis we have indeed exchanged a world threatened by Nazi domination for the present one threatened by the Communists. If the Nazis had won, the destruction of Communism would have followed, and we would now be spared the current Communist threat. Rule by Stalinist Soviet Communism or by Chinese Communism would be as bad as Nazi rule.

However serious the threat of Communism still is, however, it is no longer monolithic in character. The split between Moscow and Peking, the development of deviant forms of Communism as in Yugoslavia, have diminished the danger of outright Communist conquest of the countries which are still free. If Hitler had not been defeated, we would not have even the current opportunity to protect ourselves against the Communist threat, for Hitler would certainly have won the war without our intervention. Yet none of the denunciatory letters which I received showed any signs that the writers had considered the possible consequences of a Nazi victory.

Years later this dilemma was illustrated by my friends in the Watauga Club who expressed this belief: "If the United States had worked as hard for peace as in preparing for war, we could have avoided both world wars." I countered with the question, "Suppose we had not entered either World War I or World War II, who would have won?" No one in the club was prepared to try to defend the indefensible thesis that Germany could have been defeated in either war or even that there would have been a stalemate. Further, no one believed that a world in which Germany had won either war would have been one in which peaceful existence would have been possible. No one was willing to invoke the doctrine of total non-resistance to force.

One could, indeed, argue that if the Treaty of Versailles had not been so severe, if no heavy reparations payments had been required, if the United States had been willing to relinquish claims for the repayment of Allied war debts on condition that impossibly

2. *New York Herald Tribune,* June 10, 1940; *New York Times,* June 10, 1940.

3. I received only one commendatory letter. The writer hoped to capitalize on his commendation to borrow $1,000 to be used in starting an enterprise to manufacture a perfume which he claimed he had invented!

heavy reparations payments be foregone, then the circumstance under which Hitler rose to power in Germany would not have arisen and there would have been no World War II. Yet this offers no support to a policy of non-resistance to Hitler once he was in power.

I realized, of course, that a declaration of war against Germany by the United States immediately upon the fall of France was not a political possibility. I felt, however, that writing articles and giving lectures to speed up our preparations for what I considered our inevitable participation in the war was not enough. I re-entered government service as a consultant to the Advisory Committee of the Council of National Defense, in the role of economic advisor to Leon Henderson. I aided in staffing and in formulating the policies of "OPACS," the Office of Prices and Civilian Supply, later called simply "OPA."

In my position as economic advisor, I exerted every effort to get measures taken to increase production, particularly of strategic materials such as rubber, for I felt quite sure that Japan would be in the war against us and would attempt to seize the sources from which our raw rubber came. However, I met extreme scepticism among industrialists with regard to the probable level of demand for their products. One of the officials of a trade organization of the steel industry, for example, wrote to me following the publication of one of my articles saying that he expected a substantial slump in the damand for steel, following only a temporary spurt in demand. One of the officials of a copper mining company in an OPACS Committee meeting tried to magnify the volume of existing copper production and to minimize the possibility of increasing production by citing the amount of ore produced in pounds rather than tons! With a decade of experience during the Depression with surplus production facilities, industrialists were simply unable to visualize a state of full employment of men and of productive facilities.

In the furtherance of increasing the understanding of what full production was like and how it could be accomplished, I arranged for Dr. Otto Nathan, formerly *Oberregierungsrat* in the *Reichswirtschaftsministerium*, then a refugee in the United States, to do a study of the German experience for OPACS.[4]

4. This study was later expanded into a book under a grant of the Rockefeller Foundation and published by the Duke University Press. (*The Nazi Economic System*, Durham, N. C., 1944).

Nevertheless, I fully realized that once national resources were fully employed, too ambitious a program of production of goods both for civilian consumption and munitions accompanied by the inevitable expansion of government deficit financing would lead to inflation. Price control could not hope to cope successfully with the explosive inflationary forces which would thus be generated. I remember vividly a dinner in Washington which Leon Henderson later gave in honor of Keynes after we had entered the war. A number of the younger American Keynesians were present who favored a more vigorous expansionist program. Keynes argued for hours against his disciples, stressing his belief in the necessity for limiting disbursements of consumer income and simultaneously reducing the production of consumer goods in order to reduce inflationary pressures and to free greater productive facilities for war production. He maintained that the policy which he advocated was wholly consistent with his general theory. I fully agreed with Keynes.

In the meantime, in virtue of my position as Dean of the Graduate School of Duke University, I also served on the Educational Advisory Committee for Manpower Utilization. In so doing, I violently opposed the position of some educators that virtually no college students should be drafted for combat service. Later on in recruiting personnel for OSS, I was to find this attitude even more strongly among European refugees. They hated Hitler and expressed a desire to serve the war effort against him but usually this meant a willingness to do research or propaganda. The idea that an intellectual should undergo physical danger was utterly repugnant.

It was argued that it was folly for a highly educated individual to risk his life in combat when an uneducated man would doubtless be a better fighter. Imagine a physicist whose scarce skills were badly needed for the war effort serving in the infantry! The case of the physicist was extended to cover economists, sociologists, historians, and the whole field of the humanities. Keynes expressed the same opinion as myself with respect to the intelligentsia of the Left in Britain in a letter of October 14, 1939, in reply to an editorial in *The New Statesman and Nation:*

> The intelligentsia of the Left were the loudest in demanding that the Nazi aggression should be resisted at all costs. When it

> comes to a showdown, scarce four weeks have passed before they remember that they are pacifists and write defeatist letters to your columns, leaving the defence of freedom and of civilization to Colonel Blimp and the Old School Tie, for whom Three Cheers.[5]

I admitted the case of the physicist, but I maintained that the intellectual had an obligation to take his chance of being shot just like anyone else. Indeed, I feared the effect upon the morale of our armies if there were to be no leaven of educated men among them. I remembered too, the disastrous effect upon the morale of the Confederate soldiers during our Civil War when the larger slaveholders had been exempt from conscription.

By the fall of 1941 I had come to feel that I must participate more actively in the preparation for our inevitable participation in the war. Consequently, I left the OPA and joined the COI, later the OSS, which was just being organized by Colonel Donovan. The new organization under Colonel Donovan as Coordinator of Information was critically handicapped in the beginning by the duality of its functions. It was supposed to gather information of military value which was an intelligence function involving a high degree of secrecy. It was supposed on the other hand to disseminate information in such a way as to build up the morale of our citizenry, encourage resistance to the Nazis in occupied Europe, and encourage neutral countries to assist the Allies and resist the Nazis. This was a propaganda function. Propaganda and intelligence should never be carried on by the same organization, but at first this was attempted. It resulted in breaches of security which might have most seriously damaged intelligence operations.

Thus, news of the organization of the COI by Donovan was reported in the press, together with references to its leading personnel.[6] Thereafter, it was impossible for me effectively to conceal my connection with our intelligence operations. Fortunately, the propaganda function of the COI was soon split off and set up as OWI. After the COI became the Office of Strategic Services, its military intelligence function together with certain sabotage and guerrilla warfare activities became all important.

5. Quoted by R. F. Harrod, in *The Life of John Maynard Keynes* (London: Macmillan and Co., 1951), p. 488.

6. See p. 15 of the *United States News*, Oct. 3, 1941, for example, which not only had a news story but also pictures of Colonel Donovan, Professor J. R. Hayden, and myself, together with one of General Haushofer, head of Hitler's "Geopolitical Institute," to whom we were likened.

All of us who were to work intimately with Donovan through the years came to feel warm affection and admiration for him. Donovan had commanded the New York regiment in the Rainbow Division in World War I where he had acquired his nickname of "Wild Bill." He had been awarded the highest decorations for valor, and he was, indeed, a man without physical fear. His imagination and audacity were without limit. He seemed to us a character left over from the days of the *condottieri* of fifteenth century Italy.

A character like Donovan could not possibly be a good administrator by ordinary peacetime standards. When I joined the COI there were probably no more than fifty persons in it. By the end of the war, its successor organization, OSS, numbered thousands. It sheltered screwballs, crackpots, and adventurers along with professors from Ivy League universities, ex-diplomats and ex-soldiers, and an unprecedented number of heirs to great fortunes. Every sort of specialized and esoteric skill was represented, from professors of Sanskrit to demolition experts, cryptologists, judo instructors, sharpshooters, and specialists in guerrilla warfare. Someone even recruited a couple of safecrackers, father and son, who gave up a lucrative career as burglars to put their specialties at the service of the war effort. It is little wonder that the organization performed some incredible intelligence coups along with some amusing stumbles.

No scheme was too wild to be considered. The grandiose plan for winning the war against Japan by releasing from shipboard thousands of bats from the Carlsbad Caverns which were to have slow matches tucked under their wings to ignite when the bats sought refuge in the eaves of Japanese houses has been described elsewhere. A newspaper publisher who had joined OSS got the idea that we should have an undercover agent stationed on the Canary Islands, but no commercial steamships called there during wartime. No matter! Buy a ship! One was bought for a million dollars or so. Only after the purchase was made was it realized that it would not be the most secret way to plant an undercover agent to have a special steamship arrive to land him. I never learned what happened to the ship. Since ships were in desperately short supply, no doubt it was sold without great loss.

The State Department and the old line military and naval intelligence organizations, MIS and ONI, were bitterly jealous of

Donovan and his organization. When the COI wanted access to some State Department files, the gibe became current that the Coordinator of Information was a man who could tell you the time if you loaned him your watch. Later it was said that OSS stood for "Oh So Social!"

Hardly any real intelligence operations had been carried on prior to Donovan's setting up his organization.[7] To set up an intelligence service from scratch *after* hostilities had broken out required a man of the audacity and imagination of Donovan. An orderly administrator would never have got an intelligence organization functioning before the war was over.

During my first term of service in COI, I was a member of the Research and Analysis Branch, along with Professors James P. Baxter, William Langer, and Edward Mason, and John Wiley, on leave from the State Department. In the beginning, this branch was almost all there was to COI. A large volume of reports dealing with the military, political, and economic situation in the countries of the various theaters of war was prepared. On account of my experience in Russia and Germany, I participated particularly actively in the preparation of reports on these countries.

I had been surprised at the Nazi attack upon Russia. It was a very stupid act, with England still in the war. The failure of Hitler to take Moscow was also a surprise to me.[8] The relatively poor showing of the Soviet forces against Finland had confirmed my erroneous opinion of their low fighting caliber.

The hatred which such a large part of the Russian people felt for the Stalinist regime of which I was so keenly aware, was, it turned out, offset by the attitude of the Nazis towards the Russian people and their treatment of them. Even though a million Russian soldiers were to defect to the Nazis, confirming my estimate of the unpopularity of the Stalinist regime, the concept of the Russians as an inferior race was to prevent the effective use of these Russian soldiers under the defector, General Vlassov.

7. As an exception to this statement, ONI had broken the Japanese naval code before the outbreak of the war. The success of the Japanese at Pearl Harbor, however, tended to discredit the ONI.

8. Bill Donovan had played a crucial role by a trip to Yugoslavia, where he had been instrumental in the ousting of a pro-Nazi government and in inducing the Yugoslavs to resist the Nazi takeover in the Balkans. The time, military resources, and the paratroops which had to be used in occupying Yugoslavia, Greece, and, particularly, Crete, almost certainly were crucial in delaying the Nazi forces before Moscow until winter brought the offensive to a halt.

I had been almost alone in my correct forecast of the Nazi successes in the West. I had had lots of company in my estimate that Hitler would not attack the Russians, but that if he did, the Soviet armies would not be able to prevent the occupation of Moscow.[9] Neither the fact that the Nazis did indeed come much closer to destroying the Soviet armies than is generally realized nor that most military experts had concurred in my low estimate of the Soviet armies, cushioned the shock of realization that my estimate had been wrong. My self-confidence received a blow from which it never wholly recovered.

In spite of the stubborn resistance of the Soviet forces to the Nazis, it seems altogether probable that the Russian armies would eventually have been destroyed if the United States had not entered the war and thrown its vast resources against the Nazis. In retrospect, I realize how difficult it would have been to induce the American public to support our active participation in the war. All the efforts of the advocates of our direct participation in the war, like myself, all the somewhat equivocal efforts of President Roosevelt and Wendell Willkie might have failed, and the Nazis might have won if the Japanese had not attacked at Pearl Harbor. The Japanese victory at Pearl Harbor was a crushing blow to me which was not softened as it was to the American public by official efforts to conceal the extent of the disaster, since the real facts were available to the top echelon of our organization almost at once. I had foreseen the possibility of a Japanese attack somewhere in the Pacific, but such a defeat of our naval forces had not seemed possible. Now, for better or worse, we were in the war ourselves, and my participation in it was to change my functions in the Donovan organization.

9. I had expressed these views in a major article in the *New York Times Magazine*, Nov. 24, 1940 ("Hitler and–or Versus?–Stalin," pp. 4, 17).

Chapter fifteen. *OSS*

Following Pearl Harbor, I once more felt the emotional need for more direct involvement in the war. Psychologically, this meant the need to undergo as nearly as possible the kind of risk which our soldiers in combat would have to undergo in fighting still another war which I had advocated that we enter. I approached the War Department about the possibility of a commission in my old branch of the service, the field artillery. The officer with whom I talked smiled and commented that my artillery skills of World War I must be rather obsolescent. He suggested that I talk with a brigadier general who was in charge of statistical work. It was suggested that I might be offered a colonel's commission as a statistician. I recoiled at the thought of myself as a statistician in uniform.

Instead, I entered the branch of the OSS which had responsibility for secret intelligence, including, of course, espionage. My responsibility came to be primarily for Northern Europe and Poland and for penetration of Germany from those areas. Our system of training and our organization was modeled to a considerable extent on the British experience. We worked closely with British Intelligence, which had an office in New York.[1] We soon set up an office in London, from which, to a considerable extent, our operations on the Continent were controlled.

I began at once to recruit a corps of agents. We were anxious to operate within Germany itself as soon as possible. Contrary to

1. See H. Montgomery Hyde, *Room 3603* (New York: Farrar, Straus & Co., 1963), for an account of British intelligence operations in the U. S.

what is generally believed, it is virtually impossible for a man to be completely bilingual. For a native-born American to pass himself off as a German was thus rendered impracticable by the language difficulty, not to mention other even greater problems, including that of plausible "cover."

There were indeed, tiny cliques of German refugees who claimed that they were in touch with "underground organizations" in Germany. I interviewed a man who was the protégé of an American lady of wealth and was recommended to me as an "important leader of an anti-Nazi group" and who claimed he had returned to Germany after Hitler was in power and had been in touch with "his" underground organization, which had been turning out anti-Nazi pamphlets, phonograph records, etc. I asked whether he could offer any evidence that he had ever returned to Germany after Hitler was in power. He gave me the name of a woman who had been employed in an American consulate and who had seen him in Germany. I talked with this woman. She had indeed talked with him shortly after Hitler had come to power *but before the man in question had ever left Germany.* This individual had been born and raised in Austria, so I consulted some Social Democratic refugees from Vienna. They considered him to be totally unreliable and cited evidence to support their view. British Intelligence reported that they had found upon investigation that all the anti-Nazi pamphlets, etc., had actually been printed outside Germany before the Nazi occupation of Europe. I had our security investigators check his record further. I found it necessary, however, to call off the investigation because he was using the queries which were being made about him to build up his prestige by alleging he was being investigated in connection with a very important post which the United States government was about to offer him.

One of our newspaper correspondents who had been interned along with our diplomats when Germany declared war on the United States was approached by Nazi officials and offered a quarter of a million dollars to stay on in Germany and make propaganda broadcasts for them. He declined, although a Nazi official accompanied the train on which the Americans who were freed from internment were transported across France to Spain continuing to urge the American newspaper correspondent to accept the offer.

Now this man came to me with the proposal that he pretend

to accept the Nazi offer. He would re-enter Germany by going first to Turkey and then up through the Balkans to Berlin. He would make propaganda broadcasts for the Nazis, but he would convey vital intelligence by the use of a previously agreed upon code. I do not believe this would really have been feasible, since the Nazis would have controlled his script in advance, and it would not have been possible under such circumstances to convey information to which he would have access in sufficient detail to be useful. Nevertheless, I took the proposal up with General Donovan, who would not approve it. He was horrified at an American ostensibly betraying his country, even though acting as a double agent in our service.

In a further effort to come into contact with anti-Nazi elements in Germany who might furnish intelligence or even carry out resistance operations, General Donovan arranged to have Treviranus, a minor political figure of pre-Hitler days, brought to the United States from Canada, where the British had transported him for safekeeping. I had known Treviranus in Germany. He was indeed a bona fide anti-Nazi who had barely escaped with his life during the Blood Purge of 1934 with the aid of British Intelligence, which had smuggled him out of Germany. Treviranus was anxious to head an anti-Nazi movement in Germany. I tried to find out his plans and to see what I could do to assist through my organization, which I had by now got set up in Sweden. Did he need money? Arms? What did he propose to do with either? Incredibly enough, Treviranus proposed that his signet ring should be sent somehow to the peasants in the area in which he had been born and raised. Upon the receipt of the ring, the peasants would then rise against Hitler!

And so it went. It became clear that we were going to have to rely primarily upon an organization which could operate in neutral countries adjoining Germany. Stockholm was to become the headquarters for this organization. Simultaneously, I began to develop connections with underground national organizations operating in Nazi-occupied Europe. I found it essential to establish contacts with the various governments-in-exile with headquarters in London. I flew to London in 1942 on one of the old Pam-Am "flying boats," using the roundabout Bermuda-Horta-Lisbon-Foynes-Bristol-London route then necessary. I lived in London for a couple of months while I got in touch with the military intelligence organizations of the Polish and Norwegian governments, who in turn were in touch with the resistance movements in their respective countries.

I had previously developed cordial relations with Polish Intelligence in Washington, and I now began by having lunch with Colonel Gano at the Hotel Rubens, the headquarters of the Polish government in exile, in order to develop this liaison further. Colonel Gano had been an officer in the Tsarist army in Russia before the Revolution and had fought in the Volunteer Army against the Bolsheviks. He was the very model of an intelligence officer in charge of an espionage and resistance movement. The Poles were past masters in the invention and use of all the gadgets of espionage. They had an effective resistance network operating in Poland, some of the members of which I met.

The underground resistance groups in Poland were receiving air drops of arms and explosives from Britain. Instead of using these munitions for attacks on the Nazis by blowing up trooptrains and the like, they were caching most of the arms against the day when a general offensive against the Nazis by the Allies and Russians might give them a chance to regain Polish freedom. Any attack on the Nazis now, the Poles insisted, would only result in wholesale execution of hundreds of Poles who lived in the area of the attack, and this would inevitably mean the loss of many of their own men.

The Communist element of the Polish resistance which was connected with Soviet Intelligence insisted on the contrary that attacks should be made without delay in order to aid the hard-pressed Soviet armies. Indeed, some were made, the Communist underground specializing in making the attacks in areas where the "regular" Polish underground had larger membership. Nazi retribution then fell upon the "regular" underground and not upon the Communist underground. The split between the Communist and non-Communist resistance movements existed also in Greece, in Norway, and elsewhere and was a considerable impediment to our co-operation with the resistance movements.

The Polish officers had particular reason to be hostile to the Soviet government. Although the discovery and disinterment by the Nazis of the thousands of Polish prisoners, mostly officers, slaughtered in the Katyn massacre was yet to occur, the Polish officers with whom I was associated assumed that something like the massacre must have happened. Relatives of the Polish officers who had been in Soviet prisons received letters from them for a time. Suddenly, in April 1940, all correspondence ceased. After the Nazi attack on Russia, the Poles remaining in Russia who had not been killed at Katyn or elsewhere were allowed to leave to form a Polish army under General Anders to fight the Germans. In the negotiations prior to the formation of this army, Beria, head of the NKVD, at a conference in Moscow in October, 1940, in referring to the Polish officers said, "A grave mistake was made." When negotiations between the Polish government and the Soviet government over formation of the Polish army were begun, Stalin and Molotov in answer to repeated inquiries about what had happened to the Polish officers in three prison camps from which communications had abruptly ceased always insisted that they knew nothing of their whereabouts. Polish intelligence officers had told me about this in confidence some months before the Germans announced the discovery of the mass graves.

When the bodies of the Polish officers were exhumed by the Germans in 1943, newspapers, letters, and diaries on the bodies indicated that they had all been executed prior to the German attack. There were no newspapers or letters dated after a time a year before the German attack on Russia. After the bodies had been found, the Russians claimed that in the confusion of their retreat before the Nazi armies, the Polish officers who were prisoners of the Russians had been left behind and had been executed by the Nazis. Significantly, nothing had been said about this by the Soviet government until after the Germans announced the discovery of the mass graves.[2]

As a sequel to the above, when the Nazi armies, retreating through Poland, had reached Praga, just outside Warsaw, the Soviet armies broadcast a call to the Poles to rise against the German forces. The Poles rose under "General Bor," who was connected with my Polish friends in London. After a bitter battle, the Polish uprising was crushed by the Nazis. In the meantime, the Soviet armies simply waited in the suburb of Praga until the Poles had been crushed. The Soviet authorities refused the British request for permission for

2. For an account of the Katyn massacre written from the Polish viewpoint, by a Polish eye-witness of the exhumations, see Joseph Mackiewicz, *The Katyn Wood Murders* (London: Hollis and Carter, 1951).

British planes to land in Soviet-controlled territory, which they would have had to do in order to drop arms to the Poles who were fighting the Nazis.

As a further sequel, I was visiting an automobile plant in Praga in 1958, accompanied by an American friend. Forgetting for the moment that the young Polish official who accompanied us spoke English, I recalled the events of the Warsaw uprising and its crushing to my companion. The Polish official interrupted and justified the Soviet action on the ground that if the Polish uprising had succeeded, it would have meant the control of Poland by reactionary nationalist forces. It was experiences like these, reinforcing those of my previous visits to Russia, which enabled me to comprehend the nature of the Soviet régime.

I lived at Claridge's during my wartime stays in London since it was quite close to 72 Grosvenor Street, the OSS headquarters. I was, consequently, little limited by the strict food rationing of war time. Luxury foods available in only limited quantities on account of their high price were not rationed. If one could overlook the gamy taste and odor of birds which, to conform to British taste, had been "hung" until they were quite ripe, one could have grouse whenever one wished. Also, by confining oneself to kippers for breakfast instead of trying to get bacon and eggs, one could manage very well.

Fortunately, there were only a few air raids on London when I was there either in 1942 or 1943. It was the period in between the great fire blitz in which London almost burned down and the later period of the "buzz bombs." However, each of us had to take a turn as air raid warden for OSS headquarters at night. There was an elaborate sheet of instructions about starting ventilating fans in the air raid shelters, the proper way to use a stirrup pump in putting out fire bombs which fell on the roof, and the like. Since my whole staff consisted of one lady secretary and one corporal who knew even less about procedures than I, I devoutly hoped that the German bombers would spare us on the nights I was in charge. They did.

Since I have the poorest possible sense of direction, the London blackout was a particular trial to me. When the blackout was compounded by a London fog, I sometimes despaired of ever finding my way back to my hotel after I had been out to dinner.

When all else failed, I would illegally use my small flashlight to spot the street signs.

During my two months in London in 1942, I renewed my friendship with Keynes. His wartime insistence on limiting disposable consumer income had not changed his belief on the desirability of expanding consumer purchasing power in peacetime. After the war, said Keynes, "The answer will lie in consumption." Trying to stimulate investment by measures designed to lower the rate of interest would not succeed by itself since the motivation for investment finally depended upon the ability to sell consumer's goods profitably. He believed that after the war measures to increase the relative purchasing power of lower-income classes would be necessary.

Close contact with the various British secret intelligence and sabotage organizations had already been developed by OSS and my own relations with the personnel of these organizations became quite cordial. There were to be many examples of very useful collaboration with the British. For example, an arrangement was worked out in our Stockholm operation by means of which we were able to obtain copies of all applications of foreigners for visas to enter Sweden. These applications had to be photostated by our people and returned to the files from which they were obtained without delay. An arrangement was worked out with the British for assisting in photographing, processing, and dispatching this material to London. The British, with their larger technical staff, were in a better position to do this than were we. The British expressed keen appreciation of this material, which they had never previously been able to get.

We relied entirely upon the British for travel by air for our organization between London and Stockholm, and they were extremely co-operative in this. Although the pilots and co-pilots were usually of Norwegian or other non-British nationality, they were all officers of the RAF.

It was inevitable that the organization of intelligence operations in all countries should be quite complex. Rivalry inevitably develops between the different branches responsible for intelligence. This had been true in Washington. We were to discover that it was true in Berlin, where the rivalry between the *Abwehr*, the regular military intelligence organization under Admiral Canaris, and the Nazi *Sicherheitsdienst* became actually murderous.

Our primary contacts in London with British Intelligence were with Mi 5 and Mi 6, which were regular military intelligence organizations, particularly with Mi 5, which we ordinarily referred to among ourselves as "SI" (which was also our own designation in the OSS) or as "Broadway" from Broadway Industries, which was the cover address of British SI. We were also in contact with British Naval Intelligence.

There was in addition another quite separate British organization, under the jurisdiction of the Home Office, known as "SOE" (Corresponding to our own "SO") which maintained connections with resistance groups, carried on sabotage, and developed intelligence as a sort of by-product. We usually referred to this organization as "Baker Street," from the address of its London headquarters. This organization was quite proud that it actually had agents operating in Nazi-occupied Europe. "Broadway," the personnel of the regular British military Intelligence, made no effort to conceal the contempt which they felt for "Baker Street" as irresponsible, bungling amateurs. I was able to understand this attitude better after the war when the fact of the complete penetration of the British SOE wartime network of agents by the Nazis was exposed. Almost as fast as British SOE operatives were dropped by parachute into France and the Netherlands, they had been uncovered by Nazi counterintelligence. SOE radio operators were compelled to send messages under Nazi direction. SOE continued to drop agents by parachute, some of them women, after it should have been apparent that their network of agents was under Nazi control. Some of these women were executed in Nazi concentration camps.[3] As Walter Shellenberg, head of the Nazi *Sicherheitsdienst* boasted:

3. There is a large literature on this subject. See H. J. Giskes, *London Calling North Pole* (London: W. Kimber, 1953); Pieter Dourlein, *Inside North Pole* (London: W. Kimber, 1954); Bruce Marshall, *The White Rabbit* (story of Yeo-Thomas) (Boston: Houghton Mifflin, 1953); Jean Overton Fuller, *The Starr Affair* (Boston: Little Brown, 1954), *Madeleine* (London: Gollancz, 1952; rev. ed. titled *Born for Sacrifice*, London: Pan Books, 1957), and *Double Webs* (London: Putnam, 1958); Ian Colvin, ed., *Colonel Henri's Story* (London: W. Kimber, 1954); Gordon Young, *The Cat with Two Faces* (New York; Coward-McCann, 1957); Maurice Buckmaster, *Specially Employed* (London: Batchworth Press, 1952) and *They Fought Alone* (New York: W. W. Norton, 1958); Paul Guillaume, *La Sologne au Temps de l'héroisme et de la trahison* (Orleans: Imprimerie Nouvelle, 1950); and Elizabeth Nicholas, *Death Be Not Proud* (London: Cresset Press, 1958).

> However, these underground movements in the occupied countries were not only often traced by us, but were infiltrated by our own underground agents. There were even cases where resistance groups were jointly "directed" by the British and ourselves, and we were sometimes able to "order" from England radio equipment required by us as well as currency and explosives (these, incidentally, were superior to our own) to be dropped by parachute. Sometimes it took no more than ten days for our 'order' to be given and the necessary material to be parachuted into occupied territory.[4]

I had set my face against dropping my men by parachute into Nazi-occupied countries just to be able to say we had agents in Nazi territory regardless of their chance of survival. The discovery after the war of what happened to the British agents of SOE confirmed me in my judgment, which perhaps had been considered at one time unduly timorous and conservative.

I was unable to obtain a Swedish visa during my trip to London in 1942 as I had planned. I did have the chief of our OSS operation flown out of Stockholm for consultation with me in London. I determined to return to London during the coming year and to go on to Stockholm to survey the operation there. As will be seen, I was able to do this during the fall of 1943.

I returned to Washington in late December, 1942, on the *Queen Elizabeth*, which had been converted into a troop transport capable of moving an entire division but which on the westward voyage was only about half filled. Our deluxe cabin, originally intended for two, now had rough bunks for fifteen people. Rarely could there have been a more heterogeneous passenger list. There were several hundred Italian submariners, prisoners of war being sent to Canada, guarded by convalescent Canadian survivors of the disastrous British raid on Dieppe. There were Javanese sailors from the Dutch navy, and New Zealanders from the RAF going home on furlough. There were a number of American airmen who had ferried planes to Europe and were now returning to repeat their ferrying. Finally, there were some scores of American mechanics returning from setting up the Lockheed plant in Ireland. The ferry pilots were even hotter as crap shooters than as pilots and spent

4. Walter Schellenberg, *The Labyrinth: The Memoirs of Hitler's Secret Service Chief* (New York: Harper, 1956), p. 367.

the voyage taking the accumulated pay from the Lockheed mechanics.

After my return to Washington, I continued to recruit agents for Stockholm, which had turned out to be the center of the operations into Germany for which I was responsible. After recruitment, agents had to be sent to our special camp for training. Sometimes prospective agents lost their nerve when they began to take training and became fully aware of the risks involved in undercover intelligence operations. Such persons were always a potential threat to security, but they were so frightened that they were glad to keep quiet after being released from the organization.

For example, I prepared for the sending to Sweden of an American citizen who had spent a number of years in Germany and had been closely associated with the Hugo Stinnes industrial group in Germany. He had lived both in Berlin and the Ruhr district of Germany. He was supposed to be able to meet with certain German industrialists in Stockholm and obtain information from them. This man was one of our disappointments. He turned out to have simply no research instincts. He was quite unable to work at obtaining as large a mass as possible of definite facts. He also, to my surprise, when I met him in Stockholm, seemed frightened about trying to get any information from Germans. I would not have expected this on the basis of the man's personal history. He had been in the navy as a petty officer in the World War I, had been a successful businessman, and I had supposed would be a man of some force and vigor. After the war this man was killed, reportedly by falling off a railway passenger train under mysterious circumstances. I never knew whether his death was connected with his previous OSS association or not.

In this connection it proved absolutely essential that our agents who operated at a responsible level should be men of college or university education. The British had made this discovery long before we did. Only men of college or university education were likely to have the background which enabled them to understand what kind of information was needed, to recognize the difference between something which could be proved or documented as a fact and something which was merely hearsay, to be enough acquainted with the history and culture of the countries with which they were concerned to be able to judge of the authenticity of information. As an example, an OSS agent in Switzerland once reported in great excitement that he had learned the secret by which the Germans were able to produce gasoline from coal. It was, of course, a complicated industrial process which had been well known to chemical engineers for years, but he described it in terms of adding so many atoms of hydrogen to so many atoms of carbon, etc. This particular item, which was actually disseminated within the organization before anyone could get it stopped, aroused considerable amusement from some of the agencies which received it.

I followed a policy of recruiting major agents almost exclusively from the ranks of American citizens and preferably those of native birth. The British followed a similar practice. Again and again, in the case of men of foreign birth who were recommended to me, it developed that their loyalties and interests were divided. It was, I think, inevitable that this should be so. If one thinks, for example, of a foreign government under any conceivable circumstances recruiting a native-born American for its service, one could understand that however much an American might have had his loyalties to his country undermined by events, it would be rare if his loyalty were finally and completely destroyed. Such was likely to be the case with nationals of other countries. Something of the same thing was true of Communists or Communist sympathizers. By basic ideology, it is impossible that a Communist could be loyal exclusively to the United States government. The same thing, of course, would be true of a Fascist or anyone with similar ideology.

The results of having as an intimate part of one's organization anyone whose loyalty was not beyond question is obvious. We never employed anyone in a responsible position who was not an American citizen, but we did use one or two men who were naturalized citizens. To have employed Germans in principal positions, however, who had particular organizational loyalties, to Communism, to the German labor movement, to German nationalism, even if anti-Hitler, or what-not, would have been out of the question.

It was always a problem to find suitable "cover" for prospective agents so that an excuse could be found for their presence in the country to which they were to be sent. It was even a problem to find cover for them while they were being trained. One of my most promising agents, for whom plausible cover had been found, suddenly died while at our secret camp. It was necessary for me to arrange for the transfer of the body and to have him die over again at a different place while supposedly engaged in his regular job so that the security of the camp would not be breached. Since an intelligence organization in a free society, even in wartime, fortunately does not possess coercive powers to compel secrecy outside the organization, these arrangements presented the greatest difficulties.

After agents had been recruited and trained, we had to find means of transport for them to London and then on to Sweden. Air transport was so desperately short that I even had to resort to sending agents on the Portuguese steamship *Serpa Pinta,* which the Nazis allowed to navigate between the United States and Portuguese ports. Since I knew that Nazi submarine commanders sometimes stopped and inspected this ship, I was most reluctant to have our men take the risk of arrest and possible execution as spies. However, so anxious were the men to get at their work that we used this mode of transportation.

Difficulties of a different sort came from another source. Mrs. Ruth Shipley, head of the Passport Division in the State Department, and a political power with many congressmen, insisted that our intelligence agents should carry passports identifying them as U. S. government officials employed by OSS instead of ordinary passports! I demanded that this practice be stopped and ordinary passports substituted for those already issued, and I was successful in stopping this ridiculous and disastrous policy.

We began to have a substantial flow of information from our organization in Stockholm. One of our earliest operations was to check upon the flow of Nazi troops, arms, and other munitions through Sweden to the German armies in Norway and Finland. The Swedish government had been compelled to assent to this very unneutral arrangement during the period of Nazi victory when the alternative might well have been Nazi occupation of Sweden. The government forbade anyone to stay in the railway stations when Nazi troop trains were passing through and attempted to minimize the extent of troop movements.

Through connections arranged with the Swedish labor movement, we contrived to get actual head counts of German troops on these trains. Since our reports continually showed a troop strength about double those from other sources, I cabled our people to verify our count. Whereupon one of our principal agents, a Swedish-American professor, put on the clothes of a Swedish railway worker and went through the cars of a troop train and counted each soldier. The count was consistent with the average which he had previously been reporting. The Swedish government probably felt that it had to wink at some of our intelligence operations because of its bad conscience about this movement of German troops through Sweden.

We now began to make contact with the diplomatic and military personnel of the countries allied with Germany and with the neutrals. We established contacts within the Italian, Bulgarian, Hungarian, Vichy French, and Finnish diplomatic missions. We developed contacts among Estonian refugees in Stockholm. We purchased a diesel-powered fishing schooner manned by an Estonian crew which operated in the Baltic and caught both fish and intelligence in its nets.

I set up an "Order of Battle" section in my own office in Washington to process and evaluate the increasing flow of information which we, of course, passed on to our own military and naval intelligence organizations. This Order of Battle section was operationally separate from the selection and direction of our agents overseas. I installed as director a former German national who had been a sergeant flyer in the German army in World War I. He had come to the United States shortly afterwards and had made a modest fortune in business and had been an American citizen for years. He was Jewish and hated the Nazis fervently. He had volunteered to undergo any risk or danger, including undertaking missions in Nazi-occupied Europe. While his age precluded such a mission for him, I felt I was justified in breaching my rule against the use of former German nationals. I arranged for Professor Carroll of the Department of History of Duke University to be placed in the Order of Battle section at the Pentagon in order to have the closest possible liaison.

On one occasion a tremendous "flap" occurred because we passed on a copy of the German order of battle, showing the location of each German division and the names of the commanding generals, which we had received from the intelligence organization of a neutral country. Far from congratulating us, Military Intelligence at the Pentagon called us in great agitation. *It was an exact copy of the top-secet Pentagon estimate* of the German order of battle, right down to the misspelling of a German general's name! Fortunately, we had not had access to the Pentagon's German order of battle, so we could hardly be suspected of having leaked it ourselves. I always believed that it had originated in one of the governments in exile in London, who had passed it on to the neutral source from which we had obtained it.

While in London I shared an office with Dave Bruce, who had become the director of OSS in London and eventually was to perform this function for the whole ETO. I had previously been associated with Dave in Washington, and my stay in London was to cement the friendship and high regard I had for him. Fortunately our contacts were to continue after the war in Washington in 1947 when he was Assistant Secretary of Commerce, in Paris in 1950 where he was our ambassador to France, and in Berlin in 1958 when he had become our ambassador there.

In the late summer of 1943 I returned to London determined to go on to Stockholm as soon as I could get a Swedish visa. It required several weeks in London to arrange for my trip to Stockholm. I was able to obtain a Swedish visa, although the Swedish government must have realized that the ostensible purpose of my trip was not the real one. The Swedes no longer needed to fear occupation by the Nazi armies. Indeed, the defeat of Germany had already become practically a certainty. It was now possible for the Swedish government to show its feeling of sympathy for the Allied cause and make reparations for breaches of Swedish neutrality by the Nazis earlier in the war which the Swedes had had to suffer.

I proceeded to Edinburgh and called the telephone number with which I had been provided before I left London. It was British Intelligence at the RAF airfield at Leuchars. I was told that I would be called when the plane on which I was to go to Bromma, the airport of Stockholm, would be ready. Of course, these details were not referred to in the telephone conversation, which was in veiled language.

I had to wait almost a week until it was judged that flying conditions were most propitious for evading the *Luftwaffe* patrol. The Germans did their best to prevent air travel between Britain and Sweden, and very few planes even attempted the trip. They had recently shot down a Swedish passenger plane, and they were to shoot down another Swedish plane during my stay in Stockholm, even though these planes had tried to take advantage of the dark of the moon.

When I reported to Leuchars airfield, I knew that I would have to travel by a British Mosquito bomber, which made a speed of 350 to 400 miles per hour, the fastest plane then available. I was somewhat surprised to find that I was to ride in the bomb bay of the plane together with the United States diplomatic pouch, taking the place of the two five-hundred pound bombs which was the regular cargo of the plane. I had to perch on the diplomatic pouch with my feet braced on either side of the opening of the bomb bay. The only communication with the Norwegian pilot and radio operator was through a face mask and speaking tube which doubled as the oxygen supply. We were to fly at an altitude of 30,000 feet, a height to which the *Luftwaffe* craft would find it difficult to climb. On account of the temperature at that height, I had to wear a double RAF flying suit, together with fleece-lined boots. I also had to get into parachute harness, together with a "Mae West" life preserver vest.

I was briefed on how I was to bail out on notice from the pilot if it were to become necessary. I was first to hook on my parachute to the harness, wait until the pilot had opened the bomb bay, drop through the bay, count three (slowly!), then pull the rip cord of my parachute pack. If I came down over water (presumably in the North Sea), I was to release my parachute harness when I reached the water and then inflate the Mae West by releasing the carbon dioxide cartridges attached to it. Finally, there had thoughtfully been provided a tiny electric light to be plugged into the Mae West together with a small tin whistle to guide rescuing craft to me.

Not only was there serious doubt that I could remember to do these things in the required order, but since I was very likely to come down in German-controlled water or land areas, I was in grave doubt whether I would wish to be rescued. It was necessary for me to carry my passport in order to enter Sweden, so I could not have concealed my identity. I could imagine trying to explain to Nazi interrogators as I stood in sodden flying suit that I was merely carrying out a study of postwar international trade! If I were to be transported to Germany for further questioning, I would have been in real trouble since my anti-Nazi record had been widely publicized.[5]

I need not have worried. Our air attaché in Stockholm who was going to have to make a similar trip by Mosquito bomber told me that he had decided that if he had to bail out, the only way he could avoid having his brains batted out by being thrown against the plane's bomb bay by the air stream was to dive out head first. He added drily, however, that he did not like the idea of losing his feet.

We arrived at Bromma airport, and I went to the Grand Hotel, where my people had made a reservation for me. I met with them next day and spent the next month going over the details of the organization and reviewing what had been done.

The "cover" for my trip to Sweden was a research study of the probable status of our postwar international trade. I was carrying this study out for the Committee for Economic Development. The Committee did not know that the study was to be used as a cover, and, as I shall explain later, I did indeed carry out the projected study as planned. Consequently, during the month I spent in Stockholm, I had many interviews with Swedish industrialists, bankers, labor leaders, newspaper men, and particularly economists.

One of the economists whom I met was Professor Bertil Ohlin, who was not only a celebrated economist, but was also a member of the *Riksdag*. Ohlin was greatly disturbed by the policy of "unconditional surrender" which President Roosevelt had announced. "Do you want to destroy Germany and the German people?" he asked. I assured him that the United States government had no such goal. Actually, I knew that there were some persons in the United States government who did desire the destruction of Germany, but I was convinced that the majority of the American people did not desire this, nor did President Rossevelt or the really responsible men in his administration. When I was to be in a position to influence policy in this sphere, I felt that I could justify by my own deeds the statement I had made to Ohlin.

At another time, I was invited to lunch at the Cafe Royal of the Grand Hotel by another eminent Swedish economist. After we had sat down, another small party came in and took a table next to ours. My host arose and greeted Dr. X of the German Embassy,

5. My books had been placed on the Nazi purge list along with those of Marx and Lenin throughout Nazi-occupied Europe.

whom I knew to be an *Oberst* in the Nazi *Sicherheitsdienst*. I maintained a poker face. We had some of the staff of the Grand Hotel in our employ. So, evidently, did the Nazis.

Swedish Counter Espionage was naturally interested in my visit to Stockholm. I was able twice to recognize agents of Swedish CE who had my movements under surveillance. During my stay in Stockholm I had meetings with Dr. Erkko, former Finnish Foreign Minister and editor of one of the large Finnish newspapers, and with other prominent Finns. I learned later that the Swedish Foreign Office knew of my meeting with Erkko. They apparently had no objection to it, and indeed, regarded it benevolently. The Swedes apparently believed that I had come to Stockholm to carry out peace negotiations with the Finns. They were highly desirous that these negotiations should succeed. Actually, I did nothing of the sort. Through Erkko, the Finnish government extended an unofficial but cordial invitation to me to go to Helsinki. I would have liked to go in order to have had a look at the personnel of the German army and to look over the ground from the standpoint of our organization. I was sure, however, that Hershel Johnson, our Minister in Stockholm, would have regretted my acceptance of the invitation. At this time the United States was taking a stern attitude toward the Finns in order to induce them to get out of the war. My going to Helsinki would likely have been interpreted as a more or less friendly gesture to the Finns which would not have facilitated what was current State Department policy. The disapproval of Minister Johnson for such a trip under the circumstances was probably justified.

While I was in Stockholm, one of our agents made contact with "Dr." Felix Kersten, a Baltic German, born in Estonia, who had become a Finnish citizen. Dr. Kersten was a physical-therapist who had become the personal physician of Heinrich Himmler. He was able to give Himmler relief from the abdominal pains with which he was afflicted and thus acquired a remarkable influence over him. Kersten was then living in Stockholm but made frequent trips to Berlin to treat Himmler. An agent of ours who had heard of Dr. Kersten's connection with Himmler now became a patient of Kersten for the treatment of imaginary abdominal pains.

Our agent represented himself as the secret personal representative of President Roosevelt and urged that since it was certain that Germany would be crushed if the war continued, the last opportunity for Germany to make peace without total destruction should now be seized. Kersten discussed with our man a proposal that Himmler arrest Hitler, since the Allies would never make peace with him, and that Himmler should then head an interim government which would make peace with the Allies on terms which would be onerous but better than Germany could hope to obtain after total defeat. In discussing this proposal with Kersten, our man went beyond the instructions we had given him. When it was reported to us we were not at all sure that Kersten would make such a proposal to Himmler.

We did not for an instant really intend to deal with a Himmler government as the successor to Hitler, and certainly the United States government would not have done so. Our agent was, of course, *not* a special envoy of President Roosevelt. As far as Himmler was concerned, if the plot had been carried out, we would have been acting in complete bad faith. I felt sure that if Himmler tried to arrest Hitler, even though he would almost certainly fail, the effect upon the morale of the Nazi party and upon the German army would be shattering. Dr. Kersten communicated his proposal to Walter Shellenberg, chief of the Nazi *Sicherheitsdienst,* who took it up with Himmler.[6] Himmler was appalled at the risk involved and was unwilling to participate in the plot.

The contact with Himmler through Kersten and our agent was immediately reported to Washington. Our agent, after talking with Shellenberg, was willing to go to Berlin to talk with Himmler. I forbade him to go, at least until we heard from Washington, particularly in view of the perfectly ghastly personal danger to which he would be exposed. The senior men in my organization in Stockholm were very suspicious of Kersten. We had always to consider the possibility that the proposed plot with Himmler was actually no more than a scheme to entrap our agent and through torture to extract information from him about our organization.

We received no encouragement from Washington to proceed further with our contact with Himmler, and so the matter was dropped. The United States government was evidently very much concerned that the Soviet government would hear of our indirect

6. Both Kersten and Shellenberg have accounts of this episode, written from their individual points of view. See Felix Kersten, *The Kersten Memoirs, 1940–45* (New York: Macmillan, 1957), pp. 188–197; and Schellenberg, *The Labyrinth: The Memoirs of Hitler's Secret Service Chief*, pp. 370–371.

contact with Himmler and would conclude that we were planning to make a secret deal with Himmler and perhaps with reactionary circles in Germany. The fears of Washington lest Soviet suspicions should be aroused seemed reasonable to me, and I did not press the matter further when I shortly returned to London and later to Washington.

I have never been entirely sure that my decision to leave the matter in abeyance was the correct one. If we could have driven a wedge between Himmler and Hitler, the resulting disorganization might have resulted in the collapse of Germany a year before it actually occurred. The lives of at least a million people would have been saved. The exclusive occupation of Poland, Czechslovakia, and Eastern Germany by the Soviet armies might have been averted. The division of Germany might also have been avoided. A government similar to that which evolved in West Germany might have governed the whole of Germany.

Some eight months after I left Stockholm, Adam von Trotz zu Salz, then in the German legation in Stockholm, disclosed to my people in Stockholm the outlines of the plot by the German underground on Hitler's life which actually took place about a month later. He inquired what the attitude of the United States government would be towards an interim government. The proposal was at once reported to Washington, but no reply was ever received. After the failure of the plot in July, 1944, von Trotz zu Salz was executed.

I had expected to fly back to the United Kingdom by the same Mosquito bomber which I had used on my way in. I found, however, that one of the members of the OSS mission in Stockholm had planned to fly out at the date I had in mind, so I put off my return for a week. Unfortunately, the Mosquito crashed, and our man as well as the Norwegian pilot and co-pilot was killed. It consequently became necessary to fly out on a Liberator bomber converted into a troop carrier, larger and much slower than the Mosquito and thus more vulnerable to attack by *Luftwaffe* patrol. A larger number of passengers could be carried, however.

Our passenger list, in addition to a cabinet member from the Polish government-in-exile in London, and a Swedish industrialist, consisted of three British soldiers who had escaped from prison camps in Germany, a young and beautiful girl of Norwegian-British parentage, and myself. There was a captain from a Highland regiment captured in the Western Desert during the campaign against General Rommel, a New Zealand sergeant who had been captured while a member of the British commando force which had come so close to capturing Rommel at his desert headquarters, and a lieutenant flyer from the Midlands who had been shot down on a bombing raid over Germany. My assumption that the girl was a British agent was confirmed when I reached London by the officer in British Intelligence responsible for their Stockholm operation. The three British soldiers were naturally attracted by the beautiful girl, whom they also obviously assumed to be in the British service.

In order to circumvent local Nazi agents who might be able to tip off the *Luftwaffe* patrol of our departure and perhaps as a result of *Luftwaffe* activity, we made four false starts over several days, getting in and out of flying equipment and parachute harness before finally taking off. A Swedish plane carrying a number of passengers, including members of the Soviet Embassy in Stockholm, had been shot down in flames while attempting to evade the *Luftwaffe* on a recent night flight. This doubtless accounted for the elaborate precautions now taken.

Although our plane had intended to land at Leuchars airfield near Edinburgh, we were compelled on account of heavy fog to land at an RAF flying field near Inverness in the Highlands. The RAF fed us, put us up in barracks, and the next day we flew on to Leuchars airfield. We had by this time developed a warmly friendly feeling, and we agreed to take an apartment together on the train for London when it departed that evening. We separated in London, and I have never heard of them again, but I have rarely encountered more attractive personalities than were these young people. I reported to Dave Bruce on the status of the Stockholm operation and then flew back to Washington for a similar report to Bill Donovan.

Some years after the close of the war, the chief of our Stockholm operation wrote to me as follows:

> Viewed in retrospect, perhaps the following achievements and accomplishments were the major contributions of the Secret Intelligence Branch of the OSS Mission to Sweden during World War II. The listed items are set down more or less in chronological order of occurrence and not necessarily in order of importance.
>
> 1. The control of the German Transit Traffic through Sweden to

Norway and Finland. This control service came eventually to be recognized as the only reliable reporting service on this traffic.

2. Obtaining a *non*-Allied assessment and survey of the German military and political position in Denmark by a highly qualified observer.

3. Obtaining a survey of the German defense preparations in Norway by another highly qualified *non*-Allied observer.

4. Obtaining the German Order of Battle reports.

5. Obtaining the O.B. reports on an Allied Power which had desisted from furnishing this information to the J.C.S.

6. Obtaining the Naval Register of a Foreign Power. [The British Admiralty rated this report very highly, stating that their previous material on this navy was as 2 per cent and the new report as 98 per cent.]

7. The discovery and obtaining of evidence of a new German alloy for anti-aircraft shells, as well as location of the assembly plant. [The British rated this job as "the find of the year" in 1943.]

8. Obtaining valuable information regarding ball-bearing shipments to Germany, enabling Allied aircraft to intercept German vessels.

9. The penetration of a source which enabled access to information accumulated by Swedish Military, Naval, Political and Economic observers in all foreign capitals.

10. The uncovering of numerous Axis spy rings and their operatives in Sweden and with the cooperation of the Swedish authorities, their neutralization, incarceration and deportation.

11. The establishment of independent American Intelligence networks in Norway, Denmark and Finland.

12. The penetration of the quondam Vichy French Legation in Stockholm.

13. The special report on the German synthetic oil plants by our own observer on the spot. [This refers to the almost incredible feat by one of our agents in securing the consent of Heinrich Himmler to his visiting the principal synthetic oil plants in Germany. Himmler's consent was obtained by proposing a bogus plan for setting up synthetic oil plants in Sweden, where they would be safe from Allied bombing, and by alleging the necessity for observing the techniques of existing German plants. Our agent, Erikson, a native-born American who had become a naturalized Swedish subject pretended to be strongly pro-Nazi in order to make the necessary contacts. His intelligence, which pinpointed the location of the German synthetic oil plants for Allied bombers, was a vital factor in cutting Nazi supply of gasoline and effectively grounding the *Luftwaffe* during the Allied landings and during the Allied advance into Germany. The risks which Erikson took were hair-

raising, and his services were officially recognized and his name cleared immediately after the close of hostilities.] [7]

14. The special report on the U-Boat Schnorkel device.

15. The authoritative report on the special properties of Esthonian Shale Oil and its uses in submarine warfare.

16. The "assistance" supplied to the Opposition in Finland and facilitating of moves to bring that country out of the war.

17. The engineering of the declaration of loyalty to the King and Badoglio by the Italian Minister to Sweden; this was the first Italian Legation or Embassy to flop to the Allied side after the overthrow of Mussolini.

18. The recovery of the broken American State Dept. codes from *non*-Allied sources.

19. The recovery of the broken military, naval and secret service codes of a Foreign Power from *non*-Allied and enemy sources. These specific codes were then delivered to the Government of this Foreign Power on specific directions of F.D.R. just prior to an important conference. Subsequently, the American M.A. to the country rated this job as "the most important contribution by OSS to that Nation's war-effort."

20. The recovery of the secret codes of about a dozen other Foreign Powers.

21. The obtaining of all the most informative files of the Finnish GHQ at the time of the Armistice—including voluminous meteorological data on a certain non-communicative Foreign Power.

22. Uncovering on at least two occasions of specific evidence of the leakage of highly confidential American O.B. material through foreign channels.

23. Obtaining prior information on a projected U-Boat raid on the U. S. East Coast; these particular U-Boats were equipped to launch V-1's; they were subsequently intercepted and sunk by the American Navy.

24. Report on May 7, 1945, Jap peace-feeler.

The chief and vice-chief of our Stockholm operation had set up and directed an organization which British Intelligence referred to as the most efficient and professional of OSS intelligence operations. The warmth of the association with these men established in wartime has continued to the present time. The dedication to duty and the scrupulous concern for security of the personnel of our Washington office made the Stockholm operation possible.

7. *New York Times*, June 3, 1945. A somewhat fictionalized account of Erikson's exploits is given in Alexander Klein's *The Counterfeit Traitor* (New York: Holt, 1958). The movie of the same name, based upon the book, is even further fictionalized.

Chapter sixteen. *Germany after the Nazi collapse: I oppose a Carthaginian peace*

I returned from London in the fall of 1943 believing that the defeat of the German army was imminent. In fact, its surrender was to be delayed almost a year beyond what I had expected. How much the demand by the United States government for "unconditional surrender" prolonged the war, it is impossible to say. Because of my belief in the impending collapse of Germany, I was anxious to return to academic life. I also felt that I might be able to influence public opinion in the United States by writing and speaking in favor of an enduring peace.

In an effort to induce me to stay in OSS it was suggested that I set up an OSS mission in Moscow. I declined to do so on the ground that such a mission in Moscow would at best be in an anomalous position. General Donovan hoped to set up the mission with the agreement of the Soviet authorities. I felt that such agreement would probably not be given and that the suggestion of my appointment to the post would make Soviet refusal a certainty.

My decision to leave OSS was strongly influenced by the undertaking I had given to the Committee for Economic Development to do the study on International Trade and Domestic Employment. The Committee had had no intimation that the study was to afford cover for my trip to Stockholm. I now felt that I must complete the study. This could not be done while I still carried on my responsibilities in OSS.

I returned to my academic duties at Duke, finished the

necessary supplementary research, and began to write my report. I completed the writing of the study in the spring of 1944, but it was not in print until the fall of 1945.[1]

I pointed out in the study that in the current world to propose that we simply embrace free trade was senseless. It was widely claimed at this time that our total productive capacity was greater than our markets could absorb, so that an expansion of international trade was necessary "to get rid of the surplus." I pointed out that this also was nonsense. The real advantages of international trade consisted of the greater national product which could come about through international division of labor. Such advantages of increased international trade, however, were not great enough to compensate nations for increased unemployment if international trade took place on the basis of "beggar thy neighbor" policies of unco-ordinated national pushing of exports which had characterized the period of the Great Depression. The first requisite for increasing international trade so that it would not cause reciprocal unemployment was the institution of co-ordinated programs of full employment in all countries. Such programs would be greatly facilitated by the inauguration of certain new types of international institutions, particularly the International Monetary Fund and the International Bank for Reconstruction and Development. In the furtherance of the recommendations of the study, I gave testimony before the appropriate Congressional committees and once more gave a number of public lectures on the subject.

During the year 1944 I participated in a series of *Studies of American Interests in the War and the Peace*, under the auspices of the Council on Foreign Relations. The "Economic and Financial Series" was worked out in collaboration with Alvin Hansen and Jacob Viner, together with ten or twelve other economists, as rapporteurs. These studies were made available to the State Department to be used as background material for drawing up the peace settlement at the end of the war.

I never found much evidence that these studies had in fact been used by the State Department. They turned out to be of immense psychological importance to me, however, when by an un-

1. *International Trade and Domestic Employment* (New York: McGraw-Hill, 1945). Although the study had not been written for such a purpose, it was widely used as a supplementary text in universities and colleges. Consequently, more copies were sold than of anything else I had written up to this time.

expected turn of events I came to be responsible a year later for drawing up the details of the first reparations plan for Germany. The economists who worked on the *Studies of American Interests in War and Peace* agreed that a Carthaginian peace settlement should not be imposed upon Germany. We were agreed that the Nazi regime should be destroyed and its recrudescence prevented, that Germany should be disarmed, that German armaments and facilities for armament manufacture should be destroyed and their reconstruction forbidden. It was agreed, however, that "no good reasons existed for deliberately attempting to keep the defeated powers weak." For example, the elimination of facilities for armament production was not intended to include the elimination of the German steel industry.

At a later time I was to be confronted with a totally different kind of proposed peace settlement for Germany which would have meant the permanent reduction of German productive powers even for peaceful purposes far below their prewar level. The memory of the conclusions of my associates in these studies sponsored by the Council on Foreign Relations was to strengthen greatly my confidence in the correctness of the economic terms of a reparations program which by contrast allowed some hope of a tolerable life to the German people and, consequently, to the other peoples of Europe as well.

Following the collapse and surrender of the Nazi forces in May, 1945, I suddenly found myself projected actively into the German situation. As it turned out, I was to play a major role in working out the level of industry which was to be recommended for Germany during the period of Allied occupation. The process by which this responsibility came to be mine began with a telephone call from Bill Donovan. He wanted me to rejoin OSS and to serve as Chief of Economic Intelligence in the Economics Division of the United States Group of the Control Council for Germany, headed by Brigadier General William H. Draper. It was planned that there would also be British, Russian, and French Chiefs of Economic Intelligence. I would be on loan from OSS to the U. S. Army with the assimilated rank of colonel. For the first time in World War II, it would be necessary for me to be in uniform.

I was extremely reluctant once more to turn aside from my academic duties to governmental service. If I had known that I was to have a high degree of responsibility for recommending a program of reparations and the permitted level of industry for Germany immediately after Potsdam, I believe I would have refused outright. It was already apparent that the mood of our government and, indeed, of American public opinion at this time favored the harshest possible economic policy vis-a-vis Germany. I was convinced that such a policy would not be conducive to a durable peace settlement. I would not have been willing to take responsibility for implementing a policy which I felt was bound to be disastrous. However, the position I was offered at this time was supposed to be concerned exclusively with economic intelligence and not with the implementation of economic policy. Bill Donovan, who knew the persuasive value of the grand gesture, sent his plane to pick me up at Raleigh. The plane took me to Washington, where I discussed the proposal with him and later with General Draper. As a result, I found myself once more in OSS. I agreed to stay on the job only long enough to get the organization "off the ground," and for a maximum of four months, when I was to be free to return to my academic duties. This function of getting a new organization "off the ground" had come to be a specialty of mine which I was to carry out repeatedly in the future.

I spent a few days in Washington once more recruiting a staff, this time entirely composed of army officers. I left Washington by plane and joined our embryonic U. S. Group of the Control Council for Germany, which at that time was part of SHAEF in Versailles, in late May. Only a small part of the staff which I had recruited in Washington joined me at Versailles. The remainder, due to the vagaries of army paper work, were to join me at irregular intervals in Frankfurt and in Berlin.

We flew from Versailles to the Rhine-Main Airfield, which had only recently been taken over from the German forces and which still showed the effects of Allied bombing. We moved into Frankfurt and were billeted in German homes which had been cleared of their inhabitants, who in such cases were given two hours' notice to get out. They were required to leave beds, mattresses, and other furniture in their houses for the use of the new occupants. They were, however, allowed to take their bed clothes with them.

The center of Frankfurt had been almost pulverized by Allied bombers. This was particularly true of the oldest part of Frankfurt, the *Römer Stadt.* I used to go to my office in the morning past the ruined shell of the Opera House, of which only the stone facade remained standing. The motto carved in great letters on the facade, *"Zum Wahren, Schönen, Guten,"* remained clearly legible.

Economic Intelligence, as part of General Draper's Economic Division, had its offices at first in Höchst, a suburb of Frankfurt in which the chemical plants of I. G. Farben and its original headquarters were located. Höchst had not suffered very much bomb damage. We took over I. G. Farben headquarters for our offices. In the beginning, we functioned as an element of "USFET" (United States Forces European Theater). Soon, however the United States Group of the Control Council for Germany began to be organized preparatory to moving on to Berlin. In the meantime we had offices in the large, beautiful, and very modern office building of I. G. Farben, which had been constructed in Frankfurt immediately before the war. Most of the elements of SHAEF had moved there from Versailles, and it came to be known as the German Pentagon. The building had not suffered at all from Allied air attacks, because, according to rumor, it had been planned to use it for the purpose to which it was now being put.

The corner of one wing had been blown out, however, and I made the mistake of asking an army officer friend how this had happened. "Oh, the OSS did that!" he exclaimed with relish. "They found a locked German safe and tried to open it with a bazooka shell. They opened it all right, but they blew out that whole end of the building too!"

I had to go to OSS headquarters near Wiesbaden in order to receive my salary and allowances. Our Air Forces had their headquarters in the city, which had not been nearly as badly bombed as had Frankfurt. Allegedly, this was due to our Air Forces having scrupulously refrained from "messing up" their future headquarters. Here also there had been a small misadventure. The RAF returning from a raid on a German city had not been able to spot their target on account of fog. On the way back, the fog lifted a bit, it seemed a shame to haul the bombs back unused, and the RAF, unwittingly or not, clobbered a small section of the city in which their comrades in arms were to have their headquarters. Inevitably, the German inhabitants of the small area had got clobbered too.

We had no problem of relations with the government of the

defeated country, because that government had been destroyed and no successor national government had been recognized or was to be recognized for years to come. Not only was there no national government, there were no local governments either. General Eisenhower had proclaimed that we came into Germany as conquerors. There were indeed no indigenous governmental bodies to stand between us and the conquered population, who were wholly at our mercy. In fact, the problems of our occupational forces were much more difficult and complex than if there had been national and local governments with which to deal.

Millions of Allied prisoners had been released and were returning home. Still other millions were "displaced persons," some of them "slave labor" who had been conscripted by the Germans from their occupied territories—Poles, Czechs, Yugoslavs, Russians, French, Belgians, and others. Some had come to Germany willingly to earn higher wages. The French, Belgians, and others from Western Europe returned to their homelands as soon as they could. Millions of Russians, Poles, and Yugoslavs did not wish to return, or at least were in no hurry to do so. Hundreds of thousands of the Russians had served in General Vlassov's army as auxiliaries to the Nazi forces. The Soviet authorities took the position that the loyalty of any soldier who had surrendered to the German forces was suspect. Thousands of these Russians had to be turned over to the Soviet authorities against their will. Other thousands roamed the countryside trying to conceal their Soviet connections, living with the Poles, Estonians, Latvians, and Lithuanians who did not wish to return to their countries, which were occupied by the Soviet armies. Looting and destruction of property was widespread as caravans of these "DP's," as they came to be called, moved aimlessly about. Eventually, hundreds of thousands who could not be induced or compelled to return to their homelands were settled into barracks of the former German army. In the meantime they had to be fed by the American occupation forces. To these had been added millions of demobilized German soldiers who were trying to return to their homes and other millions of *Volksdeutsche,* expelled from Poland, East Prussia, Czechslovakia, and the Balkan countries.

A program of economic rehabilitation for our occupied areas could not be put into effect, since this was forbidden by the terms of the top-secret directive of the Joint Chiefs of Staff, J. C. S. 1067, under which we were operating. This forbade any effort to rehabilitate or even maintain German industrial production above that minimum of consumer-goods production necessary to prevent disease and unrest. No one knew what this minimum was, and no one wished to take responsibility for allowing a particular German plant to resume production. Only the absolute minimum of communication with the German population was permitted according to stringent regulations against "fraternization." The Nazi record of starting the war, of conducting the war in contravention of the rules of civilized warfare, of the torture and slaughter of millions of victims in the horror camps of Dachau, Buchenwald, and Auschwitz had put the whole German nation beyond the pale.

There was no question of "a correct attitude towards a defeated foe." On our way up from Versailles, a captain, a graduate of my own university, now an administrative officer in the 8th Air Force, boasted that he and some of his pals had taken off from England into our occupation area in a Flying Fortress immediately after the German surrender. They had put down at a former German airfield and had unloaded a jeep which they had brought with them. They then ranged about the countryside, looting cameras, radios, and anything else that took their fancy. They then flew to an airfield in France and peddled their loot on the black market.

Shortly after our arrival in Frankfurt, we carried out "Operation Tally-ho." Roadblocks were set up, and houses and persons searched by our troops in order to search for Nazi leaders who might be hiding, our own AWOL's, concealed arms, stolen governmental property, and so on. According to plan, the operation was to cover the entire population. In the process our troops quite generally looted cameras, radios, field glasses, and even personal jewelry.

French and British troops were responsible for similar acts. Indeed, I was told that British soldiers had looted the watches, rings, and other personal jewelry of the German women who had acted as secretaries to the German generals while typing out the German surrender terms.[2] The Germans were particularly outraged by the French troops who ran hoses into the warehouses where casks of *Bernkastler Doktor,* the finest of Moselle wines were stored, pumped out the rare wine, and distilled it into ordinary cognac.

2. Robert Murphy in his *Diplomat among Warriors* (New York: Doubleday, 1964) p. 244, refers to this same incident.

However, these acts were hardly comparable with those of the Russian troops in their areas of occupation. I was to learn of these in revolting detail after we moved up to Berlin.

In the early days of our occupation, almost anyone could requisition almost anything from the German population. If the owner were lucky, he might be able to obtain a signed form from the requisitioning officer, which theoretically would entitle him to some form of compensation from some as yet unknown governmental authority. However, cases came to my attention where requisitions had been signed "Captain Mickey Mouse" or "Major Napoleon Bonaparte" or simply "Captain Yur Stuk." Sometimes a lieutenant in one of our engineering battalions would take over construction equipment from some German construction company, and when he had no further use for it would simply abandon it in a wood fifty miles away. Substantially all automobiles belonging to German civilians were taken over by our troops, usually for some more or less official use. Bicycles were sometimes simply seized by our G. I's. This process of informally seizing property had begun when our troops took over occupied areas in Italy, France, or other countries after expelling the German troops. Then all property which the Germans had previously requisitioned from the native population was fair game for our troops. The process of taking over automobiles and the like under these circumstances was known as "liberating." This term continued to be used when our troops liberated German-owned automobiles. It was even extended so that it became customary for the G. I's to speak of "liberating a blonde."

In all public buildings which we took over in which there were German employees or into which German civilians came, separate toilets were set up with signs reminiscent of those in American cities in the South labeled "For Whites" and "For Colored." German demobilized soldiers who had not yet been able to replace their uniforms with civilian clothes were required to salute all Allied officers, but we were not allowed to return the salutes. A similar prohibition prevented the returning of required salutes by German policemen.

During my stay in Frankfurt, I was a member of the Intelligence Committee of USFET for our area of occupation, of which the Chairman was Brigadier General Betts. For some reason, various proposals for preventing the recrudescence of Nazi militarism used to come up for the advice of this committee. It was proposed that no former German intelligence officers, no officers of the *Luftwaffe*, and no officers of the General Staff be allowed to have any position above that of a common laborer. These disqualifications would be in addition to those attendant upon former active membership in the Nazi party. The occupational authorities were forbidden by J.C.S. 1067 to employ even skilled workers who had been members of any Nazi organization. Since almost all skilled workers had been members, this gave us serious trouble in operating the railways, for example. Eventually General Clay ordered that this particular prohibition be disregarded.

It was also proposed that the playing of martial music, and in particular *Die Wacht Am Rhein* and *Deutchsland über Alles*, be forbidden.[3] It was also proposed that all German street names associated with German nationalism, such as Bismarck Strasse, should be ordered to be changed. Finally, it was proposed that all German war memorials, including those to the war dead, should be destroyed. In general, I opposed these proposals, as likely in the long run to have an effect opposite to that desired. My memory is uncertain about the extent to which any attempt to put these measures into effect was made since final action was, of course, not the responsibility of the Intelligence Committee.

When I later made a trip through Bavaria, we began to pass on the roads the latest wave of German refugees from those portions of Thuringia and Saxony which had been occupied by American troops and which were soon to be turned over to Soviet troops. A majority of the refugees were women, often pushing baby carriages with one or more children in them, together with a few pitiful possessions piled in with them. There were many war cripples as well. I will always remember the sight of two German ex-soldiers, with one leg each and one crutch each, walking along with their arms about each other's shoulders for support.

About this time I was informed by a captain attached to the U. S. Strategic Bombing Survey that he had come across the top administrative personnel of the *Reich Gruppe Industrie*, a quasi-official body which, among other functions, compiled annual data on German industry. This administrative group, accompanied by

3. When later I was in Berlin, the playing or singing of the newly composed *Berlin Kommt Wieder* ("Berlin Shall Rise Again") was forbidden.

their families, had been evacuated from Berlin to escape Allied bombing. They had with them a half dozen Hollerith punch-card sorting machines, complete punch-card records of German industry over recent years, a ton or so of blank punch cards, and finally a payroll of some three quarters of a million marks.

If this Reich Gruppe Industrie center could not be evacuated, these records would fall into Soviet hands and would never be available to us. I asked my deputy, Lieutenant Colonel Potter, to arrange for army trucks to evacuate the center. I placed a young captain from Economic Intelligence, who had just arrived from Washington, in charge of the recently evacuated center, together with the payroll for support of the personnel, in some buildings at a nearby German health resort. I left for Berlin shortly thereafter. The young American captain traveled to Berlin a month or so later and beseeched me to relieve him of responsibility for the center. I had to tell him regretfully that the matter was now out of my hands, and that I no longer had any authority over him. I never knew what eventually happened to this group of people. At least they were out of Soviet hands, and for that I am sure they were profoundly thankful.

Our treatment of the civilian population was no worse, and in most ways not nearly so bad, as had been the conduct of the German armies, particularly SS troops, in the Nazi occupied countries of Europe. There was almost no execution of civilians by Allied troops, as had been carried out by the German occupational authorities in Czechslovakia, in Poland, in Italy, and in France. It had been expected that there might be continued resistance or even guerrilla warfare by a Nazi underground, comparable to the underground resistance to the Nazis in occupied Europe, where these wholesale executions of civilians had taken place. There was, however, no German resistance whatever. The Nazis had replaced all ethics with naked force, and that force had suffered total defeat. The population was in a state of shock from the air bombings. The German people, whether or not they had condoned the Nazi atrocities, were physically and morally utterly shaken, cowed, awaiting retribution. However brutal our occupational policy might be, the Germans knew they were fortunate in having us for their rulers instead of the Russians.

The great body of the Allied occupational forces had been

conditioned to believe that the Germans were an accursed race, inherently brutal and evil. I had, however, lived in Germany before the war and before the Nazi regime. I had many German friends. I knew that cruelty, brutality, and sadism were not exclusively German characteristics. Even though one could excuse our treatment of the German civilian population in the light of Nazi crimes, for me to participate personally in treating civilians with indignity was repulsive. I felt then, and I feel now, that it would indeed have been a grave error for us to have at once taken the position towards the German people that "All is forgiven; let us be friends once more!" I did feel that it was highly desirable to restore civilian production in Germany as a condition for stability in Germany and in the rest of Western Europe. Nevertheless, I felt strongly that the conscience of mankind demanded the earliest possible death sentences for Nazi war criminals. I felt that if some thousands of these Nazi criminals could be sentenced even by drumhead court martials, it would clear the atmosphere for harnessing a disarmed Germany to the task of rehabilitating war-devastated Europe.

General Draper now began to get urgent cables from Washington demanding information about economic conditions in Germany, particularly with reference to industrial production. However, all reporting of economic data by governmental or quasi-governmental bodies in Germany had ceased for there was no German government at any level. The intelligence officers of our combat divisions which were occupying Germany had not been required to report economic intelligence and had had no training for collecting or analyzing data. Our military governments which had just been set up in German towns and cities likewise had no aptitudes, facilities, or channels of transmission for such data.

I drew up a report based upon my own observations in the Frankfurt-Wiesbaden area, pieced out with scraps of information from other sources. This report, the first economic intelligence from occupied Germany, momentarily appeased Washington's demands. I told General Draper, however, that it was intolerable that we should not have much more and much harder economic intelligence. I determined to go and have a look myself. Our most important area outside Frankfurt and its environs consisted of Bavaria and the Bavarian Palatinate, and I arranged to visit the officers of military government in the area.

Sovereignty and police power lay in the hands of the commanding general whose combat troops had moved into a particular area. It was necessary to obtain a sort of military visa for anyone not under the direct command of a particular general to enter his area. I had to send one of my officers to arrange for such a "visa" whenever I moved about to carry out my functions as Chief of Economic Intelligence. Lieutenant Colonel Norwood Potter obtained the necessary travel orders, military visas, a SHAEF staff car, and an army driver and accompanied me on the trip.

We carried out inspection tours of Augsburg, Nuremberg, Regensburg, Munich, and the smaller towns and the countryside in between. Our military governors in these areas were just in the process of setting up embryonic forms of local government. This obviously had to be done if even the most rudimentary functions of government, such as garbage collection, sewage disposal, local police protection, and the like, were to be provided.

Although little industry was in production, I found that bomb damage was much less than I had expected. This finding was corroborated by our U. S. Strategic Bombing Survey. It had been relatively easy for the Allied bombing squadrons to locate an entire city. The bombs were then usually unloaded on the centers of the cities, which were thoroughly devastated. Industrial plants were usually located on the periphery of each city and would have required pin-point accuracy in bombing. Consequently, most of German industry had survived and could be put into production as soon as a decision was made about which plants would be dismantled for reparations purposes and which would be allowed to produce for the market. Once this decision was made, price stabilization through currency reform provided for, and the free market system re-established, German economic recovery could take place. It was not until 1948 that this favorable chain of events transpired, and the miracle of high German economic productivity could begin.

The banks in the various towns and cities had been opened on the orders of our military governors to accept deposits and to make payments to depositors, limited to some five hundred marks per depositor. Probably every one of these banks was legally bankrupt, what with the destruction of physical assets and the complete worthlessness of government securities in which other assets were invested. Fortunately, no one worried about legal solvency. The amounts deposited usually covered the restricted amounts which could be withdrawn. If a young captain or major in military government found one of his banks running short of funds, he simply instructed another bank to send money to the bank which was short. If this did not suffice, he sent a jeep to a friend who happened to be military governor of some nearby city requesting the advance of a million marks or so. It would not have been wise for a German bank official to question this highly informal transfer of funds, and I never heard of one's doing so.

The young captains, majors, and colonels of military government quickly developed a sense of personal responsibility for their German charges and showed remarkable energy, ingenuity, and efficiency in getting some faint replica of normal civilian activity under way. A few modeled themselves on the military governors in the former Nazi-occupied areas of Europe. I heard of one case where a young captain called a meeting of the heads of departments in his municipality. As the captain strode in, the municipal employees rose to their feet, all except one elderly man in frail health. The captain shouted, "Stand up, you old bastard!" The man did manage to rise, and the meeting proceeded. In another case, one of the officers of our military government in Bavaria received a feeble protest from a German civilian who claimed that there had been an infringement of his rights as a civilian in an occupied area. The military governor roared, "The conquered have no rights!"

Such cases were rare. On the contrary, the military governor of one of the cities, I believe it was Regensburg, introduced me to the German whom we had placed in charge of a sort of embryonic local government in the area. He was an elderly man, treated with kind condescension by the military governor. The man turned out to be Stegerwald, a well known political figure of pre-Hitler days, a leader of the Catholic Center party. I had interviewed him in Berlin in 1932 in his impressive office in the large building housing the head office of the insurance company associated with the Catholic trade unions. He had been confined for many months in a Nazi prison during the war, and he now appeared greatly shrunken and aged.

We ended our tour in Munich, where I had spent the last month of my stay in Germany with my wife and daughters in 1933. I had thought it the most beautiful of German cities. Now it was a bombed-out wreck. The great public park, the lovely Englischer Garten, was the encampment of one of our tank repair battalions. The beautiful little lake where my children had observed with delight a mother duck swimming with her downy brood of ducklings was now dry and being used as the dumping ground for debris from bombed-out houses.

We returned to Frankfurt to write my report, which General Draper forwarded to Washington, reporting a very low level of industrial activity in the whole area through which we had driven. I was convinced that this situation should not be allowed to continue in view of the tremendous needs of the German population, including millions of refugees from the East and the remaining hundreds of thousands of displaced persons plus the millions of soldiers of the occupying forces. I felt sure, however, that not much could be done until there could be an official determination of the kinds of industries and the level of production which would be permitted for these industries. I had no intimation that I was to have a major role in this determination.

I made one more trip, this time to observe economic conditions in the British zone of occupation. The necessary arrangements for a Command and Reconnaissance car, together with travel orders and military visas were made by Major Januarius Mullen of my Economic Intelligence unit, who accompanied me on the tour. My most vivid memory is of Cologne, the most thoroughly bombed-out city I had seen up to this time. Cologne had been the first German city to receive saturation bombing from the RAF. The moss-covered ruins from that era had been thoroughly bombed again just before the surrender. The battered shell of the burned out cathedral still dominated the skyline. In the daytime, the civilian troglodytes emerged from their cellars and cubbyholes and spread over the countryside scrounging for a bit of food. I found industrial production being carried on in the British-occupied area at a rate little above that of our own.

On August 1 we started to move up to Berlin, where an advance party had preceded us. I elected to travel in a weapons carrier with an army driver rather than by plane, together with Lieutenant Colonel Robert Bowie and Lieutenant Colonel Don McLean, who were on the staff of General Clay. I wanted to get a look at the Soviet zone of occupation on our way to Berlin.

Since we stopped for lunch in the British officers' mess in Hanover, I had an opportunity to observe the British army's cultivation of those traditions which had been of such great effect in building its *esprit de corps* through the centuries. The British officers with whom we lunched were from the Welch Fusileers. One of them remarked that it was the anniversary of the Battle of Minden fought against the French during the Seven Years' War, August 1, 1757. Their regiment had been one of the six British infantry regiments which participated in the victory. I asked whether it was a fact that these six regiments had the special right to wear roses in their garrison caps on Minden Day in remembrance of their having put roses in their caps as they passed through rose gardens on their way to the battle. He replied that this was indeed so, and that most of the Fusileers were not in Hanover since they were being sent in trucks that day to Minden so that they might put roses in their caps on the actual battlefield. We were then only five days away from the dropping of the atomic bomb on Hiroshima, which was to put a period to the millennia of warfare in which military traditions had played so vital a role. Yet even then, airpower and high explosives had already so changed the nature of warfare that the roses of Minden seemed out of another age.

Actually, there was little to be seen along the *Autobahn* to Berlin after we entered the Soviet zone at Helmstedt. The countryside seemed almost deserted. There were even hardly any domestic animals to be seen on the farms along the way. The one herd of cows which I saw was being guarded by a Soviet soldier with no one else in evidence.

The center of Berlin was an unbelievable desolation, and no area had wholly escaped severe war damage.[4] The city had not only been the object of repeated saturation air bombings, but it had been fought over street by street by the Soviet troops when they captured the city from the desperately resisting Nazis. Everywhere were enormous piles of debris from the bombed out buildings. An odor of death overhung the city, compounded of sewage backed up in destroyed sewers and of inadequately buried bodies. The Nazis had retreated to the subways in the last stages of resistance. In the

4. For a most useful description of the situation in Berlin at this time and an analysis of the whole period of General Clay's tenure of office see *Decision in Germany*, Lucius Clay, (Garden City, N. Y.: Doubleday, 1950), and Murphy, *Diplomat among Warriors*, chaps. xvi–xxii.

course of the underground fighting, the subways had been flooded, and were now choked with corpses and other debris. The German civilian population was required to clean out the subways, but it was months before the downtown sections of the subways were in operation.

The civilians had also been compelled to dig graves for the Russian soldiers who had been killed in the fighting. These had been buried anywhere they happened to fall, often at some street crossing. The German civilians had also been compelled to build neat wooden fences around these graves, to paint them, and to keep the graves supplied with fresh flowers. Such was the terror of the population that the Germans living near these Soviet graves continued to bring flowers to place on the graves after the Russian troops had moved out and we had moved in.

The civilian population was in a state of complete shock. Houses had been looted of everything to which the Soviet soldiers had taken a fancy, and there had been much wanton destruction in the process. A majority of the women from early teens to those in their sixties had been raped over a period of weeks. This was no case of troops getting out of hand. Soviet officers not only made no effort to restrain these acts but joined in them. My observations in Berlin were to confirm what I had previously observed over the years in Russia and what I was to observe there later, namely, that the disciplinary system of the Soviet army was far more severe and ruthless than that of our own or the Allied armies. The gulf between officer and soldier was also wider.

The Nazis had taught that the Slavs were an inferior race, not only without culture but incapable of acquiring it except under German direction. They had conducted themselves during their invasion of Russia on the basis of their proclaimed racial superiority, recognizing no rights for the conquered Russians. Now there was absolutely nothing to bar the Soviet troops, of lower standard of living and lower culture, from having their uninhibited way with the property and persons of a modern sophisticated urban population. The Russian troops were largely of peasant origin. The Soviet war losses had been tremendous, so that in the last stages of the war when Berlin was conquered, large numbers of non-Slavic elements had been incorporated into the Soviet combat forces. Scores of thousands of Uzbek, Kazakh, Kirghiz, Tadzhik, Tartar, and other

Asiatic peoples were still among the Soviet forces when we arrived. This added to my feeling of witnessing the immediate aftermath of the sack of a modern European city by primitive Asiatic hordes. The sack of Rome by Alaric's Goths in A.D. 410 must have been far less destructive of persons and property than was the holocaust which had just overtaken Berlin.

Ten years later when a member of the Eisenhower administration warned against too great expenditures for national defense and implied that to have inflation would be as bad as to suffer military defeat, a picture of Berlin when we entered the city August 1, 1945, inevitably arose in my mind.

The American sector of occupation in Berlin included Dahlem, Lichterfelde, and Zehlendorf, upper-class residential areas which had suffered relatively light bomb damage, although almost all the houses had been thoroughly looted by Soviet troops. By an odd coincidence, this was the area in which I had lived with my family in 1932–33 and in which I had also spent a couple of months in 1939. Indeed, the house on Archivstrasse which was given to Bowie, McLean, and myself as our billet was right beside the Podbielski Allee subway station, which in turn was the next station to Thielplatz, at a distance of only some six blocks, which had been our subway station in 1932–33.

Curiously enough, even though the subway was not in operation when we first arrived, the stations were used as centers of communication by the demoralized civil population. In the absence of all means of transport, with telephones inoperative, with no mail, no shops of any kind open, and with no local government, impromptu notices were stuck up in the stations, such as "Has anyone seen Hans Schmidt of 24 Werderstrasse, last seen just before the last big bombing?" or "Has anyone heard anything of Friedrich Schwanner, 20 Begonien Platz, taken prisoner by the Russians on the night of May 2?" There were also many proposals for barter. One of the most poignant read "Five beautifully embroidered child's undervests to exchange for bread."

As soon as possible I looked up two of the German families with whom we had been most closely associated before the war and who by great good fortune had survived. To the family of our old housekeeper, I gave a letter reading "To any Billeting Officer of the United States Forces: The people in this apartment are good people who have always been anti-Nazi in their sentiments and friendly to Americans. I should appreciate it if their apartment might be exempt from requisition." I was careful not to use official stationary and I did not use any title in signing the letter. It was effective, and indeed, the entire flat remained exempt from requisitioning as billets. The gratitude of the inhabitants was indeed warm. Similarly, I was able to help the other family, which had suffered greatly from persecution under the Nazis. From these German contacts, I got specific and detailed accounts of what had happened at the time of the Soviet capture of Berlin. Although I changed my living quarters after some ten days, I continued to have an office in the same general area.

During my last month in Berlin, I lived with Bill Draper, Bob Bowie, and Don McLean, together with a young naval lieutenant named McCormack, who was an aide to Draper, in a large villa on the Wannsee in what had been a fashionable suburb some ten miles out. The villa had been requisitioned from a German industrialist for the residence of General Draper as head of the Economics Division of the United States Group Control Council for Germany. The servants, of which there were six or seven, were presided over by Heinrich, the butler. He had been the butler of the German ambassador in Istanbul during the period, we were to learn later, when the fantastic "Cicero" operation, involving the theft of secret documents from the British ambassador, had taken place. Heinrich was later charged with having been a member of the Nazi *Gestapo* and was imprisoned but later released.

Heinrich spoke English, but since I was the only member of our group who spoke German, and since he was naturally garrulous, he talked to me whenever opportunity arose. From him and his tales of what had happened to the other servants, I got additional accounts of experiences under the Soviet occupation.

Driving out to Wannsee in the evening, we always passed a huge Soviet tank which had been placed upon a pedestal which towered over the road. A bronze plaque on the pedestal read, "To the glory of the Soviet armies." At this point this Soviet tank and its crew first breached the Nazi defenses of Berlin. It was a constant reminder of the presence of Soviet military power.

Our household was very congenial, and it was convenient for us in carrying out our work to be in constant touch with each other.

Our one problem was in inducing Bill Draper, who was a compulsive worker, to quit and come home with us to dinner, since we relied upon him for transportation. Draper carried a fantastic burden of responsibility since, as Chief of the Economics Division, he was responsible not only for the economic life of the American sector of Berlin but for the whole American occupational area of Germany. This included the feeding of the civilian population. When we arrived, each civilian was supposed to be getting 1200 calories per day but was actually getting only about 800. Laborers employed by us sometimes collapsed from hunger. An effort was made to provide one hot meal per day for the laborers employed by our forces, and the food situation, thanks largely to Bill Draper's tireless efforts, slowly improved. Nevertheless, the level of consumption of the civil population of Berlin was to remain very low for some years to come.

Bill Draper had to carry the primary responsibility for negotiating on all economic matters with the British, the French, and, above all, with the Russians. He was a superb negotiator and bargainer. I used sometimes to brief him on some complex matter on which information was incomplete, as we walked down the hall to a meeting at which he had to represent us. He would have had perhaps three minutes of briefing, yet he would absorb the necessary information and its analysis, make up his mind, and start negotiating with the appearance of complete self-confidence.

Some ten days after the close of the Potsdam Conference on August 1, the German Standard of Living Board was set up by General Clay, and I was appointed its chairman. Fortunately, this board was under General Draper as part of his Economics Division. The effective and warmly friendly working relations which already existed between us made it possible to carry out the tremendous responsibility entailed under very difficult circumstances in an incredibly short period of time.

It turned out that the German Standard of Living Board had the task of drawing up the American proposal for German reparations. This came about because of the peculiar provisions of the Potsdam Protocol. Those dealing with the reparations which were to come out of Germany were both complex and ambiguous. In general, the Protocol provided that reparations were not to come out of current German production but were to be paid by the removal of industrial capital equipment. This was to be distributed among the Russians, French, British, and Americans according to a complicated formula by which the Russians were to take their reparations out of German capital equipment in their zone and were to have in addition 25 per cent of that removed for reparations purposes from the Western zones of occupation but were to pay for three-fifths of this 25 per cent by food products from their zone of occupation.

It was the Americans who had insisted upon the payment of reparations out of industrial equipment rather than out of current production. This was a part of what might be called the "Morgenthau Effect," which was constantly cropping up in the working out of our policy in Germany. Secretary Morgenthau and his advisors had been terrified by the Nazi success in overrunning Europe. Their terror had been all the greater because they had so greatly underestimated Hitler during the days just before and just after his coming to power. Morgenthau and his advisors believed that substantially everything which could be done to weaken postwar Germany should be done lest Germany by its evil magic should regain the power to start a third world war. According to the Morgenthau doctrine, the reparations which Germany had had to pay out of current production after World War I had either actually been paid indirectly by the Allies or had merely served to build up a market for German goods.

Secretary Morgenthau and his advisors had had great influence with President Roosevelt and had been largely responsible for the implacable policy towards occupied Germany laid down in J.C.S. 1067. Secretary Morgenthau had insisted that he accompany President Truman to Potsdam and had threatened to resign if he were not invited to the conference.[5] President Truman had at once accepted Morgenthau's resignation. This, however, did not end the influence of Morgenthau's advisors. During Secretary Morgenthau's tenure of office, a process had gone on known as "Treasury Colonization" by which adherents of the Secretary had established themselves in other departments. One man who got such a position pushed for the appointment of his friends so that the colonization rapidly proliferated through the State Department, the Foreign Economic Administration, and other departments. In the U. S.

5. See also Robert Murphy, *Diplomat Among Warriors* (New York: Doubleday, 1964), p. 270.

group of the Control Council for Germany, the Financial, the Legal, and the Information Sections had been heavily infiltrated by the Treasury colonizers. The "Goat Pasture Plan for Germany," as it came to be known, was constantly revived and reasserted by the "colonizers," even though Morgenthau was no longer Secretary of the Treasury.

The French, in particular, were not happy about receiving a lot of second-hand machinery as reparations for their war losses, but could only grumble. The Russians were apparently neutral about the matter but perhaps preferred reparations in tangible form represented by capital equipment which they could immediately and directly lay their hands on. The British apparently did not wish to oppose one of the ideas which the Americans seemed always to be getting and pushing with such confidence.

According to the Potsdam Protocol, all industrial capital equipment in Germany was to be removed as reparations except that necessary to pay for the costs of the occupational forces and to provide a standard of living which was not to be greater than the average of the other European countries. The task of the German Standard of Living Board thus became that of estimating how much production was necessary to produce the stated standard of living and how much capital equipment and of what kinds it was essential to exclude from reparations in order to make this production possible. It was also necessary to compute the volume of German exports which would be necessary to provide for imports since Germany was, of course, not self-sufficient. Consequently, the German Standard of Living Board became, in effect the determiner of the level of reparations and the planning board for the postwar German economy as well.[6]

The military personnel which I had recruited for the staff of Economic Intelligence had been temporarily left behind in Frankfurt. Furthermore, top-flight economists were needed for this task rather than army officers. I was exceedingly fortunate in being able to get two highly competent economists "on loan" from other organizations. Dr. Don Humphrey, who had been on my staff when I was Consumers' Counsel in the Agricultural Adjustment Administration

6. For a most useful account of the various attempts made to work out the German reparations problem, see B. U. Ratchford and William D. Ross, *Berlin Reparations Assignment* (Chapel Hill: University of North Carolina Press, 1947), particularly chap. vii, "The Hoover Report."

was then with the United States Strategic Bombing Survey, and Dr. Edgar Hoover was then a lieutenant in the Navy on duty in Berlin. Both these economists have had distinguished careers since that time, and they did a phenomenal job with extremely limited data and very little staff and facilities. Don Humphrey directed the assembly, summations, and analysis of the data with Edgar Hoover's able assistance. I had been trying for months to have Dr. B. U. Ratchford, an economist colleague at Duke, added to my staff in Economic Intelligence, but he had been delayed by an incredible amount of red tape. He arrived in time to aid only in the final preparation of the recommendations of the German Standard of Living Board, which came to be known as the Hoover Report. He was to stay on as my successor and to bring out a more refined and complete report which was to be presented as the American position to the Economic Directorate on January 29, 1946.

It had occurred to me that the level of productivity of the German economy in 1932 at the depth of the Great Depression might be roughly the equivalent of that necessary to maintain a standard of living equal to the average standard of living of the rest of Europe in normal times. This depended upon the circumstance that the German standard of living was normally much higher than the average for Europe. The American representatives on the Allied Commission on Reparations under Ambassador Edwin Pauley had just returned from Moscow to Berlin after conversations with the Russians. Two of the economists from the Commission had come to see me. I learned to my great satisfaction that the same idea had occurred independently to them. I now proposed this solution of our problem, secure in the knowledge that I would have support, or at least no opposition to the idea, from the American representative on the Allied Commission on Reparations.

Even after this basic decision had been made, adjustments had to be made for the German loss of territory, which included the area from which a large part of the food supply of Germany normally came, for the increased population due to the influx of German refugees from the east, and for the costs of supporting the armies of occupation. It was obvious, moreover, since the production of heavy industries in all countries fell off much more sharply than did the production of consumer-goods industries during economic depressions, that it would be necessary to provide a substantially higher production for the heavy industries, particularly in the case of steel, than had been true in Germany during the Depression. While estimates had to be made for the production of each major industry, for the major exports necessary to pay for absolutely essential imports, the estimate of allowable steel production came to be the really key figure. Almost all other estimates depended upon the estimate of allowable steel production.

I took the personal responsibility for deciding that 7,800,000 tons of steel should be the tonnage for which production facilities should be retained. This meant that the production facilities for any tonnage above this amount would be available as reparations. This figure of 7,800,000 tons was only about one-third of prewar German steel production and less than one-fourth of what steel production in Western Germany was to be in 1962. Once I had chosen a figure for steel production, the level of production facilities for other industries could be set and the excess capacity made available for reparations.

General Clay was later to comment upon our recommendation on allowable steel production:

> Our experts under the leadership of . . . Dr. Calvin Hoover of Duke University, had arrived at a steel capacity of 7,800,000 tons as essential to a minimum sustaining German economy. The French experts proposed 7,000,000 tons; the Russians, 4,500,000 tons based on per capita allowance which when corrected after the population census became 4,900,000 tons; and the British, 9,000,000 tons. While we advocated a lower steel capacity than did the British, our proposed level of industry did not vary materially from their proposal in total productive output because it provided for larger capacities in other industries.
>
> Fixing the level of industry was impossible unless we could reach an agreement on steel production. I was convinced of the merits of the Hoover proposal and was amazed to receive a suggestion from the State Department that 3,500,000 tons would be adequate. This would have put the United States in favor of a more drastic program than any of the other powers. While I did not accept this suggestion, it influenced me considerably to propose figures below the 7,800,000 tons which in the hope of compromise we had settled on as the desirable capacity.[7]

7. Clay, *Decision in Germany*, p. 108.

The suggestion from the State Department that 3,500,000 tons would be adequate shows that the "Morgenthau Effect" was still operative.

None of the studies which had been made in Washington of possible levels of production for postwar Germany was available to us while we worked out our estimates. Our principal statistical source was a copy of the *Statistisches Jahrbuch* for 1943 which Lieutenant Strauss of our unit had somehow dug out of the ruins of Berlin. None of the facilities of the German universities, of research institutes, or of governmental bureaus was available to us.

Since I had assumed personal responsibility for the major decisions which had to be made in drawing up the estimates, and since I had written the text of our report, I was very conscious of the limitations of our data. When I handed the report to General Draper, I suggested that he might wish to study it for possible revisions before passing the report on to General Clay for transmission to the Quadripartite Council of the occupying powers.

Draper checked over some of the data of our report, and I called his attention to numerous points at which I had had to select a figure rather arbitrarily. "How did you arrive at the annual cost of supporting the Allied occupational armies?" he asked. "I note that you have allowed for only seven hundred and fifty thousand men, whereas there are now probably three or four million Allied soldiers in occupation." I replied, "I am sure those numbers will be greatly reduced, and besides, any larger estimate would have made it almost impossible for there to be any surplus capital equipment for removal as reparations. I got a rough figure of five dollars from our quartermaster people as the cost of maintaining one soldier for a day. I then multiplied 750,000 times 5 times 365 to get the annual cost." "Well, I am glad that you did not tamper with the number of days in the year," said Draper dryly.

When Draper had read over the report he said, "I am not going to delay handing this to General Clay while you revise it. I am going to advise that he present it without delay to the Quadripartite Council as a basis for discussion. This is a good report, and in circumstances like these, the party who gets his proposal in first has an immense advantage." Draper turned out to be right. The British later acknowledged their debt to our report in submitting their estimate, as did the French. Even the Russians, who advocated much lower figures for allowable industrial production, never tried to set up a different basis of analysis.

After General Clay had had an opportunity to read our report, General Draper asked me to discuss the report with him. I took Don Humphrey along with me since he had a more intimate acquaintance with the statistical details of the report than did I. Clay asked almost no questions but simply stated his approval of the report. Humphrey was appalled since he could not believe that Clay had had time to study the report and asked me, after the brief conference, whether we should not have encouraged Clay to ask questions. Later, when he had served as Clay's economic advisor, he fully understood why my answer was an emphatic "No!" Clay was a man of brilliant intellect and great energy who, like Draper, could absorb data and come to a decision with phenomenal speed.

Recalling the times before the war when I had seen Hitler in the Chancellory, I decided to have a look at the surroundings where he had spent his last hours. When we arrived in Berlin, an aura of mystery still surrounded the last days of Adolf Hitler. It was said that he had shot himself and that his body had been burned after it had been soaked in gasoline by his SS bodyguard just before Soviet troops captured the Chancellory. This account was later confirmed by the British writer Trevor-Roper. The Russian authorities, who were, of course, in the best position to deny or confirm this, refused to give out any information on the subject whatsoever.[8]

The Chancellory was in the Soviet sector of Berlin. Accompanied by my friend, Colonel Francis Miller, I visited the Chancellory and then went down into the underground bunker where Hitler was alleged to have shot himself. It consisted only of four or five very small rooms, quite unlike the elaborate layout which was to be featured years later in the movies.

A Polish officer who happened to be also having a look at the bunker was very insistent upon being told in precisely which one of the rooms Hitler had first shot Eva Braun, his mistress to whom he had just been married, and then shot himself. This officer could speak neither German, Russian, nor English and was quite unable to communicate with the not very bright German whom the Soviet

8. See also H. R. Trevor-Roper, *The Last Days of Hitler* (New York: Macmillan, 1947). Trevor-Roper began his investigation during the same month in which I visited the Hitler underground bunker.

authorities had installed as custodian. Since the officer did speak French, I translated his question to the German custodian, who tried to evade it. When I insisted on a reply, he replied doggedly, "I don't believe he is dead." I am inclined to believe that the Soviet authorities encouraged the doubt about Hitler's death to support their doctrine of the danger of a Nazi recrudescence.

I observed an area immediately outside the bunker where the soil had been scorched by fire and where purportedly Hitler's body had been burned. Recalling my experience on the farm of the great difficulty of burning hogs which had died of cholera, I was sure that the body could not have been wholly consumed by a fire in the open air, so that the question of the whereabouts of the remains was still unanswered. Not until 1964 did General Chuikov, the commander of Soviet troops who had taken Berlin, reveal that the charred body of Hitler had been found and removed by Soviet troops when they occupied the Chancellory.

I was particularly distressed to take leave of Bill Draper in our joint quarters on September 10, 1945, for Bill was in bed at the time with pneumonia. With some bitterness he said, "After you get home, I hope your conscience will let you sleep." I pointed out the great competence of Dr. Ratchford, whom I was leaving behind as my successor. I pointed out further that I had completed the Report of the German Standard of Living Board, that the period of four months which I had agreed to serve was at an end, and that I must begin meeting my classes at Duke almost at once. He then asked me, "Will we be able to come to an agreement with the Russians about Allied occupational policy?" I answered, "I regret to say that on the basis of my experience and recent observations, I do not think so."

It must be said that at this time all Americans in responsible positions in our occupying forces were leaning over backward to get along with the Russians. General Eisenhower was still in the state of euphoria with respect to the possibility of Soviet-American co-operation induced by the exceedingly warm welcome he had received during his visit to Moscow in August.[9] Every effort was also made by General Clay to get along with the Russians. This was likewise true of General Draper. When economist friends on the British element

9. See Robert Murphy, *Diplomat Among Warriors*, p. 280, for an account of Eisenhower's enthusiastic reception in Moscow.

of the Control Council for Germany had proposed to me that we work together informally in working out a joint recommended level of industry for Germany, I had declined on the ground that Russian suspicions might thereby be aroused. While I thus felt that we should make every effort to co-operate with the Russians, I could not honestly say that I thought this was likely. Bill Draper recovered from his pneumonia, and far from holding a grudge against me, has remained a warm friend to this day.

Ben Ratchford saw me off for Paris that same day at the Templehof Airport. It was necessary to stop off in Paris for a couple of days in order to have new travel orders cut and to arrange air transport. I felt a wave of nostalgia when I was assigned a billet in the Hotel Rue de St. Anne, which had been the headquarters of our Provost Marshal when I had checked in there on my three-day leave in Paris after the Armistice in 1918. The generally cynical black-market atmosphere in Paris in the fall of 1945 was in great contrast to the post Armistice state of exhiliration in 1918. The losses in dead and wounded of World War I had been far greater, but then there had been a sense of fulfilling the promises of Verdun, *Ils ne passeront pas* and *On les aura*. Now there was the recollection of the inglorious fall of France in 1940, and the unhappy realization of a France which had not been able to liberate itself by its own efforts.

I flew to Washington carrying official copies of my report to the State Department. I delivered copies to the appropriate officials and discussed the situation in Germany with Will Clayton, then Assistant Secretary of State. He said that he fully agreed with my recommendation for the re-establishment of civilian production in Germany as soon as possible. He pointed out, however, that in the present state of American public opinion, it was simply impossible for the State Department to take such a position officially at that time. I think he was right in his appraisal. I left Washington September 15. On September 18 I began meeting my classes at Duke. On October 8 the storm broke.

It began with the major news story in the *New York Times* of that day, starting on the front page and continuing through several columns, written from Berlin by the *Times* correspondent, Raymond Daniell. The news story was headlined "U. S. EXPERTS URGE REICH EXPORT RISE; RUSSIANS SUSPICIOUS." The basic statistics of our Report were given quite accurately, with one exception. It was implied that I had recommended the retention of 10,000,000 tons of steel making capacity for Germany, whereas our actual recommendation was for 7,800,000 tons. The basic assumptions on which the Report was based and the principles we had worked out for the relation of the German standard of living to that of the rest of Europe, the connection between the need for exports to pay for necessary imports, and the provision for an increased population in addition to the costs of the Armies of Occupation were set forth very competently. There were long quotes from the Report. The Report had been classified as "Secret," but someone had leaked it to Daniell, probably the Russians or the Morgenthau "colonizers" with the U. S. Group of the Control Council. I do not feel, however, that there was any sound reason why the Report should have remained classified and Daniell certainly cannot be blamed for his "scoop."

The general tone of the story was quite hostile. Daniell suggested that the Report indicated a joint American-British attempt to repudiate the stern terms of the Potsdam Protocol, which had been based squarely on J.C.S. 1067 and "which first appeared in rough draft at Quebec and was discussed and adopted in principle by Premier Stalin in Yalta." Daniell stated, "The group that prepared the report was headed by Calvin Hoover, Duke University. He was acting as economic advisor to Brig. General William F. Draper, American member of the economics directorate of the Allied Control Council and in civilian life a member of the firm of Dillon, Read & Co." Several individuals who had been associated with American industry in civilian life were listed as associated with me. In fact, those mentioned had not participated in drawing up the Report, although I had discussed matters informally with some of them, and it is possible that their opinion concerning the Report had been asked by General Draper. However, not the smallest detail in the Report had been altered because of any comments which these very competent men might have made.

Daniell's story caused a tremendous furor. I was widely denounced in the press. The radio commentators, from Robert St. John on the left to Fulton Lewis on the right, denounced me as an appeaser who favored a soft peace for Germany. The previous connection of General Draper with Dillon, Read & Co. was always referred to, and it became customary to refer to me as "an economist from Duke University with important Wall Street connections." To this day I have never unearthed these connections. One columnist referred to me as "the well-known reactionary celebrity."

The "Society for the Prevention of World War III" began an attack on the Report which was to continue for many months. Its publication stated, "It should also be noted that the key experts of the Hoover report are men who have personal business ties with Germany." [10] In fact, of the economists who worked on the Report and had responsibility for any of the data or conclusions in it, none of us had ever had any business connections in Germany whatever.

Leland Stowe, the European correspondent of the *Chicago Daily News,* wrote that the Hoover Report had been responsible for the collapse of the Council of Foreign Ministers in London in September, 1945. Everything had been going well until the Soviet authorities in Berlin had been handed their copy of the Hoover Report, according to Stowe. The Russians instantly became suspicious, and no progress could be made thereafter.

In a press conference shortly after the *Times'* news story, General Clay came under heavy attack. He calmly explained and defended the Report, in the face of news stories such as that of *Time Magazine* of October 22, which began: "Last week U. S. Military Government experts published an interpretation which might well wreck the policy itself." It was further commented, "Soviet tempers and suspicions flared." *Time* went on, "The Crucial question: did the Hoover report represent the official U. S. position?" Eisenhower, speaking in Frankfurt had the answer: 'No.' . . . Said he, 'I would not stay here for five minutes if I thought that for expediency it would be up to me to modify the Potsdam Agreement. . . . I say let Germany find out what it means to start a war.' "

Although I fear that I am unduly sensitive to criticism, I was fully prepared to take the major responsibility for the Report, and the almost universally hostile reaction to it. Since I was now out of the government, I was glad to be able to draw on myself the kind of blame which could be very painful to one who could be held responsible in his governmental position.

Very soon the Colmer Report, brought out by a U. S. Congressional delegation visiting Berlin, supported my general position that

10. *Prevent World War III,* No. 13, Feb.-March 1946, p. 4.

it was going to be necessary to allow the resumption of a large volume of industrial production and exports for Germany. Still later, the Herbert Hoover Report took a like position. By the time of the development of the "Cold War" and the Berlin Blockade, the whole policy of limiting production of German industry for peaceful purposes had been abandoned.

My report had materially hastened the inauguration of a policy which was essential if Germany and Western Europe were to be able to resist a Communist take-over. I was to participate later in the formulation of the Marshall Plan and in its administration. Without the Marshall Plan, free Europe would very likely not have survived. Without the restoration of German industrial production, however, we might never have got the Marshall Plan off the ground, and it might not have been successful even if we could have got it started.

Chapter seventeen. *Foreign economic aid*

My life's motivation had now become resistance to the threat of the totalitarian state to liberty. My observations in Soviet Russia and in Nazi Germany had left me with the preference for death as an alternative to life under a totalitarian regime. The prospect of the triumph of tyranny without the opportunity to risk death with any hope of winning the fight for the survival of human dignity filled me with horror. Thought and action would both be required for successful resistance to totalitarian tyranny.

If liberty were to survive, it was essential that the nature of the collectivist totalitarian state and the contrasting nature of the capitalistic, parliamentary, democratic economic and political systems should be understood. What were the economic and political forces which brought totalitarian states into existence? How could the development of these forces be prevented? Since evolution away from pure laissez-faire and individual enterprise was taking place in capitalistic countries, would a point of no return be reached, beyond which lay the totalitarian state?

My research and teaching had been devoted for years to an attempt to answer such questions. Thought, teaching, and writing were, however, not enough if tyranny was to be successfully resisted. Action was necessary to maintain and develop the economic well-being of the United States and the rest of the free world. Action took the form of participation on the national scene in the work of the Committee for Economic Development.[1] My connection with

1. After the publication of my *International Trade and Domestic Employment,* I was to serve for a number of years on the Research and Advisory Board of the

CED brought me in contact with Paul Hoffman and was to lead to my participation with him in the formulation and administration of the Marshall Plan in the United States and in Europe. On the regional scene, action took the form of directing the research of the Committee of the South, which was affiliated with the National Planning Association.[2]

However successful our economic and political system, it might be crushed by brute force. It had required World War II to protect the free world against Nazism and Fascism. Without the sacrifice of millions of lives, liberty would have been destroyed. Nazism and Fascism had been eliminated, but now once more action was required to resist the threat of Soviet miliary power. If our will and our military means to resist could be maintained, we could hope that millions of lives would not again have to be sacrificed in the resistance to tyranny.

Consequently, along with my efforts to strengthen the domestic and international economies of the free world, I devoted my energies to arousing our government to the dangers of Soviet attack and to the necessity for strengthening our armed forces. I was convinced that during the period of the disintegration of our armed forces after World War II, it was our monopoly of atomic weapons that had halted Soviet expansion by military force. I feared, however, that unless we maintained sufficient conventional armed forces to resist an attack by Soviet or satellite forces at some point in the free world, we might find ourselves in a situation in which we would not be willing to use atomic weapons until it would be too late.

Even our monopoly of atomic weapons would not have prevented the Soviet take-over of Western Europe if its economic well-being had not been restored with the aid of the Marshall Plan. Yet, without military protection, a prosperous Western Europe would have been so much the more valuable a prize for Stalin's armies. There could be no doubt that the Soviet government would also develop atomic weapons at no distant date. When this happened, we could no longer surely count upon our unilateral threat to use atomic

---

CED. For an account of the impact of the CED and of my association with it, see Karl Schriftgiesser, *Business Comes of Age* (New York: Harper, 1961, particularly pp. 64–65, 118–119, 123, 127, 133).

2. A number of research studies were brought out, including *Negro Employment in the South,* National Planning Association, 1954, and Calvin B. Hoover and B. U. Ratchford, *Economic Resources and Policies of the South* (New York: Macmillan, 1951).

weapons to stop a Soviet attack by conventional forces. I was appalled at the prospect of reducing our armed forces for budgetary reasons in view of the tense situation produced by the Soviet blockade of Berlin, and by the constant possibility of Soviet attack elsewhere. The irresponsibility of saving several billions of dollars through cuts in our military budget, which the Bureau of the Budget and the Council of Economic Advisors were urging, while risking losing a war to Stalinist Russia, horrified me. I did, indeed, favor a firm attitude in dealing with the Soviet government, but a stiff attitude supported by only weak conventional forces seemed to me to entail the greatest possible danger of a nuclear war through Soviet miscalculation.

I wrote to President Truman on April 2, 1948, pointing out the grave risks of a firm policy towards the Soviet government accompanied by inadequate military preparations on our part. President Truman replied tartly in a letter of April 6, 1948:

> In November 1945 I sent a Message to the Congress on a program for preparedness to meet any contingency. The Congress saw fit to pay no attention to that. That suggestion was renewed in the State of the Union Message of 1946—again in the spring of 1946 and on at least three occasions since then. Notably in the Message to the Special Session last fall and again in the Message of the State of the Union in January of this year.
>
> It isn't the President who needs instruction on preparedness, it's the people who control the policy and the purse strings who need it.
>
> I appreciated very much your taking the trouble to write me but you should try your persuasive powers on the Members of Congress from your State.
>
> HARRY S. TRUMAN

I acknowledged the justice of President Truman's reply. I proceeded to write to the Members of Congress from North Carolina, to my friend, Russell Wiggins,[3] now editor of the *Washington Post*, and other editors of the metropolitan press and to my friends in the Department of Defense.

In the meantime I continued my efforts through lectures and

3. I had been closely associated with Wiggins since early New Deal days. Wiggins has been a frequent recipient of my "letters to the editor." The contacts I had had with newspaper correspondents in Moscow, Berlin, London, Stockholm, as well as in Washington, had been of the greatest service to me.

articles to condition the American public to the necessity for the restoration of a viable Western Germany [4] as essential to the economic recovery of Europe. I recalled the impact of Keynes' prophetic *The Economic Consequences of the Peace,* which he had published just after the end of World War I with reference to the disastrous consequences for Europe of reparations demands in the Treaty of Versailles far beyond Germany's ability to pay. I wrote to Keynes asking whether he would be willing once more to call attention to the unfortunate consequences for Europe of a too punitive reparations policy towards Germany. Keynes replied that he was so much involved in other matters relating to international economic relations that he did not wish to intervene in the matter of German reparations.

I had been very much struck during my work in Germany in 1945 by the way our military commanders were being confronted by the necessity for making political and economic decisions. General Clay had often had to make such decisions in the absence of instructions from the State Department. He had been fortunate in having the assistance of Robert Murphy as his political advisor. Yet Clay's experience as well as that of our other commanders in Japan, Austria, and elsewhere demonstrated the urgency of providing some political and economic training for military personnel just before they moved into the upper echelons. It was particularly desirable that this military personnel should have experience in working with officials from the State Department.

It was with these purposes in mind that I participated, in 1946, with Generals Gruenther and Landon, Admiral Hill, and Professors Langer of Harvard, Baxter of Williams, Wolfers of Yale, and Wright of Princeton, in setting up the National War College. A type of postgraduate program, involving the preparation of research papers, a series of lectures and discussion by resident faculty and invited specialists, was formulated. Officers of field rank with the normal expectation of advancement to general officer or the equivalent rank, from the Army, Navy, Marine Corps, and Air Forces, together with a smaller number of officials of comparable rank from

4. For example, "The Future of the German Economy," *American Economic Review Proceedings,* XXXVI No. 2 (May 1946) 642–649; "Germany and European Economic Recovery," *Yale Review,* XXXVII (Spring 1948), 385–399; and "Germany: The Economic Problem," in *Germany and the Future of Europe,* ed. Hans J. Morgenthau (Chicago: The University of Chicago Press, 1951), pp. 40–50.

the State Department composed the student body. I was to serve on the Board of Consultants of the National War College for a number of years and usually gave at least one lecture per year.

On June 22, 1947, President Truman appointed a committee to determine the ability of the United States to give economic assistance to foreign countries. I was appointed a member of this President's Committee on Foreign Aid, which came to be commonly called "The Committee of Nineteen" or "The Harriman Committee," from the Secretary of Commerce who served as Chairman. Its members were chosen from the fields of finance, economics, business, education, and labor. Among them were Owen D. Young, Robert M. LaFollette, Jr., Paul Hoffman, James B. Carey, George Meany, Chester Davis, Edward Mason, and John L. Collyer. Richard Bissell was appointed Executive Secretary of the Committee.

In his statement setting up the committee, President Truman said that "the recovery of production abroad is a matter of concern to every American." "The non-partisan committee will be requested," he stated, "to determine the facts with respect to the character and quantities of United States resources available for economic assistance to foreign countries, and to advise me, in the light of those facts, on the limits within which the United States may safely and wisely plan to extend such assistance and on the relation between this assistance and our domestic economy."

The appointment of the committee was an outgrowth of Secretary of State Marshall's speech at Harvard on June 5, 1947, and of British Foreign Minister Bevin's acceptance of Marshall's proposal on June 14. The foreign economic aid program which the committee was to recommend consequently became known as the Marshall Plan. The Marshall Plan, in turn, was a development of the "Truman Doctrine," which had been declared on March 12, under which massive economic aid had been extended to Turkey and Greece to enable them to resist Soviet aggression. Without this aid, both Turkey and Greece would have been overrun and would have become Soviet satellites. There can be no doubt that the primary motive for the Marshall Plan was to enable Western Europe to resist Soviet aggression.[5] There was no mention of this, however, in Marshall's speech.

5. For the evidence on this point, see my article "Foreign Economic Aid and Communism," *The Journal of Political Economy*, LXIV (Feb., 1951), 1–13.

There can be no doubt that the committee was committed from the outset to recommend a substantial amount of foreign aid. Such committees may be intended to perform honest investigatory functions, as this committee certainly was, but they are appointed primarily for educative and propaganda purposes. The investigation is intended to furnish support for the necessary legislation in Congress. Such committees have now become an almost routine part of the legislative process when new programs must be put through Congress by the incumbent administration. I do not know of any case in which a committee of this sort has produced a firmly negative report.

The committee's report was sent to President Truman on November 7, 1947. After a detailed analysis of the demand and supply situation in the United States, covering food and stocks of other important consumer goods, together with those of essential raw materials and of fabricating capacities for steel and other capital goods industries, the report concluded that it would be possible to meet the minimum needs for European economic recovery. These needs would be reflected in a deficit in the European balance of payments with the United States of some 22 billion dollars over the next four years.

The committee did not attempt to recommend a definite amount of aid to be provided by the United States government during the four-year period contemplated. It was estimated, however, that aid required from the United States government would be between 12 and 17 billion dollars. The committee emphasized strongly that aid extended must be on a year-to-year basis, "subject to constant, vigilant review in Congress." It was emphasized that the annual rate of aid should taper off, with the expectation of a complete end to governmental aid at or soon after the end of the four-year period. One of the sentences in the report for which I must accept major responsibility read: "The Committee regards as nonsense the idea which prevails to a considerable degree in this country and abroad that we need to export our goods and services as free gifts to insure our own prosperity."[6] This idea, which continues to crop up to the present moment as an argument in favor of foreign aid, is, indeed, nonsense. Whenever additional purchasing

6. *European Recovery and American Aid: A Report by the President's Committee on Foreign Aid* (Washington, D. C., Nov. 7, 1947), p. 3.

power for the output of our economy is required, there is no reason why tax reduction, increased governmental expenditures, wage increases, monetary-expansion measures to encourage additional investment by domestic industry, and the like would not function as efficiently as purchasing power as dollars placed in the hands of foreign governments or their citizens. Such measures to increase either foreign or domestic demand may improve the market for our goods and services, cause inflation, or both, depending upon the moderation and technical skill with which they are carried out.

There had been some suggestions to the committee that our financial aid should be wholly in the form of grants since there was really no prospect of repayment and the overhanging weight of unrepayable loans would always be a threat to the financial stability of the countries aided. I urged, on the contrary, that a substantial portion of aid should be in the form of loans. It seemed to me that the necessity of paying interest on a portion of the aid and even of providing repayment at some future date would have disciplinary effect upon the budgetary policies of the aided countries. Further, I felt that our government might itself need financial aid at some time in the future and that it would be far better to have the promissory notes of the European governments as an asset rather than to rely upon memory of our past generosity. The very great usefulness of repayments on these loans is evident when we ourselves are now confronted by deficits in our balance of payments.

Mr. Owen D. Young had proposed in our committee that financial aid should not be given to any government which proposed to carry out the nationalization of its industries or to construct state-owned industries. I opposed this proposal on the grounds that it was highly inadvisable for the United States government to try to influence the internal policies of the countries aided. The majority of the committee agreed with my point of view.[7]

Almost six months were to pass after the Report of the Harriman Committee before the economic aid program could be

7. This policy of not interfering with the domestic policies of countries receiving financial aid was unfortunately later to be used by the underdeveloped countries to which our program of furnishing economic aid was later extended to support the doctrine of "No Strings Attached to Economic Aid." I am convinced, on the contrary, that there are many cases in which not *strings* but *ropes* should be attached to our aid. There can be no doubt, for example, that at the present moment no aid should be extended to Indonesia so long as an aggressive and expansionist policy towards Malaysia is maintained.

authorized by Congress and an Administrator appointed. In the meantime, at the request of Dean Acheson, Paul Hoffman and I had offered testimony before the Senate Foreign Relations Committee in support of the necessary legislation. We appeared in the role of private citizens who had been members of the Presidential Committee and not as governmental officials. I emphasize this point for reasons which will soon be seen.

The selection of Paul Hoffman as Administrator of the Economic Aid Administration provided for in the new legislation was most fortunate. Hoffman was a successful industrialist who had devoted much time to the study of both national and international problems. The corporation of which he had been president had always enjoyed excellent relations with labor. While Chairman of the Committee for Economic Development, he had become accustomed to working with academic economists, upon whom he would have to rely in large part for technical advice. He had no trace of arrogance and was to be eminently successful in dealing with Congressional committees.

Immediately after his appointment, Hoffman appointed three economists who had been active in the work of the Harriman Committee to act as advisors—Edward Mason, Richard Bissell, and myself.[8] At Hoffman's request, I came to Washington to aid in staffing the new organization. I remained to assist in getting the funds required for ECA through the House Appropriations Committee. The Appropriations Committee was headed by John Taber, a conservative Republican, who obviously was not happy at the prospect of his committee's allocating over five billion dollars of American taxpayers' money for the use of foreign governments. I had appeared before Congressional committees a number of times, but this was my first experience before such a committee in the role of a bureaucrat. Paul Hoffman made an excellent presentation, stressing his determination to see to it that the funds appropriated would be carefully administered, and that the maximum of self-help would be required from the European countries. He quoted with approval a statement by Averell Harriman, "The United States wants to make Europe self-sustaining and then get out and tend to our own business at home."

8. For an account of the first moments of Hoffman's organization of the ECA, see "The Administration: Man in a Hurry," *Time, LI,* No. 16 (April 19, 1948), 23–24.

I had always been and still am convinced of the vital role played by Congressional committees in their investigatory roles. The power of the Appropriations Committee to examine and cross-examine officials of the executive branch of the government is absolutely essential if the public is to have any effective control over the governmental purse. Such control is one of the most fundamental barriers to the seizure of power by a potential dictator. Of even greater practical importance is the bar which such hearings before legislative committees affords to unchecked proposals from the bureaucracy. It requires more fortitude than most administrators at successive levels possess to oppose the pet plans and projects of their subordinates in the bureaucracy, however costly, extravagant, and even outlandish these proposals may be, since they are usually camouflaged to appear laudable in purpose or are difficult of detection or both.

Yet the plight of conscientious legislators who try to scrutinize items in an appropriations bill of over five billion dollars is a serious one. We spent twenty minutes over an item of twenty tons of pulses (peas and beans) for Austria. When I volunteered to answer a question raised by Congressman Case with respect to the balance of payments of Belgium, I let myself in for very rough treatment, in which he was joined by Congressman Keith. I remained respectful and tried to withdraw from the controversy after I had supplied the requested information. The Congressmen were not willing for me to escape so easily. I was subjected to a verbal battering. Only gradually did it dawn on me that there was nothing personal in the attack. As members of the opposition Republican party, they had the *Congressional Record* in mind and the coverage they might get in the press. Even at my most uncomfortable moments, I was glad that Congressmen had this right to harass us bureaucrats.

After the hearings were concluded, I was introduced to Congressman Taber in his chambers by Congressman Judd. In the course of our friendly discussion, in which it became apparent that Mr. Taber was using the terms "economist" and "communist" as substantially synonymous, I remarked to Mr. Taber that I also was an economist. "Well," said Mr. Taber dryly, "doubtless there are some economists who are not communists."

After the hearings I returned to finish the academic year at Duke. Directly thereafter Averell Harriman, who had been placed in charge of setting up the Economic Cooperation Administration in Paris, urged me to join him as Economic Advisor and Chief of Program Planning. I stipulated that I could spend no more than four months at the task and was assured that I would be released at the end of that period. Once more the job was presented simply as one of getting the operation under way. With this understanding, I flew at once to Paris, taking with me Professor B. U. Ratchford to serve as my deputy.

The first order of business was determining how the $4,870,-000,000 of the first year's Congressional appropriation to the Economic Cooperation Administration for economic aid to Europe should be divided among the eighteen Western European countries, in addition to occupied Western Germany, represented on the Organization for European Economic Cooperation. The Marshall Plan had been "sold" to Congress largely as a program for restoring the industries of Europe, devastated by World War II. It might have been supposed that United States aid would consequently have been distributed according to the relative amount of destruction suffered by each country to its industrial facilities. In fact, such destruction had been relatively minor and offered almost no basis for determining the allocation of financial aid. Indeed, very little in the way of industrial machinery needed to be furnished by the United States. Most of such machinery had been and still could be produced by European capital equipment, which had suffered only minor damage. What was needed was liquid capital funds out of which repairs on equipment could be paid for and new and modern machinery installed to increase the productivity of European industry. Most of these liquid capital funds could be and were to be supplied out of domestic savings and investment. The need was "to fill up the depleted pipelines" of food and raw materials which had to be paid for in dollars which were not available without United States aid. Stated in another way, United States economic aid was needed to meet a deficit in the European balance of payments until increased productivity and exports brought the balance of payments into equilibrium.

Innumerable policy decisions had to be made. The amount of a particular country's deficit in the balance of payments depended upon many factors, including each country's national economic policy as well as our own policy decisions. For example, should Belgian capitalists be allowed to subscribe to an issue of dollar bonds floated on the New York market? Under normal circumstances the answer would have been an unqualified yes since this would apparently mean an addition to the total amount of international investment capital. But if this were permitted, the amount of the Belgian subscription to the bond issue would have added to the total European deficit in the balance of payments. Similarly, British external investment which had been the normal process for centuries would have added to Britain's deficit in the balance of payments. Even permitting India to draw upon accumulated sterling balances would have a similar effect.

Should OEEC countries be permitted to import American passenger cars? The question sounds absurd. But remember, the American taxpayer would be paying for these automobiles, if the deficit in the balance of payments were increased by permitting such imports. But suppose such imports were forbidden? This would please European manufacturers, but one could imagine the outraged roar from American automobile manufacturers. Should European importees be allowed to import a million boxes of American grapefruit? American grapefruit growers offered the grapefruit at attractive prices, but American taxpayers might not have been happy at having to pay for them.

It was impossible to escape entirely having to answer almost countless questions, of which the above are actual examples. For ECA to have answered all the questions would have meant taking the responsibility for planning the balance of payments of each country and a good part of its domestic economy as well. The decision was consequently made to place the primary responsibility for the division of the $4,870,000,000 of United States aid in the hands of the representatives of the eighteen countries of the OEEC.

A committee of the OEEC was set up to carry out this monumental task. At the request of this committee, Harriman asked me to serve as the chairman of an informal committee to be available for consultation with the OEEC Committee. The other members of the committee were Professor Lincoln Gordon, later our ambassador to Brazil, and Colonel, now Major General, Charles Bonesteel. The committee met at a resort hotel at Chantilly and carried out its task with rather surprising success. It is true that the representatives of some of the smaller countries attempted, in violation of our understanding, to induce me to use my influence in increasing the amount of aid going to these countries. This did not, however, present a major problem.

I had previously had to do in other governmental organizations with the problem of what came to be known as "counterpart funds." These were the local currencies which accrued to the treasuries of the individual countries when imports of commodities, say flour or steel, paid for by United States aid, were sold to importers. These funds in local currencies could be used to a limited extent in paying for expenditures by the United States government in these local currencies. The much larger amounts remaining could be spent by the recipient governments only for purposes intended to promote price stability and increase productivity, but only with the agreement of the United States government.

We now worked out a system of "drawing rights" by which a country such as Britain undertook to allow, say, the Greek or Turkish government to pay for needed imports from Britain out of these counterpart funds. These "drawing rights" amounted to some hundreds of millions of dollars and were a substantial addition to the total of economic aid received by the countries which received the "drawing rights." The donor country was credited with the amount of the drawing right and had no further liability with respect to the United States for these funds. The recipient country in turn assumed the liability of these funds in respect to the United States government. Such a use of these counterpart funds had not been contemplated in the authorization and appropriation of funds for the ECA—indeed, such use, narrowly construed, may have been illegal. The arrangement was so obviously in our national interest that I gladly assumed my share of the responsibility for working it out.

On July 4, 1948, I flew with Harriman to Vienna for a conference dealing primarily with counterpart funds with representatives of the Austrian government. I was pleased when we were joined by my old friend Bill Draper, now Under Secretary of the Army. The conference with the Austrian government was quickly and satisfactorily concluded. I had the misfortune to come down with a severe attack of hay fever and had to spend a week in one of our military hospitals, staying on after the rest of our delegation had left.

My stay in Vienna enabled me to compare the status of our occupational forces vis-à-vis the Russians with that in Berlin. The arrangements in Vienna worked more satisfactorily, largely because our right of access had been formally recognized by the Russians. Vienna, although suffering some war damage, had not had to undergo anything like the air bombing which Berlin had undergone. Neither had Vienna been defended street by street against Soviet ground forces as had Berlin, and the damage from this source had thus been escaped. The civilian population of Vienna had, however, suffered very much the same looting and rape from the Soviet occupying forces as that of Berlin.

The relations among the economists of ECA, those who represented their countries on the OEEC, and those of the secretariat of OEEC were most cordial. Robert Marjolin, the Secretary General of OEEC, carried out his administrative and liaison functions with admirable efficiency. All our opposite numbers, however, complained at the mass of reports and statistical data which ECA required. No other country possessed a substantial fraction of the number of economists and statisticians of the United States. The country representatives complained that they had to send out our questionnaires to their home offices, then leave over the weekends and go home to answer the questionnaires before returning to Paris. Often the data asked for did not exist and the answers simply had to be guessed at. This passion of our economists and statisticians for voluminous and frequent reports was commonly referred to as the "American disease." Apparently this was based on an analogy to the "Italian disease," under which name syphilis was first known when it was widely spread throughout Europe after the capture and sack of Rome by the troops of the Constable de Bourbon in 1527.

Our statisticians continually pushed to get more statistical information from the countries receiving aid. How was it possible to determine the proper level of food imports and hence the allowable deficit in the balance of payments without knowing the average number of calories in the Italian diet as compared with the Swedish one? I did not improve my standing among our statisticians by refusing to press for an added volume of statistics, but instead I ordered that a number of reports be dispensed with altogether. My order did not eradicate the "American disease," but it was at least a palliative which was gratefully welcomed by the country representatives on the OEEC. I did manage to get the quality of the remaining reports improved.

It had originally been understood that I was to set up program planning sections in the eighteen ECA missions in the various European capitals. With the exception of the trip to Vienna, I never got out of Paris. Averell Harriman always insisted that I was needed in Paris. Officially we worked six days a week, but almost invariably on Sundays my phone would ring about ten o'clock and Averell would ask whether I could step over to the Annex of the Embassy, which was just next door to the Crillon, where I lived. We would then work all day on some pressing problem.

To a greater extent than with any other cabinet minister or chief administrator with whom I worked, Harriman insisted on being familiar with the details of the problems which he had to decide. Furthermore, he would sometimes consult with the heads of OEEC delegations and make decisions without the immediate personal presence of his advisors. Many claimed that he did not adequately delegate responsibility. For myself, I felt this insistence upon doing work and taking responsibility personally was admirable. It reflected, in part at least, the revulsion which Harriman had developed as a young man to a life of idleness and luxury. He had seized the opportunity of public service when he had been offered the job of assistant to General Hugh Johnson, the first Administrator of NRA. Thereafter he had remained in governmental service almost continually. I believe that he actually cherished the *work* that went along with a governmental post.

Now that the allocation of funds among the OEEC countries had been made, the system of reciprocal drawing rights worked out, and the most pressing of the policy questions dealt with, I began the process of getting relieved from my post. The customary difficulties arose. Paul Hoffman called Dean Wannamaker at Duke asking that my leave be extended. Wannamaker coldly but quite correctly said that that was up to me. I told Harriman and Hoffman that I did not want to ask for a further extension of leave since I had been gone so much from my classes. Fortunately a successor, Dr. H. B. Arthur, was found and I returned to Duke in time to resume my fall classes.

Following the inauguration of the Marshall Plan, it became the policy of our government to encourage the economic and political unification of Europe in every possible way. Indeed, the Organization for European Economic Cooperation, through which our financial aid was administered, was looked upon as a prototype of an economic chamber for Europe. A major motive for our encouraging European integration was the belief that a united Europe could resist Soviet aggression more successfully. Unification was also counted upon to improve greatly European productivity through the removal of trade barriers and thus to eliminate need for further United States financial aid.

With the motivation of providing unofficial encouragement for European unification, Bill Donovan, Ken Galbraith, and I were appointed by the Council on Foreign Relations as United States observers at a meeting of the European Movement in London in April, 1949. Characteristically, Bill Donovan chose at the last moment to aid in the investigation of the assassination of an American newspaper correspondent in Greece and so did not attend.

The European Movement was a non-governmental organization with representatives from all the countries of Western Europe dedicated to European economic and political integration. It was this organization which gave the impetus to the Schuman Plan for the confederation of French and German iron, steel, and coal interests and eventually for the Common Market.

The Conservative party took part much more actively in the meetings than did the Labour party, which was then in power. Churchill and other Conservative leaders participated in the meeting, while only minor officials from the Labour government were present. (I came into momentary contact with Harold Macmillan again at this conference and found him the same cold fish whom I had met ten years before.) I had supposed that the Conservatives would be more nationalistic than the Labour party and hence less willing to submerge British interests in a united Europe. Labour representatives indicated privately that they feared that European unification would hamper their plans for a planned and socialized national economy. I note that the relative attitudes of the British parties is still reflected in their attitude towards joining the Common Market.

Since I was deeply concerned about developing European economic viability, I now agreed to participate in a study sponsored by the Twentieth Century Fund and the National Planning Association of the ability of the United States to absorb additional imports from Europe. It appeared that only in this way could the European deficit in the balance of payments with the United States be corrected and the need for financial aid ended.

My concern with the unfavorable balance of payments of Europe with the United States seems almost comical now that the imbalance has been for some years sharply in the other direction. At this time, however, no one considered a United States deficit in the balance of payments remotely possible. We had no premonition that massive United States financial aid would begin to be extended to underdeveloped countries even before aid to Europe had come to an end, that these underdeveloped countries would begin to demand the continuance and even the increase in the amount of our aid as a matter of right, and that the United States would pay such a large part of the military costs of the coming NATO Alliance. We could not foresee that by the year 1963 the United States financial aid would have proliferated into numerous additional forms and would be extended to 105 countries instead of to the 20 countries of the original foreign economic aid program.

Thus the implicit assurance given by our Committee of Nineteen to Congress and the public in setting up the Marshall Plan that foreign economic aid would be temporary proved abortive. We should have realized that once a bureaucracy of the size necessary to administer the Marshall Plan got established it would inevitably find arguments to justify its continuance and even its expansion.

The study of imports was planned jointly with Professor Don Humphrey.[9] In the course of our study I spent the summer of 1950 in Western Europe analyzing the prospects for enlarging European exports to the United States. I had conferences with governmental officials, industrialists, bankers, with our own diplomatic representatives, as well as with our ECA staff.

European industrialists were not optimistic about their ability to increase sales in the mass markets of the United States in spite of a number of ingenious governmental devices for the subsidy of dollar-earning exports. Nevertheless, it was plain that European

9. I had to withdraw from our joint study when the Korean War broke out, and I had to return to the intelligence service. I continued to confer with Professor Humphrey as the study developed, however, and contributed a chapter to the book, *American Imports* (New York: The Twentieth Century Fund, 1955).

economic recovery was already well under way. Prewar levels of productivity had already been surpassed. The real difficulty in building up exports to the United States lay in the still unsatisfied demand of European consumers for goods. Why try to sell goods in the United States when the domestic market was still unsatisfied?

Nevertheless, the balance of payments was about to turn in the opposite direction, as the immediate postwar need for abnormally large European imports from the United States began to subside as European productivity improved. This increased productivity was facilitated not only by financial aid from the United States, which aided in rebuilding European industry with the most modern equipment, but by technological advice from the United States. During this period teams of European industrialists traveled to the United States and were encouraged and given financial aid to visit American plants and to familiarize themselves with the latest techniques. It was already apparent that the Marshall Plan was going to be an outstanding success in facilitating the economic recovery of Europe.

I took the occasion of this trip to spend a few days at Bussieres-le-Belmont, in eastern France, visiting Madame Victor Amiotte, mother of the French family with whom I had lived just before going to the front in 1918. I had a look at the local industry of basket weaving, which had formerly had an export market in the United States. This market had now disappeared. Of greater interest were the talks I had with the village grocer who had been the leader of the local *maquis* during the Nazi occupation. He spoke with nostalgia of those times when all Frenchmen were united in the resistance against the Germans—even the Communists, he said.

Madame Amiotte took me to see the monument which had been erected over the graves of two French girls who had been nurses serving the *maquis*. They had been caught by the Nazi SS troops, who had tortured them to death and buried their bodies under stable manure. The resistance leader told me with grim satisfaction that they had captured and executed the Nazi officer who had been responsible for the murders. He added grudgingly that the SS officer had refused to beg for his life. The incident helped to place in perspective the atrocities which had been inflicted upon the German people by the French troops in our forces of occupation. Doubtless the Russian troops in Berlin had also heard of similar atrocities by the Nazis in Russia. Such incidents were to come to mind when later I heard the argument in the United States that defense expenditures on so high a level as to produce inflation would be as bad as losing a war.

Chapter eighteen. *Return to intelligence; a grand design, the Soviet Union revisited*

I received the news of the outbreak of the Korean War in Rome in late June, 1950. The North Korean attack confirmed my expectation of a series of probes to test our willingness and ability to resist Soviet expansion. The breaking of the Soviet blockade of Berlin by our air lift had been a plus for us. However, our failure to smash the blockade on the ground by sending an armed detachment to Berlin over the *autobahn*, accompanied later by cuts in our military budget, had led Stalin to believe that we would not employ our armed forces to save the government of South Korea from defeat if his satellite forces attacked.

My prognosis of the probable reaction of our government to the North Korean attack agreed pretty closely with that of Stalin. However, neither Stalin nor I had given sufficient weight to the determining factor in the crisis, namely, President Harry Truman's guts. Our early military reverses, following so closely upon the boasts of Secretary of Defense Louis Johnson about what we would do to a North Korean attack, confirmed my worst fears about what the budgetary cuts had done to our military strength.

I expected momentarily to be called back into governmental service, so I hastened the rest of my economic survey of Western Europe as much as I could. I had planned to attend the sessions of the International Economic Association, which was meeting on the Riviera, but I cut short my trip and returned to resume my academic duties in the fall. I was not actually called back into the intelligence services until December, 1950, immediately after the Chinese Communist forces entered the war and inflicted crushing reverses upon our forces along the Yalu River.

I had made up my mind that if I once more had to enter the intelligence services, I would not again undertake to operate an intelligence network in the field or personally take on intelligence missions. I felt that by reason of age, experience, and special training, it would be more appropriate for me to analyze intelligence data and to draw conclusions from such analyses than to carry out more active roles as I had done in OSS. Fortunately, General Walter Bedell Smith had also come to just this conclusion. I agreed to serve as a member of a board of national estimates, composed largely of professors, generals, and admirals. It was a pleasure to find myself associated once more with Allen Dulles and with other friends of OSS days.

It was the responsibility of our board to produce intelligence estimates which could be used as the background by the appropriate agencies of our government for decisions on long-term international policies and on current action required, particularly those within the competency of the National Security Council. National intelligence estimates had to be provided covering a very large number of countries and particular situations, all involving in some fashion the threat of Soviet aggression. For example, how explosive was the political, social, and economic situation in Iran? When Mossadegh came to power, to what extent was he under the domination of the local Communist party and was the Communist party effectively controlled by Moscow? If the oil resources of Iran were nationalized, would they be made available to the Soviet government and could they effectively be utilized? How serious would be the loss of these resources to the West?

The national intelligence estimate with respect to the Soviet Union itself was obviously of the greatest importance of all. Beyond the necessary information with respect to Soviet armament and the size and efficiency of Soviet military forces, economic intelligence was absolutely essential.

The competition between the Soviet economic and political system and our own will be profoundly affected by their comparative growth rates, almost regardless of the extent to which the contest is one of military or only of economic strength since both are intertwined.

The rate of Soviet economic growth depended upon the proportion of the Soviet gross national product allocated for consumption, for further investment, and for the current production of armaments. In turn, these depended upon a host of other factors. Consequently, the most intensive study of all sources of information on the Soviet economy was necessary. Naturally this field was one of great concern to me. Through the years it was of the greatest usefulness to me to have this information available in carrying out my own studies of the Soviet economic system, always with due care for the classified character of some of the sources of data.

Intelligence data were presented to us by representatives of the component units of the intelligence community and from our own staff. It is one of the first rules that intelligence officers should not be policy makers. A second rule is that intelligence estimates should be arrived at independently of their probable effect upon policy. It is not easy to hold to either rule, but the second one presents particular difficulties. In estimating the capabilities and intentions of the Soviet government in the military and political fields, it was inevitable that the various agencies presenting data would often have their special interests involved.

The possibility of a deliberate decision by the Soviet government to carry out a large-scale surprise attack would be an argument for a major build-up of our own air forces in order to resist successfully. On the other hand, those who had the responsibility for the readiness of our ground forces would naturally be inclined to estimate the number of Soviet divisions on the high side and perhaps to underestimate the number and effectiveness of the divisions in the armies of our European allies. In a certain sense it would be the duty of the different agencies to take these particular positions since each had a peculiar responsibility for our national capabilities for defense in these special areas.

The representative of a civilian agency might likewise be tempted to select and emphasize intelligence which would induce support for a maximum program of economic aid to foreign countries. The temptation to compromise the various positions so that everything would be left in a sort of gray zone which would afford no firm basis upon which decisions of national policy might be based had constantly to be guarded against.

The most crucial question of all with which our board of national intelligence estimates was confronted during the years immediately following the outbreak of the Korean War was "How great a risk of becoming involved in general war will the Soviet government take?" At the one extreme were those in the early days who believed that the Soviet government might even deliberately launch a surprise assault with overwhelmingly large forces in the expectation of being able to overrun Western Europe and perhaps the Middle East as well. Remembrance of Pearl Harbor and the shock of our recent military reverses in Korea were responsible for this extreme view.

At the other extreme were those who argued that the Soviet government would never risk general war since such a war would be a nuclear one, accompanied by universal devastation. If this extreme view were to hold true for all situations, then there would be no risk of general war, however "hard" our national policy towards the Soviets might be. According to this argument, whenever firmly confronted, the Soviet government would always retreat. This view that the Soviet government would never risk general war was based in part upon the belief that Stalin was, after all, a cautious, shrewd, unwarlike man who would never risk the destruction of the new Soviet industry built up at so great a cost to the Russian people. Moreover, even as late as the Korean War, there still lingered something of the picture of Stalin which had been built up while Soviet Russia was our ally in World War II. It was further argued that Stalin was no dedicated Communist, no wild-eyed advocate of bloody "World Revolution" on the Trotskyist model but, on the contrary, had always proclaimed "the possibility of building socialism in one country."

Stalin had indeed never been primarily concerned with World Revolution in the Marxist-Leninist sense. It was forgotten, however, that while he was not dedicated to a bloody international Communist revolution, perhaps no one in history had had a greater thirst for power, pursued with a taste for blood which had grown through the years. My intimate connection with the Russian scene over the years had made me fully aware that he was essentially a man of violence. The disclosures by Khrushchev of the bloody deeds of Stalin which were to be made in 1956 only added details as far as I was concerned.

I insisted that while the World Revolution was, for Stalin, not a major goal, World Revolution would and could be used as a means for the expansion of Soviet power, which in turn meant the power of Stalin. I did not believe that Stalin planned general war, but I was convinced that only military force or evidence of our will to use military force could stop Soviet aggression. I did not believe that Stalin could be counted upon to avoid all risk of war by retreating at every confrontation. I was to continue to hold this view even after Khrushchev succeeded Stalin, although Khrushchev was eventually to enter the path of possible peaceful coexistence as Stalin never would have done.

The unconscious feeling that nuclear war could not really happen was a baffling element in making an intelligence estimate of the risk of war in any particular situation. This feeling was rooted in the realization that war in a certain sense has always been illogical, if the premise is accepted that life is always better than death. Since in the nuclear age, death is raised to the nth power in the equation, it was assumed that war was finally excluded from the calculations of rational men. I never accepted the premise that life in all circumstances is better than death. Further, I was not convinced that raising the exponent attached to death totally altered the equation which expressed the probability of war.

I had not fully realized the strain involved in arriving at these national intelligence estimates until I found that I had developed a heart condition which made it imperative that I leave the board of estimates and try to restore my health. For once the problem of how to obtain my release from government service was solved. Bedell Smith asked that I continue to serve as a consultant to the extent my health would permit. I agreed and continued to serve in this capacity during succeeding years.

In the summer of 1953 I was once more called back into government service to participate in a review of our foreign policy, including national military strategy, on behalf of the National Security Council. This confidential review of national policy was given the code name of "Operation Solarium." At the time, its procedures and its conclusions were highly classified, but after eleven years I do not believe that some general observations concerning it violates security considerations, particularly since Joe Alsop referred to "Operation Solarium" in his column within weeks.

Some fifteen generals, admirals, officials of the State Department, and several of the leading specialists on Soviet Russia participated in an analysis of our national foreign policy. Everyone was or had been in government service. We were divided into three teams, with each team assigned a particular strategic policy to be examined and the case for its adoption developed. The three alternative policies were (*a*) the continuation of our present strategic policy; (*b*) the drawing of a line of defense beyond which the Communist powers should be notified that an advance would mean nuclear retaliation; (*c*) a policy of pushing back Communist power by the support of popular uprisings in the satellite countries such as had occurred in East Germany in 1953 and were later to take place in Poland and in Hungary in 1956.

We had no choice of the team on which each of us was to serve, and the three alternative policies were arbitrarily assigned among the teams. We carried out an intensive analysis of the particular strategic policy to which we had been assigned. All members of the teams had the highest security clearance and, consequently, had full access to all relevant data.

My team had been assigned the task of making the best case possible for the "drawing the line" strategy, designed to avoid the situation which had confronted us in Korea, where we had become involved in a bloody local war from which we could not withdraw and in which we could not use nuclear power to force a decision. The North Koreans might never have attacked if it had been clear that the frontier of South Korea were part of the line which the United States would certainly defend against attack. It at once became apparent that "drawing the line" was not at all a clear-cut alternative. "The line" might simply be drawn around the Western Hemisphere. It might be drawn to include Western Europe, Japan, and India, or it might be extended to include all the world not yet under the domination of the Communist countries. It was this widest alternative which my team chose to defend, although I would have preferred a more restricted one.

It became apparent that there could be no definitive strategic decision with respect to the area which would be defended by nuclear weapons, unconditioned by the particular circumstances under which an attack might take place. Would Hong Kong be included in the automatic defense area, and if so under what circumstances? Would Cambodia, Laos, and Viet Nam be so included? Further, would an attack by local guerrilla forces with logistic support from Soviet Russia or Communist China be considered an attack by Soviet Russia against which we should be prepared to use nuclear weapons? Numberless variants obviously might arise which could never be dealt with by advance push-button decisions, and we pointed this out.

All three teams were briefed one day by the Secretary of the Treasury on the limitations which the dangers of inflation placed upon the volume of our defense spending. I recognized that such limitations might become operative, but I always insisted that our national resources were such that there could be no doubt of our ability to support any necessary defense expenditures. Above all, I insisted that the dangers of inflation could not be weighed in the same scales as the dangers of losing a war.

After some six weeks the teams made a day-long presentation of the three alternative strategic policies at the White House before President Eisenhower, the National Security Council, most of the other members of the Cabinet, and the Joint Chiefs of Staff. It became apparent in the course of our presentation that President Eisenhower had been so deeply shaken by the prospect of a nuclear cataclysm that he could hardly contemplate the actual use of nuclear weapons even in self-defense. In one comment he implied that our team must not realize the horrors of nuclear war if we proposed the use of nuclear weapons in defense of any "line." We were somewhat annoyed since this alternative was not our choice but had been assigned to us. Nevertheless, the attitude of the President only underlined the proposition that no Chief Executive could really undertake an immediate nuclear reaction to an attack unless such an attack was of such a nature as to endanger irrevocably our national security.

After the three teams had made their presentations, President Eisenhower suggested that we extend our period of study long enough to amalgamate the three alternative policies and present him with an agreed-upon recommended strategic policy. The members of the teams respectfully declined the suggestion. They had been none too happy at having been required to analyze our strategic policy by arbitrary assignment to three alternatives. Furthermore, we could not see how we could possibly strike a sort of average of three policies, many of the elements of which were mutually exclusive.

Our alternative of "drawing the line" did appear to become partially embodied in our strategic policy during the immediately succeeding years under Secretary Dulles. One could maintain that it played a role in putting a period to Soviet expansion. Yet our involvement in South Viet Nam at the present moment shows how difficult it is to "draw a line" which would always prevent our involvement in small but long and dirty wars.

I was now able to turn back from my commitment to intelligence to resume my analysis of national economic and political systems. My election as President of the American Economic Association gave me the opportunity to undertake a "grand design" which I had had in mind for many years. I wished to make a comparative study of the economic and political systems of totalitarian countries with those of the countries of the West which were still considered capitalistic. It would, however, have been useless to make a comparison of the totalitarian systems with capitalistic economic systems characterized by pure and perfect capitalism and complete laissez-faire. In fact, such systems had never existed in a pure form even under old-style capitalism. Still less did such systems closely resemble the mixed economic systems of Europe, where elements of socialism were intermingled with those of capitalism. Likewise, the economic system of the United States with its large corporations, its powerful labor unions, and with the legislative inheritance of the New Deal, assuredly departed from either the theoretical or historical model of capitalism.

Yet there was by no means agreement among American economists with respect to the fact or the degree of departure of the current economic system from capitalism as that term had been traditionally understood. For a time, the majority of American economists had accepted the decline of competition and the growth of monopoloid market arrangements as a fact. They had debated only about whether competition could be restored by drastic legislative and judicial action against these monopoloid arrangements or whether comprehensive governmental controls or even the nationalization of large-scale industry might not be required. Now there was a resurgence of the belief among some economists that the American economic system was still effectively competitive and had not undergone basic change. There had never been an opportunity for a full confrontation between these conflicting views. I felt that before I could proceed further with my "grand design" such a confrontation involving a survey of the major elements of our economic system was required. An occasion for this confrontation was provided by the publication of Galbraith's book, *American Capitalism: The Concept of Countervailing Power*, which assumed the emasculation of old style competition and its replacement by the operation of countervailing power of large corporations and labor unions. Sometimes these large corporations bargained with each other as buyers and sellers, sometimes they bargained with industry-wide labor unions. Where the market could not be so organized, as in the case of agriculture, the government provided countervailing power. This doctrine was, however, by no means generally accepted by economists.

Substantially all the meetings of the American Economic Association in December, 1953, were devoted to a survey of our economic institutions with respect to whether or not they had undergone fundamental alteration. The confrontation among the economists was vigorous, not to say violent. No consensus was reached, but the survey left no doubt that while competition had indeed survived, the process had undergone very great changes as the importance of individual enterprises had declined and that of large-scale organizations of capital and labor, with large-scale government intervention and control, had grown tremendously.[1]

With the *Proceedings* of the 1953 meeting of the American Economic Association available as background, I wrote an article, "The Relevance of the Competitive Laissez-faire Economic Model to Modern Capitalistic National Economies." This article was published in *Kyklos*, an international economic journal published in Switzerland and was designed to induce European economists to do a survey of the economic system of each European country. This project was carried out under the direction of Dr. Edgar Salin and

1. *Papers and Proceedings of the American Economic Association, American Economic Review*, Vol. XLIV, No. 2, May 1954.

Dr. Rudolf Frei. The surveys covered the economic systems of fifteen countries of Western Europe, plus those of Canada and Japan. *Economic Systems of the West* was published in two volumes by the *List Gesellschaft* with the aid of a subsidy from the Twentieth Century Fund. The findings with regard to the economic systems of these seventeen countries were, of course, diverse. Nevertheless, a general picture emerged. The nationalization of industries had apparently come to an end. There were even some cases where governments were divesting themselves of industries previously acquired. The role of government was, however, increasing everywhere. The share of national income passing through the governmental budget had been increasing, governments were participating in arrangements for wage settlements between organizations of employers and labor unions, and governments were trying to co-ordinate fiscal policies and controls of the volume of public and private investment with these wage settlements. Expanded social insurance and public welfare programs were universal.

Since I now had available these analyses of the economic systems of the United States and of Western Europe, it was essential that I have another close look at the Soviet economic system. I had followed events in Soviet Russia as closely as possible through the years, but I had not been in Russia since 1939.

I spent a month in Russia in the summer of 1956. I knew that I was taking a serious risk in entering Soviet Russia. My past connection with OSS was well known. It seemed likely that my later connections with the intelligence services of the United States government were also known to the Soviet authorities. I was not in the employ of our government during any of my trips, nor were any part of my expenses paid by our government. The Soviet government could not be expected to know this, however. I simply gambled that when the Soviet government had the alternative of refusing me a visa, they would not choose to arrest me without cause after I was in the country. Any advantage which the Soviet authorities might expect to obtain through extracting information from me under pressure would be more than offset by the uproar that my arrest might be expected to cause. My estimate seemed correct, for I was not arrested. Since Professor Barghoorn's arrest in 1963, I am no longer sure that my gamble was a reasonable one.

I entered Russia after spending a few days in Helsinki. I

traveled by train to Leningrad. I was interested in seeing whether war damage in the area which the Soviet government had annexed from Finland had been restored. Contrary to what I was to observe elsewhere in Russia, where almost all war damage had been repaired, this particular area still showed extensive scars of war. It appeared that the Soviet government regarded the area primarily as a buffer zone against a possible attack on Leningrad.

The Finnish frontier was marked by a single strand of barbed wire, alongside which stood a Finnish soldier in a thoroughly relaxed attitude. A hundred yards further was a wide bristling belt of barbed wire which marked the Soviet frontier. As our train slowly crossed the frontier, a Soviet patrol with two German police dogs on leash and with submachine guns at the ready was conducting a security check. At that moment I asked myself, "Was this trip really necessary?" However, the menacing appearing security patrol was probably staged to coincide with the moment of the train's crossing the border.

In Leningrad I visited the construction sites of a large number of apartments in the company of the Secretary of the Chamber of Architects of Leningrad. These apartments were being built in an effort to cope with the great housing shortage. However, the cement blocks of which some of the apartments already completed had been built were beginning to crumble. When I asked how long the apartments had been built, the answer was, "Two years."

I also visited a cotton textile mill and had a long conference on technical and financial problems with the manager and chief engineer, both of whom were women. The mill compared fairly favorably with our plants in North Carolina. However, in this plant as well as other non-textile plants in Kharkov and Moscow, I noted the much larger number of workers than one would see doing similar work in American plants.

I revisited the points connected with the February and October Revolutions which I had seen when I had first visited Leningrad in 1930. I was particularly struck by a bronze plaque which still remained on a building next to the Winter Palace. "From this building Lenin and Stalin directed the attack which overthrew the Kerensky government and established the Soviet power." There were two remarkable things about the plaque. In fact, neither Lenin nor Stalin had directed the attack from the building in question.

Lenin had provided leadership for the October Revolution in the Smolny Institute, a mile or so away. The actual attack had been directed by Antonov-Ovseenko, who was liquidated years later by Stalin. Where Stalin had been at that moment, I do not know. This was some months after Khrushchev's speech on the crimes of Stalin, yet the plaque had not been removed.

I also saw the cruiser *Aurora*, which had fired the last shot in the struggle for the Winter Palace in 1917, anchored in the Neva. I did not go on board, but I heard later that where once there had been companion statues of Lenin and Stalin, only the statue of Lenin and a scarred surface where the statue of Stalin had stood remained. I was to note numerous examples of this ambivalent attitude towards Stalin's memory during further stages of my journey.

I traveled from Leningrad to Kiev by plane, but thereafter traveled by railway as much as possible in order to observe the countryside more closely and in order to have some opportunity to talk with my fellow travelers. I visited a number of collective farms and factories at Kiev and Odessa. I had planned to take ship at Odessa for a trip to Sochi in the Caucasus. At the last moment, however, I was informed that since the ship would stop for a few hours at Sevastopol, I would have to join the ship later at Yalta, since Sevastopol was a naval base closed to foreigners. Doubtless this decision was connected with Soviet knowledge of my past intelligence connections. I had to fly to Simferopol and then take a taxi for some seventy miles to Yalta. While we drove through the beautiful Crimean hills, my taxi driver furnished me with an appreciated travelogue.

I took the opportunity to visit the palatial homes of the former Russian nobility, now converted into convalescent homes for those fortunate enough to be selected for this privilege. I had stepped out of my hotel on one occasion and had returned after being gone only a few minutes. I found a man and a woman sitting in my bedroom looking over my baggage and making entries in a large book. I realized at once what was going on, and I did not really mind since there was nothing incriminating in my baggage. The man and woman did not speak a word and paid no attention to me whatever; I decided that it would appear strange if I did not protest. Since the office of Intourist happened to be in the hotel, I went to the local director and complained. "You must be mistaken," he said. "Perhaps you got in the wrong room." "That is hardly likely," I said, "since the man is sitting on my sweater." "Would you like me to go with you and investigate?" he said. "Certainly," I said. He went with me and strode confidently into the sitting room of the suite and started to go into the bedroom. I have rarely seen a man stop so quickly. Apparently he was really surprised. Still no words were spoken. The Director of Intourist backed hastily out of the room. "Think nothing of it," he said. "They are only counting things." "You mean they are taking inventory?" "Yes! Yes!" he cried, pleased at my apparent acceptance of his explanation. "Well," I said, "see that they are out of here by the time I return." In fact, I considered this episode and others somewhat like it only the normal security precautions which it was not unreasonable for the Soviet government to take.

I traveled to Sochi on the *Rossia*, a modern, well-appointed ship which had been built in Germany as part of the reparations payment to the Soviet government. It was interesting to observe the differences between the first, second, and steerage classes, much more marked than on an American or Western European ship.

From Sochi I went on to Tiflis and took the occasion to go by auto to Gori, the birthplace of Stalin. There the tiny cottage in which Stalin had been born had been enshrined in a marble pavilion. There was a large Stalin museum, and a still larger one had been under construction. Construction had now been stopped, and it was said that it would not be resumed. There were only a young worker and his wife being shown through the old museum, where doubtless crowds would have been in evidence only a few months earlier. The custodian who gave us the routine tour of the museum was extremely nervous, obviously dreading embarrassing questions. I did not ask any.

After a stop at Kharkov, where I visited more factories, I went on to Moscow, where I was joined by Professor Warren Nutter of the University of Virginia. He accompanied me to a number of conferences which I had with officials of *Gosplan* and others. I called on my old friend "Chip" Bohlen, now our Ambassador to Russia, whom I had first known as one of the secretaries of our Embassy in 1939. I had been so much impressed by his facility in the use of the Russian language and in his knowledge of the situation at that time that I had written a letter of commendation to Secretary of State Hull.

Ambassador Bohlen told me that the top Soviet "brass" had been invited to attend the Fourth of July party at the Embassy in a couple of days. He asked me to come and promised to introduce me to those of the Soviet hierarchy who attended. In fact, Khrushchev, Malenkov, Molotov, Bulganin, Shepilov, and Benediktov did attend the party. Bohlen introduced me to Khrushchev, Malenkov, Molotov, and Bulganin. All except Khrushchev greeted me politely. Indeed, Bulganin chatted with me genially for some ten or fifteen minutes. Fortunately Bulganin had a very good interpreter, for my Russian was by no means up to a prolonged and relaxed conversation. I also had an informative discussion with Benediktov, at that time head of the Ministry of State Farms. Khrushchev shook hands but only gave me a tough, hard look. I thought it barely possible that this was because he was aware of my identity. Several years later, it became clear that this was not true, since in a speech before the Supreme Soviet, he referred to "the bourgeois economist Hoover, in his day," as though I had been dead many years.

A little later Warren Nutter called my attention to one of the Soviet officials accompanying the cabinet ministers. "Do you know that man?" asked Nutter. "Why, he does look very familiar," I said. "He should," said Nutter; "he is your chauffeur." I then recognized the driver who had repeatedly given me near heart failure as he passed other cars just at the brows of hills. I recalled how when a traffic policeman had stopped us and had ordered us to pull over to the side of the road, my driver had got out, given the traffic policeman some sign, and had been instantly waved on. In conversations when my Intourist guides were not present, I had learned that several of my drivers had been lieutenants in combat outfits in the war, as had been true of this man. Apparently it was these drivers who had primary responsibility for keeping track of me. They were efficient, friendly fellows who did their job well.

A great deal of statistical data was released almost coincidentally with my arrival in Russia that had not been given out since before the war. Yet my experience on this trip to Soviet Russia clearly demonstrated the necessity for continuous personal contact in order to retain an intimate understanding of a different economic and political system, however closely one followed developments from other sources. I found that much had changed in the Soviet after seventeen years. The Russian standard of living had substantially improved over what it had been in 1939. The improvement over the war and immediate postwar years must have been very great.

I did a series of spot checks on prices and availabilities of food and clothing in most of the cities which I visited, as I had in 1939. I did a more limited and less dependable check on average wages paid. While there had been some increase in real wages since 1939, the increase did not approach the fantastic Soviet claims. I concluded that the lower range of estimates by Western economists of the annual rate of Soviet economic growth of some 6 per cent was reasonably accurate. This was almost double the rate of growth for the United States. Subsequent observations in 1958 confirmed my conclusion. However, both 1956 and 1958 were years of exceptionally good harvests, and subsequent years were not to maintain this rate of growth. Both on account of a declining rate of increase in industrial production and a catastrophically bad harvest in 1963, the Soviet annual rate of growth has at least temporarily fallen by now to some 2 per cent or 3 per cent, substantially lower than the current rate for the United States.

There had been a great relaxation in tension since the death of Stalin. Thousands had been released from prison camps after his death. Secret arrests and executions had apparently almost ceased, once the partisans of Beria had been disposed of. Yet the essential character of the police state remained. It was quite impossible for any foreigner to have relations with individual Russians on a basis of friendship and confidence. No freedom of the press had developed. The Party was once more the source of all power after its decline under Stalin's personal tyranny. Khrushchev ruled the Party by dint of the expulsion of party leaders who opposed him. Substantially all the institutions and procedures by which individual liberties are protected in the West were still lacking in Soviet Russia. It was evident, too, that a ruling class had developed and was becoming solidified. Its position was even strengthened by the absence of the bloody purges which under Stalin had repeatedly decimated its ranks. The Soviet form of the totalitarian state now gave evidence of having developed a permanent form.[2]

2. See chap. iv, "The Soviet Totalitarian State after Stalin," and chap. v, "Soviet Economic Growth," in my book *The Economy, Liberty and the State.*

Chapter nineteen. *The prospect for the transformation of the Soviet totalitarian state*

Many intellectuals of my generation came to idealize revolutions. While their violence might be deplored, it was assumed that revolutions were always directed against reactionary tyranny. The lessons of the French Revolution had been forgotten. There was much truth in Danton's bitter observation made shortly before he was guillotined: "In times of revolution, power will always go to the worst scoundrel." Revolutions do indeed sometimes produce economic and political reforms. They also are very liable to produce tyrants.

Now that the real face of the Stalinist regime has at last been authoritatively revealed by Khrushchev, there is some indication that intellectuals are rediscovering what liberals of the nineteenth century had fully realized, the complex reciprocal relation between revolution and tyranny.[1] Even if a dictator is overthrown by revolution, another dictator may be produced by the new revolution. Liberty and stability once lost may require generations to be regained.

It is inherent in the nature of a totalitarian state that only the most ruthless personalities can attain the highest power. Inevitably this conditions the character of the society over which the dictator rules. The Soviet Union, as a Marxist-oriented society,

1. Thus the dictator-tyrants, Pisistratus and Dionysius, Caesar, Robespierre and Napoleon, Stalin and Hitler, Peron, Batista and Castro, came to power through radical revolutionary movements. See my "Revolutions and Tyranny," *The Virginia Quarterly Review*, XXXVI (Spring, 1960), 182–194.

is further characterized by the absence of a moral philosophy. As Lenin put it, "We do not believe in eternal morality, and we expose the deceit of all legends about morality." Marxist doctrine assumed that neither law nor morality would be necessary under full Communism since substantially all evil stemmed from capitalism. When full Communism had been attained, the state would be unnecessary as a restraint on anti-social behavior and would have "withered away." In the words of Pashukanis, who wrote the first draft of the Soviet Constitution of 1936 before Stalin made him an "unperson," and who maintained that the need for criminal law would wither away along with the state itself in the final stage of Communism, "While certain crimes against personality and so forth will not disappear, such crimes should be regarded *per se* as a task of medical pedagogy." In actuality, the Soviet state had become, in Stalin's words, "The most potent and mighty of all state authorities that have existed down to this time." Far from the state having withered away, today the Soviet Union, unlike capitalist countries, frequently applies the death penalty even for crimes against property.

It is striking, too, that full collectivization of society has resulted in the Soviet Union in almost complete fragmentation, indeed, atomization of society. There is no private philanthropy, since the state is supposed to provide whatever aid is necessary. There are almost no voluntary organizations of individuals. Even personal friendships seem less frequent and less close, and family relations are less intimate than in other societies, although this may, in part, reflect urbanization of society rather than purely reflecting collectivization. This atomization of society makes the individual far more vulnerable to the ruling power of the totalitarian state.

Doubtless the foreign policy of Soviet Russia is not uniquely determined by its moral philosophy or its absence. However, a totalitarian state will be less inhibited in the use of force than will a democratically controlled country, even though the rulers of Soviet Russia are no longer dedicated revolutionary Marxist-Leninists. Consequently, the maintenance of world peace depends ultimately upon the eventual escape of the Russian people from the present totalitarian economic and political system. The same conclusion follows with respect to China. But how can a break-out from the politico-economic totalitarian state ever come about?

The evidence is clear that command economies, that is, fully planned and directed national economic systems, have never existed in the absence of political absolutism. Stated in another way, economic totalitarianism has in the past been associated with the Soviet, the Fascist, or the Nazi state, but never with a democratic, parliamentary state characterized by individual liberty. Historically, too, civil liberties, parliamentary institutions, and democracy were bourgeois concepts, even though the capitalist classes eventually only grudgingly shared the advantages of these concepts with the masses of the population.

Paradoxically, the evidence with respect to the increased roles of the state in the economic system of the United States and in the "mixed economies" of Western Europe shows no net erosion of individual liberties thereby. This conclusion had been fully substantiated by the studies of the economic systems of the United States and of Western Europe which I had just carried out.

Before developing a comprehensive theory of the relation between the economy, liberty, and the state, I wished to tackle the problem from the other direction: Was it possible for a command economy ever to develop a set of democratic, parliamentary institutions, accompanied by procedures for protecting the civil liberties of individuals? Could a totalitarian economic and political system shed its political totalitarianism while retaining completely centralized state planning and control of the economy? Or, if this were not possible, how much centralized control and direction of the economy would have to be relinquished by the state in order for democracy and civil liberties to come into existence?

In the hope of finding some evidence which might aid in answering these questions, I felt that it would be essential to have a look at the economic systems of the present or former Soviet satellites, particularly Yugoslavia and Poland, where it was claimed that steps were being taken to change the economic and political systems away from the fully totalitarian model. I wished also to have another look at the Soviet economic system. In 1957 Khrushchev had decreed a plan for the decentralization of industrial controls and had even talked vaguely of bringing labor into the management of industry. Was it possible that this move had anything in common with the claim of the Yugoslav government that control of the nationalized industries was to be placed in the hands of workers' collectives rather than in the hands of state-appointed managers? To gather evidence bearing on these questions, I returned to the Soviet Union during the summer of 1958 and also visited Poland, Czechoslovakia, and Yugoslavia.[2]

I stopped for a week in Berlin on my way to Poland. I had revisited West Germany in 1950, but I had not been in Berlin since 1945. I at once got in contact with my old friend, David Bruce, our ambassador to the West German government, to get a "fill in" on the current situation. Since there had been a "foul-up" on my hotel reservations, I lived with the German family whose apartment I had saved from our billeting officers in 1945. Another family whose apartment had also inadvertently got saved at the same time furnished me with a car. I was, consequently, able to get a quick picture of life in a free enclave within the Soviet orbit.

The physical recovery of Berlin from the utter destruction of 1945 was simply unbelievable. The standard of living was superior to what it had been in 1939 on the eve of the war. Civilian morale was good, and relations with the American Occupational Forces excellent. All this was in contrast to conditions in the Soviet sector of Berlin and in Soviet-occupied East Germany as described by my German friends. A glimpse at the bleakness of the Soviet sector on my way to Schöneheide, the airport at which I boarded my plane for Warsaw, was confirmatory.

I was joined by my friend Harold Linder in Warsaw. We had a series of conferences with members of the Polish government, with economists, with newspaper correspondents, with foreign diplomats, and of course, with our own diplomatic representatives. We visited several factories and villages in the countryside.

There was substantial evidence that the uprising at Posnan in 1956, followed by Gomulka's successful resistance to Khrushchev's threat of the use of Soviet troops against the new Polish government, had greatly shaken the Soviet hold on Poland. Individual Poles would now talk more freely to foreigners than would people in any of the satellite or former satellite countries which I was to visit. I was surprised and pleased when in a private conversation the Polish Minister of Commerce gave the major credit for an improvement in

2. I was accompanied by Mr. Harold Linder, formerly Assistant Secretary of State for Economic Affairs, at the present time Chairman of the Export-Import Bank. Mr. Linder participated in many of the conferences with the economic administrators of these countries.

living conditions to American surplus grain made available substantially without cost by our government.

The Polish government, as apparently did the public, fully recognized the necessity for continuing as a sort of Soviet protectorate, yet dislike of the Russians was more noticeable than dislike for the Germans, from whom the Polish people had suffered so much. This was reflected in a minor way by the willingness to converse in German and a complete unwillingness to use Russian. This, however, may have reflected primarily the fact that both the Poles with whom I came in contact, as well as I, knew German much better than Russian.

The Polish planning authorities were making great efforts to substitute to some extent a market economy and a rationally determined price system for an arbitrarily planned and directed command economy. They were having heavy going of it, since the two systems inevitably are in some degree in conflict. The system of factory management by workers' councils which had been inaugurated after the revolution of 1956 had been largely suspended since the effect upon industrial discipline and productivity and upon the price level had showed signs of becoming catastrophic.

The Polish effort to move away from both economic and political totalitarianism since this survey in 1958 has not had much success down to the present moment. Governmental restrictions on intellectual freedom have once more been tightened. The relinquishment of forced collectivization of agriculture by the government has not brought about adequate levels of food production. The attempt to marry a collectivist economic system with a market economy has been accompanied by a discouragingly low rate of economic growth.

Moscow in 1958 revealed the usual contradictions. The plumbing and furnishing of our rooms in the monumental Leningradskaya Hotel were beginning to run down, although the hotel had been built only two years earlier. Yet the subways of both Moscow and Leningrad were far superior both in construction and maintenance to any in the Western World. Totalitarian regimes have demonstrated their efficiency in those areas which are given the highest priorities, be it the construction and maintenance of subways or carrying out programs for the exploration of space.

The customary series of conferences with Soviet economists and governmental officials, visits to factories, and reading of the press revealed that Khrushchev's scheme for the decentralization of industry was in trouble. The hinted-at intention to bring labor into the management of industry had not even been attempted, as it had in Poland and Yugoslavia. What was more important, the conflict between local autonomy in industry and central planning had become acute. While I was in Moscow, there appeared on the front page of *Pravda* a decree authorizing severe punishment for the many cases of favoring local interests over the national planned program. When I clipped this article out of *Pravda* and passed it around at a conference with Soviet economists, requesting comment, the clipping was handed about as though it were red hot and returned to me with no comment whatsoever.

Subsequently, almost continuous reorganizations of Soviet industry have taken place. The number of *sovnarkhozi*, the semi-autonomous economic areas, has been reduced greatly from the original 105.[3] *Gosplan*, the State Planning Committee, has been reorganized again and again. The fearfully slow rate of construction of capital equipment was causing Khrushchev and the planning authorities great concern in 1958, and this is still true. The advantage of a totalitarian state in its ability to withhold consumption goods from its people to facilitate greater capital investment was consequently offset, and a serious shortage of capital began to appear. This shortage was, of course, sharply accentuated by the large expenditures for armament and on the space program. Yet the greatest vulnerability of the Soviet economic system was concealed by the excellent harvest of 1958. Only in 1963, when tremendous imports of grain from Canada and the United States had to be authorized in order to prevent famine, was the deep trouble in the Soviet economy revealed.

Our stay in Czechoslovakia, accompanied by visits to factories and collective farms, did not offer evidence of any effort to move away from the totalitarian economic and political model.[4] Instead, the collectivization of agriculture was being relentlessly pushed against the crumbling resistance of the peasants. I was surprised at

3. Since the removal of Khrushchev from power in 1964, it has been announced that the *sovnarkhozi* are to be abolished. The dual control of industry and of agriculture by the Communist party which Khrushchev had inaugurated was also to be abolished and a single system of control restored.

4. Since the removal of Khrushchev, the Czech Communist party has announced a reversal of previous policy which is intended to permit decentralization and to allow a much greater role for profit in the economy.

Prague's Western look and at how much the standard of living surpassed that of Soviet Russia. Nevertheless, a couple of Czech citizens took the risk of expressing their despairing discontent with the régime.

We found evidence in Yugoslavia of progress in moving away from a fully totalitarian economic and political system. The customary round of visits to factories and state farms and conferences with economists and governmental officials showed that a real effort had been made at setting up workers' collectives which hired managers to run industrial and commercial establishments. How effective the supposed worker control, in fact, was, it would be difficult to say. It may have been of about the same order as the control of the management of a large American corporation by its stockholders.

Substantially the whole apparatus of authoritative planning directives to industrial units had been dismantled. As one Yugoslav economist put it, "We decided to do away with a state-directed economy, not because it did not work—it did. But we felt that we could never have personal freedom in a state which carried on substantially all economic activity on the basis of command and obey."

The effort to substitute a free market for authoritative state planning and direction in a system without private ownership of industry had not been wholly successful. Price controls had had to be retained for some of the most basic commodities. There has been a constant struggle by interested individuals and groups to manipulate wage rates, prices, investment policies, and the division of profits in their favor. Now and again an inflationary wave has necessitated quite comprehensive re-establishment of state controls. Yet some success had been attained in developing autonomy in the investment and production processes of industrial plants. Concurrently, at least lip service has been given to the goal of reducing political totalitarianism. The promise was even held out that at some future date the monopoly of political power of the Communist party (now called the Yugoslav League of Communists) would be relinquished. Measures eventually to prevent the permanent tenure of office holders were called for. Significantly, Tito was exempted from this prohibition of permanency. In belated recognition of Milovan Djilas' warning of the danger of a new ruling class taking for its own use the former surplus value of the capitalist class, excessively large salaries and perquisites of industrial managers and governmental officials were currently being frowned upon.

Yugoslavia, nevertheless, remained a police state, with almost no freedom of the press, with few of the safeguards traditional in a Bill of Rights, with the state and economic apparatus still in the control of one party. Yet no one who had lived in a fully totalitarian state could doubt that people were much freer, had less fear of arbitrary arrest, had less fear of association with foreigners, and were generally more relaxed in Yugoslavia than in Soviet Russia or in Czechoslovakia. Consequently, Yugoslavia did offer limited evidence for the possibility of reducing the totalitarian economic and political aspects of an economy without the restoration of private property in industry.

Immediately after my survey of the economic and political systems of the present or former Soviet satellites, I published my study on the relation among economic systems, liberty, and the state.[5] In this book I had a chapter entitled "The Prospect for the Survival of Liberty." I came to the conclusion that the survival of liberty depended upon the evolution of the modified and mixed forms of capitalism in the United States and Western Europe. The use of economic and political power on the part of the managements, of corporations, and of labor unions, together with the failure of the automaticity of full employment of human and capital resources, has partially supplanted the free market and necessitated the intervention of the state. Yet, in the United States and in Western Europe there is good ground for hope that the role of the state will not have to become either so powerful or so comprehensive as, on balance, seriously to curtail our liberties.

Writing five years ago I could feel little hope for either the disappearance or the substantial modification of the Soviet economic and political system. As long as the Soviet system remained unchanged, it constituted a threat to the liberties of the peoples who

5. *The Economy, Liberty and the State* (New York: Twentieth Century Fund, 1959, and Doubleday, 1961). My study of economic systems has continued and now includes surveys of the economic systems of underdeveloped countries. Studies of the economic systems of Australia, Britain, Canada, Ceylon, Ghana, India, Malaya, New Zealand, Pakistan, South Africa and the West Indies were carried out by economist of each of these countries and published as *Economic Systems of the Commonwealth*, ed. Calvin B. Hoover (Durham, N. C.: Duke University Press, 1962). Studies of the economic systems of Tanganyika, Tunis, Chile and Mexico are now being carried out by my graduate students. Other studies are in the planning stage.

yet remained free. However, in the last two or three years the prospect for the survival of liberty in the world has greatly improved.

The Soviet rate of economic growth has fallen substantially. This reflects not only the inability of the Soviet government to carry on agricultural production successfully; it also reflects an inability to carry out the fearfully complicated task of planning and directing capital investment and industrial production in a society which finds it necessary to produce something other than the most basic and crudely fabricated commodities. No Communist country has been able to produce a really adequate food supply for its people. Meanwhile, the economy of the United States, which had momentarily faltered in its rate of economic growth, now shows a rate of economic growth comparable to that of Western Europe, while both currently equal or even exceed that of the Soviet Union.

Shortly after the removal of Khrushchev, far-reaching changes in the organization of the Soviet economy were inaugurated by the new regime. In part these changes reversed the organizational policies of Khrushchev. One of the policies which he had tentatively favored was, however, further developed and vigorously championed by the new leaders. This was the policy originally proposed by Liberman of according a much greater role to profits while increasing the autonomy of plant managers and diminishing the role of centralized national planning. Simultaneously a great relaxation on the restraints on production by individual peasants on their individual plots was announced.

In addition to the economic difficulties of Soviet Russia, which are a force pressing towards change in the economic and political system, the whole ideological structure upon which the system has rested has been severely shaken. Foremost in undermining Soviet ideology has been the great Soviet-Chinese Communist conflict. This flaming controversy has hopelessly divided the Communist forces of subversion which appeared for a time to be likely to turn the underdeveloped and less developed countries of Africa, Asia, and Latin America against the West. Communist parties throughout the world have had their loyalties divided between Moscow and Peking. The Communist party in many countries has become split into Soviet and Chinese factions. In conjunction with the economic difficulties facing both Soviet Russia and Communist China, this ideological split has greatly limited the possibility of joint Sino-Soviet economic and military assistance to these underdeveloped countries.

Even more important is the disintegration of the Marxist-Leninist image of a world-wide socialist society which would be erected upon the wreckage of capitalism. In this society there would be no more war between nations, since the state would have "withered away." With the withering away of the state, the coercive power of men over men would disappear. There would be no more "surplus value" for capitalists, and hence no exploitation of the workers. Now that this myth has been shattered, even warfare between the two great Communist powers cannot be excluded as a possibility.

This Marxist-Leninist image of an ideal society attainable only through revolution and the temporary dictatorship of the proletariat had had its most critical influence outside Communist circles and precisely upon those intellectuals who had only the vaguest knowledge of Marxist-Leninist doctrine. These had been able to escape the difficulties of trying to resolve the internal contradictions of the doctrine or to reconcile the realities of the Soviet and Chinese regimes with the doctrine. So long as the chief of the Soviet regime was accepted as the infallible fountain of authority, realities could be denied, and ideological differences resolved by the firing squad after branding the dissidents officially as "enemies of the people."

Now that the ideological monolith has been broken, the image of a Stalinist society which had begun as an alleged dictatorship of the proletariat and which had become a tyranny in the guise of "the cult of personality," and the ever-present possibility of the "New Class" taking for itself the "surplus value" which formerly went to the capitalist, cannot any longer be effectively concealed from intellectuals throughout the world. The spectre of this fouled image cannot be suppressed even within Communist countries.

The proclamation of the crimes of Stalin by Khrushchev, the shooting down of the insurrectionary workers in Budapest by Soviet tanks on the orders of Khrushchev, the building of the Berlin Wall have further contributed to the irreparable damage which the Communist *mystique* has suffered.

The writer witnessed a curious reaction in a movie theatre in Leningrad in June, 1956. Before the feature film began, a newsreel of the current visit of Marshal Tito of Yugoslavia to Leningrad was shown. Tito was accompanied by Khrushchev, Bulganin, and other Soviet dignitaries. At one point in the newsreel the narrator announced, "And now Comrade Khrushchev comes forward."

> Khrushchev, a rather fat man, walked into the center of the picture with a slightly clowning sort of strut, and a look of jocular good humor. There came a half chuckle, half snicker from the movie audience. Twenty-seven years earlier when I first lived in Russia there had been a few surviving "anecdotes" told about Stalin; but for at least twenty-five years the writer had never seen or heard of a Russian laughing at or with Stalin. He had been too greatly feared for that. It flashed across the writer's mind that if Khrushchev were to try to continue to rule without the legitimacy supplied by some sort of popular electoral process, he would feel the need to make himself feared by much the same sort of terror that Stalin had wielded.[6]

Khrushchev did manage to rule for some eight years thereafter. In 1957 only the support of Marshal Zhukov had been able to save him when a majority of the Party Praesidium turned against him. When Khrushchev was ousted in 1964, his clowning and boorishness constituted one of the charges brought against him.

The removal of Khrushchev in 1964 still further weakened the chain between the mythical dictatorship of the proletariat and the personality of the Communist rulers. Although the change, at least in its early stages, was bloodless, the secrecy surrounding the process of Khrushchev's removal and the selection of Brezhnev and Kosygin as his successors underlined the complete absence of either the dictatorship of the proletariat or any form of a democratic process.

This series of disasters to Soviet ideology outside the Soviet Union may be expected substantially to weaken the domestic resistance to the kind of changes in the Soviet system towards which current economic difficulties are pressing. Would it be possible for the Soviet economic system to evolve into something more nearly resembling that of the United States or those of Western Europe if the economic difficulties became so great as to require fundamental change? All large and complex organizations of human beings to carry on economic activities have certain characteristics in common. This is true of Soviet and American industrial organizational forms. The differences are great and complex. There are no private stockholders in Soviet industry, but the stockholders in the typical large American corporation have only vestigial control over corporate management. The role of stock ownership in channeling investment and in influencing the management to maximize profits is not

6. *The Economy, Liberty and the State*, pp. 113–114.

negligible, yet it is obviously far different from that of our earlier economy of individual enterprise and ownership. Whatever the effect of the partial divorce of stock ownership from corporate management may be, the American system does produce a high degree of industrial autonomy with a substantial amount of competition among corporations supplying the market. The result is a complex of reasonably flexible prices which does a much more efficient job of allocating resources and controlling the kinds and volume of production than the Soviet state-owned, -planned, and -directed economy has been able to do.

While there is an inevitable conflict between central direction of an economy and the autonomy of corporate units producing for a free market, we have many different cases in capitalistic countries where some form of planning has been married to corporate enterprise and a partially free market. The Netherlands and France afford such examples. The proposed "incomes policy" in Britain, or even the "guide lines" for wage increases in the United States are lesser examples.

How much change would be required in Soviet industrial organization to approach the modern corporate industrial organization in the countries characterized by modern capitalism? It is not easy to see how such a change could come about, but it does not seem that it would be impossible. A reorganization along the lines of the Yugoslav economic system would be a step in this direction.

If a large degree of autonomy could be worked out for enterprises in large-scale industry, while permitting private ownership and operation of small-scale and service industries, a system somewhat like that set up by Lenin under the New Economic Policy in 1921 would exist. It is significant that during this period of NEP, which endured until brought to an end by Stalin in 1929, there was a general relaxation of terror and far more personal freedom than before or after. There was a substantial relaxation of the arbitrary methods of the policy state under Khrushchev. There has also been some relaxation in the rigid control over literature. Some divergence in editorial policies of newspapers now occurs occasionally. Under a "Newest Economic Policy" this gradual liberalization might develop further. Early pronouncements on economic policy by the successors to Khrushchev indicate intentions to proceed in this direction.

The transformation of the Soviet totalitarian state might be delayed if a pronounced improvement in economic conditions in Russia came about. One of the most important forces pressing towards change is the dissatisfaction of Soviet citizens with their standard of living as they have become more familiar with life in Western countries through cultural exchange and other means. The difficulties which the Soviet economic system has encountered as it has had to try to provide a greater variety of goods and services has aroused the impatience of the consuming public even as their appetite has been whetted by a taste for better things inadequately satisfied. The lag in production in Poland and in Czechoslovakia accentuated these difficulties for the Soviet bloc and was a factor in bringing pressure for a change away from centralized planning.

The most crucial factor is likely to be whether or not Soviet agriculture can produce an adequate supply of food. Khrushchev had planned a huge increase in the production of fertilizers in the hope of increasing agricultural production. If long-term credits under the guarantee of capitalistic governments were given to the Soviet government for the purchase of capital equipment for the chemical industry and for other purposes, the pressure for the transformation of the Soviet economic system might be postponed, perhaps indefinitely.

The current bitter Sino-Soviet conflict serves as a deterrent to both governments against aggression (except perhaps against each other!), which holds an obvious threat of general war. Anti-government riots by Czech and Bulgarian students in the spring of 1964 likewise limit the aggressive capabilities of the Soviet bloc. The critical agricultural difficulties, as well as the fall in the rate of economic growth, have compelled the Soviet government to curtail the volume of resources which it can commit for either conventional or nuclear weapons and their delivery systems. Thus, the Soviet military threat is somewhat diminished, although it certainly has by no means disappeared. The danger of miscalculation which would lead to nuclear war will always exist as long as a major power retains the totalitarian state form. Only the transformation of both Soviet Russia and Communist China from a closed and totalitarian form to a freer and more open society could afford an eventual escape to mankind from the continual threat of nuclear war. Recent events in Soviet Russia afford at least some hope.

Index